TROUBLE
WITH THE LAW?

TROUBLE WITH THE LAW?

A LEGAL HANDBOOK
FOR LESBIAN & GAY MEN

CAROLINE GOODING

GMP

First published October 1992 by GMP Publishers Ltd
P O Box 247, London N17 9QR, England

World Copyright © 1992 Caroline Gooding
Immigration chapter — Copyright © 1992 Sue Shutter

A CIP catalogue record for this book
is available from the British Library

ISBN 0-85449 156 2

Distributed in North America by InBook
P O Box 120470, East Haven, CT 06512, USA

Distributed in Australia by Bulldog Books
P O Box 155, Broadway, NSW 2007, Australia

Printed and bound in the EC on enironmentally-friendly paper
by Nørhaven A/S, Viborg, Denmark

To my family, real and pretend.

ACKNOWLEDGEMENTS

A great debt is owed to Paul Crane's ground-breaking book, *Gays and the Law*, and to the numerous gay and lesbian agencies which have sprung up since that book was published, particularly Dai Harris of Terrence Higgins Trust, Phillip Derbyshire of GALOP, Gay Switchboard and LER/LAGER. Also to Maureen O'Hara from the Children's Legal Centre and Russell Campbell from the National Housing Law Project, Fran Stone, Angus Hamilton, Marilyn Howard, Lucy Nuttall and Anne Kane for their comments and criticisms.

Thanks to Kathleen Marshall, of the Scottish Child Law Centre, Alistair Brownie and Paul Burns, for their comments on the Scottish sections.

Thanks also to Emily Driver for her help, and Sarah Beskine for sharing the initial enthusiasm and planning.

And finally I owe a great debt to, and to some degree share authorship with, Sue Shutter, of the Joint Council for the Welfare of Immigrants, who wrote the chapter on Immigration, and to Nicola Donbridge who wrote all of the Scottish sections found in this book. Without them this project wouldn't have been possible.

CONTENTS

INTRODUCTION

This book aims to provide lesbians and gay men with an overview about how the law affects them.

We do not attempt to provide a theoretical analysis of the law's treatment of sexuality, nor proposals about how the law should be changed to counter discrimination. Many different books could be and need to be written about these subjects. Instead, we attempt an equally ambitious project: to compile a legal handbook to guide lesbians and gays in dealing with the law in every area of their lives. Precisely because laws are devised and applied within a framework which assumes the normality and superiority of heterosexuality, the situations in which we are not "all equal under the law" are myriad — from having visiting rights to your sick lover to protection against discrimination at work, keeping your children or remaining in your house after your lover has died, the law will treat you differently because of your sexuality.

In some instances, laws have been deliberately designed to suppress or contain gay and lesbian sexualities. The criminal law with regard to gay sex and the notorious Section 28 are the most obvious examples. In many other instances it is the law as it is put into practice which directly discriminates against lesbians and gays — arrests of lesbians and gays for public displays of affection and the courts' bias against awarding custody of children to lesbian mothers, for example.

A more subtle form of discrimination stems from the law's unwritten assumption that everyone is heterosexual. In many cases there is also an explicit purpose to promote heterosexual marriage. To remove this form of discrimination requires a fundamental reorganization of the law, not simply removing discriminatory features. Some lesbians and gays would argue in favour of retaining the framework of the law but allowing lesbians and gays to enter it by permitting lesbian/gay marriage. Others (myself included) seek a more fundamental restructuring of society and laws, to reflect the differences in lesbian and gay lifestyles.

Even when we are unaware of the legal position, the law provides the framework within which we operate. When you move in with a lover sharing the rent or the mortgage you will both have assumptions about what the legal position would be in the event that you split up. These assumptions, whether verbalized or not, will determine the sort of agreements you reach, as well as how you act in the event that you fail to reach an agreement.

As well as having this practical effect on our everyday lives, the law also affects us in a more indirect way, by the ideological messages which it carries. When a court rules that a lesbian cannot inherit the flat of her long-term cohabitant because she does not count as either a "spouse" or "a member of the family"; when gay teenagers are prosecuted for having consensual sex; when the sacking of a gay employee is upheld by a tribunal on the basis that it is "reasonable" for an employer to believe that all homosexuals are predatory dangers to youth, these decisions have a powerful impact in increasing the homophobic attitudes which surround us in our everyday lives. Thus, whilst the criminal law has a powerful practical effect, particularly on teenagers attempting to understand and give expression to their sexuality, it also carries an immensely powerful ideological message. This is why it is in the interest of lesbians to campaign for reform of the criminal law despite the fact that it does not control lesbian behaviour to the same extent.

Because the law provides the framework within which social institutions exist it is difficult to draw a line as to where "the law" ends and social life begins. Similarly, because the law does not operate in the abstract but through a myriad of institutions from the police and the courts to social services and local authorities, it is constantly changing, and these shifts are, in a broad sense, political. This book presents a snapshot of the legal position of lesbians and gays at the time of writing, but to understand this fully you have to see it in a historical and political context.

On the formal level, in terms of the laws on the statute book, the only progress since the "Reform" of 1967 has been the extension of that measure, originally applying only to England and Wales, so that it now covers Scotland, Northern Ireland and the Channel Islands. Indeed in these terms the legal position of lesbians and gays has actually worsened since 1967. A series of Parliamentary assaults began in the late 1980s with Section 28, and continued with the Human Embryology Act's attempt to control lesbians' fertility, Section 30's tightening of sentencing guidelines for consenting gay sex-crimes, and attempts in the Children's Act to prevent lesbians and gays from fostering and adopting. If we add to these the "Operation Spanner" which criminalized consensual sado-masochistic sex and a series of measures tightening up the censorship of "pornography" then the legal situation of lesbians and gays looks as if it has significantly worsened since 1967. To complete the picture we can point to figures concerning the enforcement of the criminal law against gay men, which show that the number of convictions has increased to the level of the 1950s.

However, this one-sided picture illustrates the dangers in looking at law in a formal way, divorced from the broader social context. Without underestimating the ferocity of the assaults in recent years, it would be absurd to deny that there has been substantial progress in the social and political position of lesbians and gays since 1967. Undoubtedly the most evident change in the daily lives of lesbians and gay men is the opening of social spaces where it is possible to be comfortably and confidently "out". This is interestingly paralleled by changes in media stereotypes. These stereotypes remain vicious and damaging, despite the development of a few spaces which accurately reflect our lives. However the images are not now of lonely, pathetic individuals, but of "fanatical" activists.

Perhaps the most symbolic signs of change (and at present they remain merely symbolic) are those at the heart of the authoritarian state: the Lord Chancellor's statement to *Gay Times* in October 1991 that "homosexuality per se would not prevent a person being appointed a judge", may not lead to a spate of out lesbian judges but is an interesting sign of the times, as are the establishment of an association for lesbian and gay policemen, and the government announcement, also in 1991, that lesbians and gay civil servants would not automatically be denied security clearance. Indeed, the most powerful factor behind the attacks of the late 80s and early 90s was a backlash against the progress of lesbians and gays during the 70s and 80s in establishing ourselves on the social and political agenda, despite the lack of any substantive law reform. Starting from the growth of open lesbian and gay lifestyles, advances were made in the arts, media and particularly in the unions and labour movement. The numerous organizations specifically addressing the needs of lesbians and gays (see Listings), are themselves powerful testimony to our social progress.

The fundamental driving force behind this progress was the same broad social shifts which had brought about the series of modernizing social reforms in the late 1960s, of which the "decriminalization" of gay sexuality was part. These social developments included the increasing numbers of women in the work-force, allied to contraceptive developments and changes in the abortion laws, the massive decline in the birth rate and, through an escalation of illegitimate births and a soaring divorce rate, the crumbling of the traditional heterosexual family.

It is a curious irony that as some sections of the lesbian and gay community are clamouring to be allowed to take part in the institution of matrimony, heterosexuals are deserting it in droves. This breaking up of the conventional family structure has increased the social space within which lesbians and gays can operate.

It was precisely this dissolution of the "traditional family" and the rise in the social and political prominence of the lesbian and gay movement which Section 28 was specifically tailored to counter. For the first time in British law we have a measure aimed not at sexual acts per se, but at sexual lifestyles and their defence and promotion.

In the narrowest context Section 28 was a response to the policies of a sector of the labour movement. The Greater

London Council and Greater Manchester Council, in particular, introduced attempts to integrate the concerns of their lesbian and gay voters into the agenda of municipal socialism. In targeting these policies the Tories were calculatedly reacting to a split between the leadership and left wing of the Labour Party: the Labour leadership having expressed (through a well publicized press leak) its intention to distance itself from lesbians and gays.

The practical effects of Section 28 may in fact have been more limited than its opponents claimed at the time of the great struggles surrounding its Parliamentary debate (although it is very difficult to chart its precise effect because of the extent of informal self-censorship by local authorities). However its ideological effect was a powerful assault on lesbian and gay claims to equality. The law reform in 1967 had been carefully tailored to contain gay sexuality at the same time as decriminalizing it within narrowly drawn confines. The concept that homosexuality is alright in private, behind closed doors, coupled with an extraordinarily high age of consent, makes the point that this activity is offensive to the public order, and that the public, especially the young people, must be protected from it.

Lord Reid succinctly expressed the legal system's attitude towards "homosexuality" in his House of Lords judgement (1973) at the trial of *International Times* for conspiracy to corrupt public morals (see Crime chapter): "There is a material difference between merely exempting certain conduct from criminal penalties and making it lawful in the full sense . . . indulgences in these practices . . . is corrupting."

Section 28 was a resounding legal reinforcement of these attitudes, and this is its chief danger. However, the Section must be seen as a contradictory success for the right-wing homophobes. By rallying support for lesbians and gays from leading figures in the arts, media and establishment, as well as provoking the mobilization of the lesbian and gay communities on an unprecedented scale, many have commented that Section 28 may itself have had the effect of actually "promoting homosexuality".

Out of the struggle around Section 28 have come a number of promising political developments for lesbians and gays, despite a failure to maintain that level of activism. In spite of some disputes, the campaign has provided an added impetus for lesbians and gays to work together. This is reflected in the three most prominent politically active groupings of the early 90s: OutRage, Act-Up and Stonewall.

The Stonewall group, launched in 1989 by Ian McKellan (a prominent establishment actor whose coming out and political involvement with lesbian and gay issues was a direct result of Section 28) is modelled on US lobbying organizations. It is neither an activist nor a democratically accountable organization. Despite Sir Ian McKellan's much publicized chat with John Major, Stonewall's value remains to be proved.

An indication of the limitations of their reformist approach was shown around Section 30 (see Crime chapter).This Section encourages judges to hand down more severe penalties for crimes which have been labelled as serious; these just happen to include a number of the consensual sexual acts which have been criminalized between men. Stonewall claimed that they had achieved a lobbying success because the Clause had been amended to specify that it should only apply where "serious harm" was likely to be caused. However as we discuss in the Crime chapter, it seems likely that because of their homophobic attitudes many judges will conclude that gay sex crimes automatically fall into this category. Moreover, by announcing this "success" a few days before a planned protest demonstration, Stonewall surely fell into the trap of demobilizing the very forces which they need to exist in order to win concessions.

This danger, that a self-selected group of reformist gay men and lesbians are used to exclude the broader community from political influence, was also apparent in the Labour Party leadership's luke-warm, and profoundly ambivalent, response to pressure from its own rank and file. Although committed by Conference decision to lowering the age of consent, in early 1992 Labour's leaders announced their intention to leave the vote to the consciences of individual MPs, treating the issue as one of morals rather than of civil rights. They went further and announced that if they won office they would not even introduce such a bill, but leave it to an individual MP to introduce it as a Private Member's Bill.

When OutRage complained about this "profoundly insult-ing" treatment, the Deputy Leader, Roy Hattersley, declined to discuss the issue with them. He claimed that he was "committed by resolution of the Labour Party to discuss our policy on these matters with Stonewall — the group which the National Executive judge to be the most representative and most influential amongst gay men and lesbians." The Stonewall group had the grace to comment: "Whatever you may think of Stonewall we are careful not to use the term representative."

OutRage is a loose collection of grass-roots, direct action groups around the country, organizing popular and imagina-tive protests against instances of homophobia. They are the diametric opposite of Stonewall, not only in their composition and organizational form, but in the thrust of their politics. While few would disagree with the list of reforms for which Stonewall claims to be working (anti-discrimination legisla-tion, equalization of the age of consent, partnership recogni-tion and acceptance of homosexuality in the armed forces, amongst others) the challenge which OutRage (and the section of lesbian and gay opinion which they represent) presents to society cannot be satisfied merely by a shopping list of reforms. The subversive energy which underlies the camp humour of gay nuns canonizing Derek Jarman, or the mass weddings of "queer" activists, challenges heterosexual institutions and gender roles. Chris Woods of OutRage at Charter 88's convention on constitutional reform, after rec-ognizing the need to "deal with oppression as it now exists" by "clear legal reforms which acknowledge our oppression as lesbians and gay men", also stressed the need for a broader perspective: "Concepts of sexual orientation, of lesbian and gay sexuality, of gender preference, must be replaced with a new model which acknowledges sexual diversity across per-ceived boundaries."

Despite its openly unaccountable nature, Stonewall's emphasis on equality and acceptance into existing institu-tions probably expresses the dominant mood amongst lesbi-ans and gays — we are after all part of the broader society, and these are not the radical 70s. However, in practice, to improve the position of the mass of lesbians and gays there will need to be broader and more fundamental changes — including increased legal protection for employees, fairer and non-racist immigration laws, a mass building programme of affordable housing, more self-determination for young people, an education system which genuinely promotes toleration of diversity and provides for the needs of its different pupils, protection from police abuse and local accountability of the police force and a good national health system.

This brings us to the third group, Act-Up. A direct action group, in the same mode as OutRage, it focuses on the issue of Aids. Undoubtedly the greatest set-back in recent years for both the lesbian and the gay communities has been the Aids epidemic and the virulent homophobia which it has fostered, particularly in the press. Act-Up fights these homophobic responses, but without ignoring the wider issues raised by Aids — the rights of prisoners to confidentiality, adequate care and access to outside help; patient control of medicine; the need for decent housing and state benefits for disabled people; and, of course for a decently funded NHS.

If gay men are left to die from Aids because they are viewed as bringing this punishment on themselves by their sordid lifestyle, and as intrinsically less valuable human beings, this is the most enormously important message concerning the status of lesbians and gays in society. This, and the life and death nature of the issue, makes the fight for funding to fight Aids and help those with the disease, a key issue for us all in the 90s.

* * *

Before continuing with the main body of text, a few words of explanation and warning. Firstly, this book offers an overview to enable readers to broadly understand their legal options in particular situations. It is not intended to replace good legal advice or specialized text books, and when appropriate you should consult these.

The Scottish legal system differs substantially from that in England and Wales. Wherever the laws of Scotland differ from those of England and Wales this is expressly indicated.

Unless there is such an indication you should assume that the law applies to all three countries.

We were unable to directly address the laws of Northern Ireland. However, while these do differ at some points from those of England and Wales, and therefore readers in Northern Ireland should check this out, the legal situation is broadly similar.

The text covers the situations of lesbians and gay men equally, and we indicate when the legal positions of lesbians and gays differ. (In general we use the term "gay" to refer specifically to gay men as opposed to lesbians.)

This book states the law as of August 1992. It is wise to check that no alterations have been made since this date.

EMPLOYMENT

Employment is an area in which lesbians and gays continue to suffer extensive discrimination. Many respond by hiding their sexuality, at the expense of considerable stress and a rigid division between work and private life. These who cannot or will not deny their identity frequently face victimization, harassment and even dismissal. The law unfortunately provides little protection. On the positive side, however, many unions are developing encouraging policies in relation to their lesbian and gay members.

LEGAL OVERVIEW

In British law employers are permitted to freely decide the terms of employment of their employees — except where legislation or case law provides specific protection or rights. There is no law which specifically bans discrimination on the basis of sexuality. Therefore, unless one of the legal protections described below applies, an employer can dismiss, refuse to employ or otherwise harass you simply because you are lesbian or gay.

The main protection in law for employees is against unfair dismissal, but this will only apply if you have been with the same employer for at least two years.

There is no adequate protection against forms of discrimination other than dismissal (e.g. harassment or lack of promotion). You may be able to seek legal protection in these situations by resigning and applying to an industrial tribunal on the basis that you have been "constructively dismissed", but this is a very risky course of action.

It may be that you have some protection under the Race Relations Act 1976 or Sex Discrimination Act 1975. These Acts do not require a minimum period of employment and so you could, for instance, bring a case if you felt your job application had been rejected for discriminatory reasons related to your race or sex. They provide protection from discrimination in all aspects of employment, including dismissal.

The only other legal remedy available is for breach of contract. However this usually provides very limited compensation.

We consider these remedies in the various sections below. The cases which we consider reveal that even these limited measures tend, in practice, to be enforced in the courts and tribunals in a way which favours the employers. Undoubtedly the most important lesson for lesbians and gays is to get into unions and work to strengthen your rights before trouble brews.

APPLYING FOR A JOB

As we state above, unless you can show that there has been discrimination on the basis of sex or race you will have no legal protection against employers who choose not to employ lesbians or gay men. If the employer has an equal opportunities policy, which includes lesbians and gays, then it may be possible to use this, either by getting the union involved to enforce the policy or possibly by claiming that the policy is a form of contract which the employer has breached. As far as we are aware this approach has not yet been tried in the courts.

We consider below two particularly common problem areas when applying for jobs — health and criminal records.

HEALTH

Employers will often ask you to consent to them contacting your doctor to check that you are healthy. You may be worried about this if your sexuality has been recorded on your medical records. However if you refuse access to your records you will almost certainly be rejected for the job.

Until recently you were not entitled to know the contents of medical reports to employers. However the Access to Medical Reports Act 1988 now provides a right of access to medical reports for employment (and also insurance) purposes. If you wish to take advantage of this right you should notify your doctor that you wish see the report and then contact him/her within 21 days to arrange access. You can then discuss with the doctor any amendments which you think are needed, although s/he is not obliged to make these. If you do not like the report you can refuse to allow the doctor to supply it, but that may well be the end of your job application.

In addition, the Access to Health Records Act 1990 enables individuals to request in writing access to their health records from any holder of such records. Applicants can ask for corrections to be made if they consider the record to be incomplete, misleading or incorrect. If the record holder refuses to make the requested alteration s/he is obliged to make a note of the information regarded to be inaccurate by the applicant, and to supply a copy of the note or alteration to the applicant. The chief restriction to the scope of this Act is that it will only apply to records kept after 1 November 1991. In addition, access to any part of the record can be denied where it may cause harm to the health of the patient.

This is a particularly serious problem for gay men because of the current Aids panic. Employers who become aware of their prospective employee's sexuality may well insist that he is tested for HIV, despite the fact that this is no measure of one's present health condition (see Aids chapter).

The story of Geoff Brighton will both illustrate the potential dangers and possible ways of fighting discriminatory employers. In 1980 Geoff Brighton applied for admittance to a Certificate of Education course and had to have a routine medical examination. He was passed but then recalled because they had realized that he was gay and wanted him to undergo a psychiatric examination before passing him as fit to teach. He refused and it was only after a year-long campaign that the University backed down, accepted him on the course and even added a clause to its Charter banning discrimination on the basis of sexual orientation. During the ordeal the National Union of Teachers refused to back Brighton on the basis that he was not a member at that time, but he did receive support from local NUT branches which contributed to his success.

In a similar case the National Council of Civil Liberties intervened on behalf of a gay applicant and lobbied the Polytechnic governing body, which eventually overruled an earlier decision to ban the student from teacher training because of his sexuality.

Therefore it seems that public pressure from campaigns and distinguished organizations can help overcome discrimination where employers are image-conscious and legal action may be unavailable or ineffective.

CRIMINAL RECORD? — REHABILITATION OF OFFENDERS ACT 1974

The criminalization of gay sexuality means that the common practice of employers asking whether a job applicant has any criminal convictions can pose serious problems for gay men. The Rehabilitation of Offenders Act provides some protection, since it states that after a certain period (which varies according to the seriousness of the penalty received) convictions do not need to be declared for employment purposes — they are said to be "spent".

If you receive a prison sentence of two-and-a-half years or more this must always be declared. A prison sentence which is less than this but more than six months is spent after ten years. Prison sentences of under six months are spent after seven years. A fine is spent after five years. A conditional discharge is spent one year after the end of the conditional discharge period. An absolute discharge is spent after six months. For young offenders under the age of 17 the time periods are slightly shorter.

The Act does not apply to certain occupations: doctors, lawyers, accountants, dentists, nurses, midwives, opticians, chemists, employees of the courts and prison services or insurance and trust companies, civil servants subject to positive vetting, some social workers and childcare workers. People applying to work with children and young people are particularly vulnerable to discrimination on the basis of criminal convictions. Not only are they almost invariably asked about their record, and obliged to report even "spent" convictions, but also the Department of Education and Science has a list (called "List 99") of people not allowed to be employed anywhere in Britain as teachers or youth workers. This list is not confined to people with convictions; it also includes people who merely have allegations of misconduct made against them. If the DES considers placing someone on List 99 that person has the right to make representations. It is worth exercising this right. According to NCCL in virtually every case where submissions were made the DES did not continue to include a person on the list.

There is yet another check available to certain statutory bodies: Social Services, Local Education Authorities, Regional/District Health Authorities and probation services. These bodies can check directly with police headquarters the criminal backgrounds of applicants for posts involving substantial contact with young children. They must have the written permission of the applicants but refusal to give this consent will mean that you will not be appointed. The police list includes not only all convictions, spent or otherwise but also any bind-overs or bye-law offences (see Crime chapter).

UNFAIR DISMISSAL

The law against unfair dismissal only protects full-time employees who have been with their employer continuously for two years, and part-timers (working more than eight but under 16 hours a week) if they have been with their employer continuously for five years. (A note of warning: you may think that you are an employee but legally you may be termed self-employed for the purpose of this legislation. If in doubt, take legal advice.)

CONSTRUCTIVE DISMISSAL

The term unfair dismissal is a bit misleading, because a claim can also, in some circumstances, be made if you have resigned because of the unfair way in which you were being treated at work. The legal term for this is "constructive dismissal". It could be that the employer has changed the fundamental terms of your contract, or that you were being harassed so much that it was not possible for you to continue working. In these circumstances you may be able to claim that the employer made or allowed the situation to become so bad that you had no choice but to resign and that s/he has effectively "dismissed" you unfairly. However, because such claims can be difficult to win, it is essential to take legal or union advice before you resign.

PROVING UNFAIR DISMISSAL

Your case will be heard at an Industrial Tribunal. Here three people (a lawyer, a union representative and one of employers) will decide your case. The proceedings are supposed to be more informal than court proceedings.

The law requires you to prove that the dismissal was unfair but, in practice, once you have shown that you were dismissed, the employer must prove that you were dismissed for a reason which the law regards as fair and also that a reasonable employer would have regarded this reason as sufficiently serious to justify dismissal. If s/he fails to show this, then the dismissal was unfair.

For the employer's reason to be accepted in law as justifying dismissal it must fall into one of the following categories:

- a reason related to the employee's capacity (i.e. skill, aptitude or health)
- conduct
- redundancy

- employer cannot continue to employ the worker without being in breach of a statutory requirement
- some other substantial reason.

The employer then has to show that in the particular circumstances the decision to dismiss was one which a reasonable employer might have made. This is quite different from having to show that the decision was fair. Tribunals will look at all the circumstances of the dismissal, including the contract of employment and whether any disciplinary or grievance procedures were followed. If there are no agreed procedures the tribunal will usually take the ACAS Code of Practice 1977 as a guide to good practice. They will also take into account the size and administrative resources of the employer.

If the tribunal decides that the dismissal was unfair it can order that the employer reinstate you but may just order that s/he pay you compensation. On average the compensation tends to be quite low but on occasion it can amount to several thousand pounds.

If the employer refuses to reinstate you the tribunal cannot force him/her to do so. It can merely award more compensation.

PROCEDURE

You need to apply to the Industrial Tribunal on form IT1 (available from your union or local Job Centre). You must apply within three months of being dismissed. This time limit is strictly adhered to. Although it is technically possible for you to conduct your own case, it is very important to get as much help and legal advice as possible. Although legal aid is not available to pay for a solicitor to represent you at the tribunal, you may be entitled to legal advice under the Green Form Scheme, depending on your financial resources (see Legal Aid chapter).

You should always try to get your union to back you. It will also be useful to contact Lesbian and Gay Employment Rights (LAGER) or Lesbian Employment Rights (LER) as they specialize in giving advice on this topic. They can discuss tactics with you and, if it seems helpful, may help you co-ordinate a campaign. If you have a local law centre or Citizens Advice Bureau you should contact them.

The Industrial Tribunal can order a pre-hearing assessment to test the strengths of both sides' cases. This will be a mini-hearing at which the main lines of argument and disputed facts will be outlined. This can work in favour of the employee. In Ray Moore's case, discussed further below, the tribunal indicated at an assessment that it was likely to decide against the employers, who then agreed to settle.

If you lose your case at the Industrial Tribunal you can appeal (within 42 days of the receipt of the decision) to the Employment Appeal Tribunal, but only if you can argue that the law was misinterpreted, not just because you think the tribunal got the facts wrong. You may be entitled to legal aid for the appeal.

THE LAW IN PRACTICE

The decisions of one Industrial Tribunal do not have to be consistent with those of other tribunals — in legal jargon they are said not to create "binding precedents". However tribunals do have to follow the guidelines for interpreting the law set out in the decisions of the EATs. The 1980 case of John Saunders (see below), where an Industrial Tribunal upheld the dismissal of a man who worked in the proximity of young people solely on the basis that he was gay, is a particularly important case because it was decided by an EAT.

However each case is always supposed to be looked at on its own particular set of facts. So do not despair if your case seems exactly like one which has lost! You may still have a good chance of success. For example, when Ray Moore was sacked from his job as a training officer in May 1988, after being convicted of gross indecency, the bare facts seemed similar to the Saunders case. Nevertheless his employers gave him a substantial out of court settlement ("a four figure sum"). Because this settlement was "out of court" it does not create a precedent for other tribunals, but is clearly encouraging for gays and lesbians.

All too often tribunals have accepted that employers need

just look at the general characteristics supposedly pertaining to "homosexuals", rather than looking at the characteristics of the particular individual involved. Nevertheless they are supposed to follow the latter approach and it is generally worth stressing the particular merits of the individual rather than allowing yourself to become caught up in abstract arguments.

This was the basis on which Mr Davies won his case (Davies v. L.B. Tower Hamlets 1976, unreported). He was a senior social worker with 12 years excellent work record who was sacked after a conviction for gross indecency. The tribunal said that the conviction was not enough to justify the dismissal of someone with Davies' work record.

The other aspect to which you should pay close attention is whether your employer has followed the correct procedure. This is discussed in more detail below but it should be stressed that cases can be won because of procedural irregularities which would not succeed on the tribunal's assessment of the merits of the ultimate decision.

Conduct — working with children

Many of the cases which have gone to tribunal have concerned men who have been convicted of sexual offences. In some cases the police have contacted the employer direct, in others press publicity has alerted the employer. The employer is entitled to dismiss someone on the basis of his/her "conduct" (even where the alleged conduct took place outside work hours) provided it has some impact on the employer's business (e.g. reputation of the firm).

The other common feature of many cases going to the Industrial Tribunal is that the employee was working with children. This need not even be part of the job description in order for the tribunal to regard it as a relevant consideration. One leading case involved John Saunders who was a maintenance man in a camp ground where young adults stayed (Saunders v. Scottish National Camps Association Ltd 1981 IRLR). When his boss discovered that he was gay he was sacked. At the tribunal the employer argued that because he was gay he represented a threat to young people — the sexual predator/child molester stereotype which is unfortunately widespread. The tribunal accepted that "whether that view is scientifically sound may be open to question." However they considered that it was, nevertheless, a commonly held view, and one in which this employer genuinely believed. That was enough to convince them to uphold the dismissal.

In Mr Wiseman's case (Wiseman v. Salford C.C. 1981 IRLR) the tribunal's decision spelt out this biased approach even more clearly. They said that the question before them was not whether someone who had been convicted of gross indecency was a threat to the young adults that he was lecturing, but whether the argument that he was not a risk was a "self-evident proposition". They concluded that it was a highly controversial subject and went on to say: "In our judgement the disciplinary bodies, and the majority of the Industrial Tribunals, are not making a error of law if they do not accept that view but conclude that there was a risk. Short of the proposition being self-evidently right then it is for the Industrial Tribunal to evaluate the reasonableness of the employer's action in treating Mr Wiseman's conduct as a reason for dismissal in the circumstances, having regard to equity and the substantial merits of the case."

"Having regard to the merits of the case" is precisely what neither the employers nor the tribunal appear to have done in Mr Wiseman's case. He was a highly respected lecturer with a national reputation as a leader in his field who was dismissed for conduct which took place outside his employment and had no bearing on his capacity to perform his job.

Teachers should also see the chapter on Section 28 (page 290) for the effect the law has on what it is permissible to teach, and for a case where a teacher successfully sued for unfair dismissal and was awarded £12,000 damages — only to have the case overturned on appeal.

Public prejudice

The tribunal in the Wiseman case also felt that the employer was entitled to take into account the possible prejudiced reactions of the young people's parents. It has been established in cases not involving gay workers that customer prejudice and fears can legitimately be taken into account by an employer if they are likely to have a strong impact on his/her business. However, considerations of the impact on the employer's business must be weighed against the degree of unfairness to the employee — such factors as the individual's service to the firm, their work record, whether or not they are "to blame" in some way for provoking public prejudice (sexual offences generally being regarded as blameworthy) and any difficulties they might have in obtaining another job — must also be taken into account.

In practice there have been cases where the tribunal did not even require any evidence that clients actually held these views, merely accepting the employer's assertions, and sometimes even ignoring evidence to the contrary. In a case which did not actually reach a tribunal a bus driver/conductor was suspended without pay for wearing a badge reading "Lesbians Liberation". She had never received any complaints but when an inspector noticed the badge she was suspended without pay for refusing to remove it. She collected a petition of 1,000 passenger signatures in her support. But the company refused to alter their decision. She might have had a good chance of success at the tribunal but did not take it that far. Many other employees with strong cases against their employers do not take them to the tribunal for reasons varying from fear of publicity, particularly as it might effect future job prospects, to intimidation and lack of faith in the remedies offered by the law.

Co-workers

Some gay and lesbian workers have been dismissed, and their dismissals upheld as fair by the Industrial Tribunal, because of the antagonism of their co-workers. The rationale is that conflict within the workforce can disrupt the smooth running of the business. Where this is the case, and if the person being harassed is regarded as in some sense to blame, then the tribunal will accept that the employer is justified in dismissing him/her. However the tribunal would normally expect an employer to attempt first to defuse tension in the workforce and also to consider alternatives such as moving the employee to another position before dismissing him/her.

This approach was spelt out by the tribunal in McCormack v. TNT Sealion Ltd (Central London IT Case). The employer selected Mr McCormack for redundancy because his fellow workers objected to his presence on the pretext that he was gay and that they were afraid of "catching" Aids.

Despite upholding the employer's decision the tribunal made a statement describing good employment practice which may be helpful to other employees facing a similar threat. "The innuendo behind the complaints of lack of personal hygiene is that Mr McCormack was a homosexual and suspected carrier of the Aids virus and this led to an unjustified and emotional reaction against him by the Chief Officer. This is a problem that is likely to arise with increasing frequency and a good employer who is fair to his employees must be seen to act promptly to lay at rest all unfounded suspicions. He has an obligation to safeguard the health and safety of his employees on the one hand which must be balanced against his obligations to deal fairly with the individual employee on the other."

The tribunal stated that to dismiss purely on the basis of an unfounded complaint from the workforce linking a gay man with Aids, without proper investigation would be "plainly unfair". They specified that they upheld the dismissal because the degree to which a worker got on with the rest of the workforce was a relevant consideration in deciding who should be selected first for redundancy. They went further and said that it was also significant that the man was employed on a ship; had he been a sales representative, or a shop floor worker where good working relationships were less significant, then it might not have been reasonable to attach such weight to this factor in making the selection.

Employers should be encouraged to tackle the problem at the source, by taking firm action against homophobic employees rather than blaming the victim of harassment. In one such case an employer's decision to sack two employees for victimizing a gay employee as an alleged "Aids carrier" was upheld (Philpott v. North Lambeth Law Centre). (We should add that there were other reasons which the tribunal accepted as fair for this dismissal.)

National security

Lesbians and gay men have traditionally been seen as security risks, both because of infamous figures such as Guy Burgess and Anthony Blunt, and because lesbians and gays are supposedly vulnerable to blackmail. Security clearance is required for a wide range of jobs within the civil service, and used to be routinely denied on the basis of homosexuality. When Andrew Hodge informed his employers at the Government Communications Headquarters that he was gay they immediately removed his security clearance. He appealed to the High Court to quash this decision, arguing that because he was open about his sexuality the basis for blackmail had been removed. GCHQ acknowledged that the risk of blackmail was slight but said they were worried about the frequency of his relationships (four) and his lifestyle (he visited gay clubs). The judge praised Andrew Hodge for his honesty but ruled that the courts were not entitled to review this decision because it concerned questions of national security.

However in 1991 the trade union for senior civil servants (the First Division Association) managed to lift the ban on lesbians and gays in the intelligence services. In a written answer to a Parliamentary question the Prime Minister said that homosexuality would no longer be a bar to being employed in government jobs involving access to classified information. Susceptibility to blackmail remains a factor in security vetting, but this should be assessed in a similar fashion as for heterosexuals.

Other reasons

Sometimes the reasons given by employers for their actions are not overtly homophobic, but nevertheless reflect a strong prejudice against lesbians and gays. Lesbian Employment Rights were contacted by a woman working in a hostel. She was sacked when she started having a relationship with another lesbian who was living in the hostel. Her managers refused to see their actions as anti-lesbian, insisting that the employee had been unprofessional in "taking advantage" of the other woman who they felt was "vulnerable". The hostel resident objected to being labelled by the management in this way. She had a strong lesbian identity and also worked in a voluntary organization. Both women were prepared to undertake not to have a relationship before the resident moved out of the hostel. However the management did not settle until they had been taken to an Industrial Tribunal. They then agreed to pay £300 in compensation.

GRIEVANCE PROCEDURES

If you have been sacked it is vitally important to investigate whether the employer has any disciplinary procedure laid down. If s/he does, the tribunal will look carefully to see whether the employer has complied with these procedures. If s/he has not then the tribunal will measure up their actions against the ACAS Code of Practice on Disciplinary Practice and Procedure.

If an employee is dismissed without the proper consultation procedures then this will almost certainly lead to a finding of unfair dismissal, even if the employer shows that it was likely that such a meeting would have made no difference. It is only if consultation would have been utterly useless, such as where a firm is insolvent, that a dismissal might be upheld. This principle was established by the House of Lords in 1987 (Polkey v. Drayton Services Ltd.).

Michael Buck, a cinema projectionist, was sacked after his second conviction for a cottaging offence because of his colleagues' fears that he might "have Aids". Initially the tribunal upheld this decision because they argued that Michael Buck, who was "out" at work, realized what the attitudes of his colleagues would be if they also knew that he was engaged in "promiscuous sex". He appealed against the decision and his employers conceded the case, as it was clear that there had been no discussions with him nor any attempt to resolve difficulties before dismissing him. The initial hearing took place before the House of Lords' decision (mentioned above) and the settlement was reached after it, which helps point out the significance of the principles set out in that case.

RACE AND SEX DISCRIMINATION

You may face prejudice based on race or sex as well as homophobia. If this is the case you can take proceedings against your employer under the Race Relations Act 1976 or Sex Discrimination Act 1975. Unlike the rules concerning protection against unfair dismissal, you do not need to have been employed for a minimum amount of time before becoming entitled to protection; indeed you are entitled to protection if you feel that you have not been offered employment because of your race or your sex.

The only time limit that you need to watch out for is the rule that you must apply within three months of the last discriminatory act against which you are complaining. You need to apply on form IT1 to the Industrial Tribunal, in the same way as for unfair dismissal. It would be advisable to contact your union, the Equal Opportunities Commission or the Commission for Racial Equality for assistance. They may fund your case or even undertake their own investigation. At the very least they can provide you with useful advice and case law. Otherwise if you have a local law centre or citizen's advice centre contact them. If you are within the financial limits, you will be entitled to advice, but not representation from a solicitor under the legal advice and assistance scheme.

WHAT IS THE LEGAL DEFINITION OF RACIAL OR SEXUAL DISCRIMINATION?

In law sexual or racial discrimination can be either direct or indirect.

Direct Discrimination

You need to show that less favourable treatment has occurred (for example, being denied promotion or access to benefits and services) and that the reason for this less favourable treatment is your sex or race.

Indirect discrimination

You may be able to show that although, on the face of it, a requirement stipulated by the employer applies equally to men and women, or to people of different races, in practice the proportion of women, or people from racial minorities, who can meet the condition is substantially less than the number of men or white people who can meet it.

If women or people from ethnic minorities are put at a disadvantage because they cannot meet the condition, and the employers cannot show that the condition is justified, then this is indirect discrimination and illegal.

Men can also bring cases under the Sex Discrimination Act in appropriate circumstances. Dan-Air, the airline, had a policy not to employ male stewards. Their rationale for this was that male stewards would be likely to be gay, and therefore a high risk group for Aids. The Equal Opportunities Commission took them to the Industrial Tribunal and had the policy overturned.

Sexual or racial harassment can also legally constitute discrimination, if, in the tribunal's consideration, it is serious enough. Harassment from fellow workers as well as from the employer can constitute unlawful discrimination, if the tribunal decides that the employer did not take sufficient steps to prevent it.

You can take proceedings for racial discrimination at the same time as for sexual discrimination or unfair dismissal.

WRONGFUL DISMISSAL

Even if you cannot claim the legal remedies set out above, you may still be able to sue your employer in the courts, where proceedings are more formal than in the Industrial Tribunal, for breach of your employment contract. The proceedings and grounds for "wrongful dismissal" are completely different from those required for "unfair dismissal" claims. The most significant difference is that there is no minimum period of employment required before you are entitled to claim. You will need legal advice on your particular circumstances, but in broad terms if your employer has sacked you without the right amount of notice or still owes you holiday pay then you may be entitled to compensation.

The amount of compensation to which you will be entitled is unlikely to be large unless you have a fixed term contract. There are two types of contract — those which will expire on a fixed date, specified when you enter into the employment contract, and the more common type which can be ended by either the employer or the employee giving a period of notice. If you do not have a fixed date for ending work and there is no period of notice specified in your employment contract then the law will imply a right to a fixed amount of notice. The length of this implied notice period will vary according to how long you have been in your job — one week for every year of employment up to a maximum of 12 weeks, with a minimum of one week.

DEFENDING YOUR JOB

It will only be a minority of those discriminated against because of their sexuality who can, or will want to, go to a tribunal. The application to the tribunal will generally take months rather than weeks to be heard. As we have seen, the tribunals themselves often have prejudiced attitudes, which make it harder for gay and lesbian employees to win. You may not get back your job, even if you win. There may be quite a lot of publicity, which might make it harder for you to get another job.

Having said this, a worker who takes his/her employer to the tribunal, is a warning to other employers even if s/he loses. Most employers do not like legal proceedings or bad publicity.

We want to stress that the time to start changing things and making your job more secure is before any trouble starts; it may help avoid the need to go to a tribunal, and in any event will undoubtedly help your case if you do have to bring one.

The Davies case is an example of the importance of

building support in your workplace and union. Although the tribunal ordered Mr Davies' reinstatement the employers at first refused. However, supportive strike action made them change their minds.

PRACTICAL WAYS TO PROTECT YOUR JOB

Join your union

Members should push for unions to take equal opportunities seriously. This means equal opportunities for people from ethnic minorities, women and people with disabilities as well as lesbians and gays. A united front is vital, and many of us are affected by more than one form of discrimination.

Great progress has been made by lesbians and gays in getting unions to take our rights seriously. In 1991 the Labour Research Department found that 21 out of the 25 unions which it surveyed included sexual orientation in their equal opportunities statements or had specific policies on lesbian and gay rights. Some of these unions are also beginning valuable campaigns to extend to gay and lesbian partners the same benefits and services which are available to heterosexual partners. If your local branch does not seem co-operative you should contact the national office to see if there is a lesbian and gay group (see Listings).

Unions can sometimes help sort out harassment from fellow workers. An explicit union policy of support can help warn off employers from harassment and unions may even be able to negotiate an equal opportunities policy from employers. They can also negotiate with an employer over a threatened dismissal and represent you at the tribunal.

Read your contract

With a few exceptions employers are obliged to give workers a written statement of the main terms of their employment. Check whether your employers have an equal opportunities statement, and if so whether it includes lesbians and gays. If not you may be able to get your union to take this up.

Act on the first signs of trouble

a) Discuss the problem with the shop steward. LAGER or LER are always willing to chat over a problem, even if it has not become very serious yet. Always check your employment rights before taking any action.

b) If discussing the problem with your employer and the union does not help you might contact the Equal Opportunities Commission or the Commission for Racial Equality if relevant.

c) Keep a written record of incidents or events, as this can be useful at disciplinary hearings or tribunals.

d) Follow through any disciplinary or grievance procedures (look at any agreements with the union, the staff handbook or contract of employment). If there are none try to get the ACAS Code of Practice 1977 implemented, as the employers should follow this. Use all negotiating forums to impress on the employer the seriousness of the situation.

e) If you are dismissed ask for written reasons for the decision — this is very important. Provided that you have been with your employers for two years they are obliged to give you written reasons for your dismissal within 14 days of your request and are obliged to pay you compensation if they fail to do so. Employers quite frequently try to bring in spurious reasons at a later date when they realize that their real reason is not legally valid. They are not allowed to do this, and must defend the dismissal in front of a tribunal on the basis of their reasons at the time of the dismissal.

f) Campaign! If the issue is sufficiently serious (i.e. dismissal) consider launching a campaign to publicize the injustice. Always keep the union as involved as possible.

g) Get legal advice either from your union, a local law centre or a recommended and sympathetic solicitor. You can represent yourself or have a friend represent you but it is best to have someone who know the legal complexities.

h) Union action — such as a walkout, a threat of non-co-operation or strike — can be pursued at the same time as legal proceedings, and can be a valuable back-up to them.

i) If you do end up at an Industrial Tribunal, you should always check to see whether you can show any breach of the disciplinary rules or grievance procedures by your employer. For instance, you should know the nature of the charge being made against you, and have the chance to put your case to your employer, before any final decision to dismiss is made. Another possible line of attack, if you think that the dismissal is due to your sexuality, is to show that this is irrelevant to your job. Try to get the support of your colleagues at work, and if possible the company's clients.

j) Even if you cannot claim the legal remedies set out above — unfair dismissal, sexual or racial discrimination — consider suing your employer for breach of contract in the civil courts.

ARMED FORCES AND MERCHANT NAVY

If you are discovered to be lesbian or gay this will lead to your automatic discharge from the armed forces. In June 1992, the Ministry of Defence announced that "homosexuality in the armed forces" would no longer be a crime. Previously sex for lesbian and gay members of the armed forces could lead to imprisonment as "disgraceful conduct of an indecent kind." About ten people a year were imprisoned for this offence. The Ministry stressed that this was a "tidying up" measure, to bring the military law into line with the civil law, and that "homosexual activity" would still lead to an automatic discharge from the forces.

About 100 people a year have been discharged from the services because of their sexuality. Despite the fact that they will no longer face the threat of criminal charges, or a "dishonourable" discharge, lesbians and gays in the armed forces will continue to suffer gross discrimination.

HOUSING

The housing options for lesbians and gay men, particularly for those who are young and/or unemployed, are often very limited. In recent years, Tory attacks on public housing have created a crisis of homelessness, and increased lesbian and gay dependence on the private sector. With restricted access to public housing and insufficient resources for buying property, most single people (and therefore many lesbians and gays) have historically lived in the private rented sector. This has been the worst housing sector in terms of security and standards of accommodation. It is likely to get worse with the recent changes in housing law (some of which we mention below) which overwhelmingly favour landlords.

Within this general picture of gloom there are some disparate signs of progress, as some local authorities and housing associations begin to address the needs of lesbians and gays by, for instance, providing protection from harassment, rehousing partners upon the break-up of relationships and extending the right to inherit a tenancy (legally conferred only on heterosexuals) to lesbian and gay partners. These practices provide models which need to be struggled for nationally.

OBTAINING HOUSING

We discuss the particular problems of lesbians and gays who live together in owner-occupied property in the second half of this chapter, but first we consider housing options for those who cannot afford to buy. Tory attacks on local authority housing provisions have restricted the availability of council housing so that in many areas you will only be rehoused if you come within the categories of people which they are legally obliged to house (see section on Homeless, below). Even if you do not fit into one of these categories it may be worth applying to the local authority, as in some areas of the country local authorities do have more vacancies, and therefore more flexible policies.

If the local council are not prepared to house you it may be helpful for you to contact local housing associations, as these provide good quality housing at reasonable rents. Local Housing Advice Centres should be able to advise you on both the local authority's policies and those of local housing associations. You can get their address from the telephone directory or Citizens Advice Bureau. If all else fails you could consider squatting, and we set out the legal implications of this below.

LOCAL AUTHORITIES' DUTY TO PROVIDE HOUSING

The Housing Act 1985 gives local authorities a duty to house people if they are "homeless and in priority need", provided that they are "not intentionally homeless" and that they have a "local connection" with that particular area (or no local connection with another housing authority in the United Kingdom — a provision which refers to recent immigrants. But there are many complications involved in such circumstances, and you should seek specialist advice). We will consider these different terms below.

If you fail to qualify under this definition the local authority will only be obliged to provide you with "advice and assistance", which nowadays may not amount to much. If you satisfy these conditions apart from the fact that the council considers that you are intentionally homeless then the local authority should provide you with temporary accommodation.

HOMELESS

You will be considered homeless if you have no legal right to stay in accommodation or if there is no accommodation in which it is reasonable for you to reside. If the physical conditions are extremely poor then the council might agree that it was not reasonable for you to live there, but be warned: the standards which have been considered reasonable by the courts are unbelievably low. If you are suffering violence or serious harassment the council may accept that you satisfy this condition, but many local authorities will insist that you exhaust all legal remedies (see Life, Love and Other Problems chapter) before they will accept you on this basis. You may be able to argue that it is not reasonable for you to stay in the accommodation because of your particular circumstances — possibly a medical condition or perhaps that the accommodation is prohibitively expensive.

The local authority must also consider whether the accommodation is reasonable for your cohabitant to live, but only if they accept that either s/he is "a member of your family" or that it is reasonable for you to live together. Most local authorities will not accept that it is reasonable for you to live with your gay or lesbian partner, despite the fact that they would always accept that it was reasonable to live with a husband or wife.

You do not have to be literally homeless in order to apply. You can also apply if you have been threatened with homelessness. If you are staying with family or friends it may be difficult to persuade the council that you cannot continue to live there. They may ask for written proof that the regular occupier of the home has asked you to leave. It is wisest to co-operate or they will probably decide that you are not really threatened with homelessness.

Sometimes local authorities will insist on your friend/family getting a court order for possession against you before they will accept that you are homeless. If they try to insist on this provision you should consult legal advice because in nearly all cases no possession order is legally required either to end the right you had to share with your friends or family, or to establish that you are legally homeless. Most courts would not approve of local authorities forcing parents to take court action against their children, however the situation may be more complicated if you have been living with a friend or lover.

PRIORITY NEED

Only certain narrow categories of persons are legally considered as having a "priority need" for housing. If you are caring for a child you will be accepted as having a priority need for housing, otherwise you must convince the council that you are particularly vulnerable in the context of housing. This normally means that age or physical or mental disability makes finding and keeping adequate housing more difficult. If you are trying to establish your need for housing on this basis you will need good medical evidence. Some, but not all, councils accept HIV-positive people under this category (see Aids chapter).

If people with physical or mental disabilities apply for re-housing they are entitled to accommodation for themselves and anyone else with whom it is reasonable to live. If you have been or intend to provide care which is essential for such a person then you should be rehoused with them.

Some local authorities accept that young people leaving care are vulnerable and the official Code of Guidance states that this term should include "homeless young people who are at risk of sexual or financial exploitation". It will be hard to convince the local authority that you are "vulnerable" on any other grounds.

Intentionally homeless

This refers to a situation where the local authority claims that you have brought your homelessness on yourself. You may face difficulties if you have had to leave your family or some other shared accommodation because of other people's hostility to your sexuality. The local authority may insist that you are "intentionally homeless" unless you can convince them of the seriousness of the harassment. This is a very contentious area of the law and you should seek specialist legal advice if you are having problems.

LOCAL CONNECTION

A local connection is established by length of residence or
employment in an area or if you have strong family connections in the area. One problem for lesbians or gay men may
be that the local authority will not accept gay or lesbian
lovers or friends as being in effect the family of lesbians and
gays, who may of course have been rejected by their "natural"
family.

If you think you may qualify as homeless check first with a local advice agency.

They will be able to give you further information about your
particular situation, the policies of the local council and
indeed the address and opening hours of the appropriate
council offices.

How long will a decision take and what will happen in the meantime?

The length of time will vary according to the local authority
and on the extent of enquiries which they are conducting to
satisfy themselves that they are under a duty to house you.
If you are already homeless and appear to be in priority need
the local authority will have to provide you with temporary
accommodation while they make a decision. This may be a
hostel or bed and breakfast accommodation. Even if they
accept that they have a duty to provide you with permanent
accommodation it may take them some time to do so and you
will have to wait in temporary accommodation.

If you are turned down seek advice about taking the matter further.

This can be done through either the council's own procedures
or the courts. (There is no automatic right to appeal to a court.
For court action to be considered you would need to show that
the local authority had misinterpreted the law.)

SQUATTING

The term "squatting" refers to people who occupy empty property without the consent of the owners of that property. In England and Wales, squatting in itself is usually not a criminal offence unless you use force to enter the building or have an offensive weapon with you. You will also be committing an offence if you refuse to leave when asked to do so by a "displaced residential occupier" (i.e. someone who was living in the house immediately before you occupied it). Similarly it is an offence not to leave when requested to do so by a "protected intending occupier", or someone acting on his/her behalf. This means someone who either owns the premises and is planning to live in them or who is a prospective tenant of the premises (but in this case the landlord must be a local authority, housing association or trust). These last two offences will only be committed if the person requesting you to leave has shown you a statement indicating that they are a protected intending occupier.

If any of the above situations apply the owner or prospective occupier may be able to get the police to assist him or her in evicting/arresting you. If none of the above situations apply then you have not committed a criminal offence. The landlord does not have to get a court order to evict you but s/he will commit an offence if s/he attempts to use force or threats of force against you or your property in order to evict you. This means that eviction while all of the squatters are out of the premises will be legal. Otherwise the owner of the property will need to go to court before evicting you. There is a procedure relating specifically to squatters which enables the owner to get an order very quickly. If a bailiff is evicting you as the result of one of these court orders you will commit an offence if you obstruct or attempt to obstruct him/her.

In Scotland, squatting is a criminal offence under the Trespass (Scotland) Act 1865, and criminal charges are brought against squatters from time to time. Further, as in England and Wales, squatters have no protection against eviction by the owner of the property, although it is a criminal offence for the owner of the property to use excessive force, or threats of excessive force, to evict you. S/he is probably entitled to use "reasonable" force.

Squatting can provide temporary accommodation if you have no other alternative — it is likely to be particularly successful if the property is owned by a local authority or housing association which is intending to redevelop the property but it is lying empty until they have obtained sufficient funds to do so.

RENTED ACCOMMODATION

We do not attempt to consider here the very detailed laws governing rented accommodation. Instead, after a brief consideration of problems of discrimination and harassment, we consider the particular problems facing lesbian and gay couples who are living together.

Can a landlord refuse to rent to me because I am gay?

The short answer is yes, landlords are entitled to choose their tenants on whatever basis they choose unless the refusal is on account of racial or sexual discrimination, in which case you will be protected under the Race Relations Act 1976 or the Sex Discrimination Act 1975.

Harassment from the landlord

If a landlord (or someone on the landlord's behalf) evicts or attempts to evict you without a court order then this is a crime, unless you have an "excluded tenancy" which has come to an end. Probably the most common category of "excluded tenancy" is where accommodation is shared with your landlord. It will be worth investigating your rights even in this situation.

You should immediately report the offence to the Tenancy Relations Officer of the local authority, whose job it is to prosecute private landlords. You should also consult a solicitor as you will probably be able to apply for a court order (injunction, or interdict in Scotland) forcing the landlord to allow you back into the building. You may also be able to get an order stopping him/her from harassing or attempting to evict you in the future, as well as compensation for any losses which you have incurred or hardship which you have suffered because of your landlord's action.

Harassment with a view to persuading you to leave your tenancy or give up any other sort of right (for instance to stop you complaining about disrepair) is also a crime. Harassment in this context is anything that is intended to interfere with your peace and comfort, or that of the other occupants of your household. Even if you cannot show that your landlord committed his/her action with this specific intent, an offence will still have been committed if the landlord has reason to believe that the harassment is likely to make you quit or give up the exercise of a right. Once again you should contact the Tenancy Relations Officer of the local authority as well as consulting a solicitor about obtaining an injunction/interdict and possibly compensation from your landlord.

Harassment which does not fall into the above definition may not be a crime but you may still be able to sue for an injunction/interdict and compensation because your contract to live in the premises always has an implied term that you should be allowed peaceful enjoyment of them, and by harassing you your landlord will be in breach of contract.

Trouble with the neighbours

The remedies for violence and harassment are outlined in general terms in the Life, Love and Other Problems chapter. If you are having trouble with your neighbours you may be able to apply for an injunction (or interdict in Scotland) to stop them on the grounds of "nuisance" and/or "trespass". In order to take action for trespass your neighbours must have intruded onto your property, while nuisance may be committed without physical intrusion — perhaps by noise or verbal abuse or threats.

Other remedies may be available if the people who are harassing are also tenants of your landlord. Your landlord may be able to bring possession proceedings or apply for an injunction against them because most tenancies include clauses in which tenants promise not to cause "nuisance". It will probably only be local authorities or housing associations who will be prepared to take such action on their tenants' behalf.

If you are living in council or housing association accommodation, and suffering severe harassment you may be able to persuade your landlords to give you a transfer to another property.

LIVING TOGETHER IN RENTED ACCOMMODATION

The chief legal problems that arise through living together occur when a couple split up or when one partner dies. Here the situation will vary according to whether the property is owned by a private or public sector landlord, what sort of an agreement there is with the landlord (i.e. whether it is a licence or a tenancy, and what sort of a tenancy it is) and what sort of arrangement the couple have between themselves (i.e. are they joint tenants or if only one of them is a tenant is the other a sub-tenant or a licensee?). The law in this area is incredibly complex and changes fairly frequently. This brief section is therefore intended only as a rough guide and you should consult a legal adviser if you are actually experiencing difficulties.

Licences and leases

The distinction between a lease and a licence is complex and has very important effects. If you and your lover have exclusive occupation of at least part of your home then this will probably mean that you have a lease rather than a licence. Conversely, if there is no part of the home to which you have exclusive right then this will be a licence — for instance, if you share a bedroom with your "landlord".

The term "licence" is not often used in Scotland in the context of residential housing, although in practice the distinction between people with the benefit of a lease and those without is the same as in England.

If you live together under a licence this is essentially a personal relationship between you and the landlord. The law provides few extra rights. Thus if you are both licensees (i.e. both of you have agreements with the owner) then what happens in the event of one of you dying or the relationship splitting up will largely depend on the terms of the agreement and, in the absence of prior agreement, on the desires of the owner of the property. If only one of you has a licence from the owner then the other member of the couple will have no right to stay if the relationship ends or if the licensee dies (apart from a "reasonable" period of time to find somewhere else to go). The rest of this section only applies it you have a tenancy rather than a licence.

Security of tenure

In very many cases the landlord does not have the power to end your tenancy at will. S/he must go to court and establish that certain circumstances (known technically as "grounds") exist (for example, that you are in rent arrears) and get an order before s/he is able to make you leave. Your protection against your landlord ending your occupation of the premises is known as "security of tenure". The laws concerning security of tenure are very complicated, and therefore we will not attempt to outline the different types of security that exist or the different grounds which a landlord must establish before getting a court order.

Basically your landlord must always get a court order before evicting you unless s/he shares the accommodation with you. If your landlord is trying to make you leave the premises get legal advice immediately.

In the sections below we discuss the rights of the couple when splitting up or if one of them dies. In these situations the joint-tenant, sub-tenant or licensee can only inherit a tenancy subject to existing restrictions. Thus if the landlord has a possession order against the tenant, any sub-tenants or licensees will also be evicted. Similarly if one joint tenant has committed a breach of the tenancy on the basis of which the landlord can claim possession, then s/he is entitled to evict both tenants.

Splitting up

If you live with your lover in rented accommodation the tenancy can either be in both your names (a "joint" tenancy) or in only one of your names. This distinction will affect the person who has the right to remain in the property. Often the situation will be clear (e.g. if you move into someone else's flat and s/he continues to have all the dealings with the landlord). However if you move in together or you take over responsibility for dealing with the landlord then it may be possible to establish that you are joint tenants. On the other hand, if there is a rent book or written agreement in one person's name it will be difficult to establish a joint tenancy. If in doubt get legal advice.

Joint tenants

If you are joint tenants neither of you can force the other to leave; you both have a right to be there. If one of you wants to leave s/he will still be liable for rent unless the tenancy is ended. If the tenancy is for a fixed period of time then one person cannot surrender (end) their share of the tenancy, you both must do this and the landlord must accept the ending of the tenancy. Obviously the remaining tenant will not want to do this unless the landlord is willing to grant a new tenancy on equally favourable terms. If you are in this situation you should take legal advice before surrendering the tenancy, as many new tenancies have less legal rights than previous ones.

If your tenancy is not for a fixed period of time (such tenancies do not exist in Scotland) then one person alone can give notice to the landlord that s/he intends to leave; this will then end the whole joint tenancy. The other tenant will only be entitled to stay if s/he can get a new tenancy agreement with the landlord. If you wish to leave a joint tenancy you should ensure that before doing so you end your part of the tenancy with the landlord, otherwise you will continue to be liable for the rent and for any other breaches of the tenancy conditions which the remaining tenant commits.

Sole tenants

If only one member of the couple is a tenant then the other partner is either a subtenant or a licensee. This is a complicated area of law and you will need legal advice to determine your exact status.

If you share meals and living accommodation aside from the bathroom (as do most couples living together) the arrangement is almost certainly a licence rather than a subtenancy.

Sub-tenants: The exact situation will depend upon the terms of your "tenancy" with your cohabitant but usually the "tenancy" will be one which is excluded from the normal Rent Act protections. This will mean that the amount of notice that is required before the "tenant" can force the "sub-tenant" to leave will depend upon the arrangement for paying "rent". If rent is paid on a monthly basis then a month's notice is required, while if rent is paid on a weekly basis a week's notice will suffice. If the tenant leaves and you wish to stay you will not usually have the right to do so without the landlord's agreement.

Licensee: The legal position is similar to licensees of owner-occupiers, as described below. The amount of notice depends, in England and Wales, on whether it is a bare or contractual licence and if contractual on the terms of the contract.

If you refuse to leave the tenant can evict you without going to court only if s/he does not use violence or threats of violence. If the tenant leaves you will have no right to stay and the landlord can evict you in the same way. In Scotland they must obtain a court order.

Council/housing association tenants

The legal position if you have a public sector landlord is basically the same as outlined above but, in addition, these landlords may have specific policies about rehousing their tenants in the event of a break-up of the relationship. In the past, where such policies existed they only applied to married, or at least heterosexual, couples. However an increasing number of housing associations and local authorities do now recognize gay and lesbian couples so it will be worth investigating their policies.

DEATH OF THE TENANT

Joint tenants

On the death of one joint tenant the other tenants inherit the entire tenancy. For this reason it is advantageous to have a joint tenancy. You may wish to ask the landlord to transfer the tenancy from one of your names into both of them (i.e. create a joint tenancy out of a sole one). However, they are not obliged to do so. A local authority or housing association is more likely to agree to do this if they know that you are involved with each other.

Sole tenant

If the sole tenant dies then his/her partner will not be entitled to inherit the tenancy and can be evicted. This is an area of law which has been interpreted by the courts in an extremely unfair manner, since unmarried heterosexual cohabitants are in some circumstances allowed to inherit tenancies from each other. Indeed prior to 1989 members of the tenant's family with whom s/he had been living for a certain period of time were entitled to inherit.

The case of Harrogate B.C. v. Simpson 1984, involving a lesbian who lived with her lover in a council flat, established that homosexual cohabitants were not legally regarded as "living together as man and wife", nor as members of each other's family, and therefore the council was entitled to evict Ms Simpson on the death of her lover.

In reaching this cruel decision the judge pronounced that: "The essential character of living together as husband and wife . . . is that there should be a man and a woman." Despite the discriminatory legal position, some councils and housing associations have policies extending the right of lesbian and gay couples to take over tenancies on a partner's death.

One situation in which a lover can inherit from his/her lover is where s/he has a fixed term tenancy which has not expired (for example, the lease is for five years and only two years have elapsed since the tenancy started). In this circumstance the tenant is able to leave the remaining period of the tenancy in his/her will.

In other circumstances you will only be entitled to inherit a tenancy left to you in a will if your landlord consents.

OWNER/OCCUPIERS

The section below discusses shared living arrangements when one or more of the occupants owns the property. It applies whether or not the people living together are lovers and whether or not the people moved into the property at the same time. Where these factors make a difference we will point this out. The most important advice we can give is to discuss fully beforehand your expectations of the living arrangement, and preferably record these in writing.

PURCHASE

Very few people will be able to buy a property without a mortgage. A mortgage is a form of loan which is secured against the property which it is being used to purchase. This means that if you fail to repay the loan or the interest on the loan, the institution which gave the mortgage (the mortgagor) can take legal action to gain possession of the property, sell it and use the sale proceeds to reclaim the money owed to it (any surplus money belongs to the owner of the property).

Most mortgages are given by banks or building societies. Nowadays it is possible to obtain a mortgage for the entire purchase price of the property, but generally mortgagors prefer the borrower to have a deposit of at least five per cent of the purchase price. Mortgages are usually repayable over 25 years.

The two most common types of mortgages are endowment and repayment. Endowment mortgages involve the borrower taking out an insurance policy to cover the full amount of the loan. Every month the borrower pays interest on the loan plus a premium for the insurance policy. The insurance policy will mature at the same time as the loan becomes due to be repaid. (It may produce more or less than the full amount of the loan depending on the investments of the insurance company.) If you die before the loan becomes due the insurance policy will pay off the full amount of the loan.

A repayment mortgage involves paying monthly interest on the loan and at the same time paying off a small part of the loan. At first the monthly payments will consist almost entirely of interest, but gradually the repayment portion will increase.

If you get a repayment mortgage you may still choose to take out an insurance policy at the same time. You may wish to do this if you have any dependants, and mortgagors will almost certainly insist that you take out such a policy if you take out a very large loan or a 100 per cent mortgage. Generally however you can avoid taking out an insurance policy on other loans by shopping around.

For gay men in particular this is an important advantage of repayment mortgages. The advent of Aids has made insurance companies very wary of giving insurance policies to gay men, or indeed to single men over a certain age, especially if they are co-buying with other men. (We go into this in more detail in the chapter on Aids.) For up to date advice telephone Gay and Lesbian Legal Advice (see Listings).

BUYING JOINTLY

The law of property in Scotland is different to that in England and Wales, and we will therefore deal with it separately below.

ENGLAND AND WALES

The law assumes, in the absence of any evidence to the contrary that land belongs to the person, or persons, whose name is on the title deeds (the legal documents with which land is purchased). However historically there have been two ways of "owning" land. The "legal title" — that is whose name is on the title deeds — is the primary form but, because there have always been classes of people (including married women until 1882) who were not able to legally own property, another form of property developed in parallel. This is a system of "trusts", by which one set of people ("trustees") hold property for the benefit of another set of people ("the beneficiaries").

Generally a trust is established by a formal document known as a "trust deed". In some circumstances, even in the absence of written evidence, the law will imply that the holder of the legal title holds it on trust for another person (see below, section on Implied Trusts). We would advice you strongly not to rely on these hazardous and expensive legal proceedings but to set out your agreement in writing from the beginning.

Assuming that all the people who it is intended should own the property have their names on the title deeds there is a further crucial legal distinction to be considered. There are two ways by which the legal title of a property can be owned by more than one person. You can either own the property as "joint tenants" or "tenants in common". Unless you are a lawyer it will not be obvious which applies in your case. The difference is crucially important: if you hold the property as joint tenants and one of you dies the other co-owner(s) will automatically inherit his/her share of the property, regardless of any will that might have been made. Moreover if you have a joint tenancy it is legally assumed that you both own the property in equal shares.

On the other hand where you own the property as tenants in common the individual shares of the property do not pass to the other owner(s) of the property on the death of a co-owner. They can be disposed of in a will and if the deceased co-owner has not left a will their share passes by the rules of intestacy (see Life, Love and Other Problems chapter). This means that it is very important to consider and protect the position of a co-owner in the event of death by drawing up wills, otherwise part of the house may become owned by a hostile relative of the deceased co-owner, who may then enforce a sale of the property.

You can convert a joint tenancy into a tenancy in common without the consent of the other co-owners, simply by giving a written notice that you wish to do this. It is only if a joint tenant alters the way in which s/he holds the property, and becomes a tenant in common (the legal term for this is "severing the tenancy") that s/he can leave his/her share of the property to someone else in his/her will.

In the absence of an explicit statement of the terms upon which the property is to be held (i.e. who owns how much of the property) a court can interpret the terms as we consider below in the section concerning implied trust (i.e. it can postpone the sale and alter the shares of the parties to reflect their respective contributions to the property). It is therefore wise, even if all the co-owners' names are on the title deeds, to have a trust deed drawn up setting out the terms on which you agree to share the ownership of the property.

Trust deeds

We would strongly advise you not to draft a trust deed yourselves. You should instruct a solicitor as this is a complex area of law, where misdrafting could lead to consequences which you do not intend. However it helps to have discussed between yourselves beforehand exactly what you want to include in the trust deed. You should discuss how you wish to share the mortgage payments and other outgoings, the shares of the property which you will each own and under what circumstances one of you can force the sale of the property. For instance you will probably wish to set out a minimum notice period before a sale can be forced by one of the owners.

Apart from these basic considerations you might wish to set out other details — for instance the process by which the house should be valued (one, two or even three valuations) for the purpose of buying out someone's share, or restrictions on inviting other people to stay for more than a certain period of time. When you consider what to include in the deed you should assume that you will have fallen out by the time that the trust deed comes into effect — as this is the practical purpose of having such a document.

Splitting up in England and Wales

Sale

If both your names are on the title deeds then neither of you can sell without the other's consent. If one of you wants to sell against the wishes of the other s/he can apply for an order that the property be sold. If you have a trust deed the court will order that its provisions be complied with. In the absence of a trust deed it is very exceptional for a court not to make an immediate order for sale. The only justification for delay would be if the purpose for which the house has originally been bought has not come to an end (see section on Implied Trusts).

If the shares in which you own the property are set out in the title deeds or in a trust deed this can only be varied by an agreement in writing. We explain in the section on implied trusts below the principles which the courts will apply in deciding shares in the absence of a written agreement.

Rent

If one owner voluntarily leaves the property the remaining owner will not have to pay rent to him/her, in the absence of agreement to the contrary. On the other hand, where a co-owner has been forced to leave the remaining co-owner may be legally liable to pay him/her rent for occupation of the premises.

Mortgage

Even if a co-owner leaves the property s/he will continue to be liable for his/her share of the mortgage. If one co-owner pays more than half of the mortgage s/he should be entitled to an increased share of the sale proceeds of the property.

BUYING JOINTLY IN SCOTLAND

In Scotland the system of land ownership is in many ways more straightforward than in England and Wales, and in particular, the device of the trust has substantially less

significance. Broadly property in Scotland may be owned by
one person alone, or by two or more people together. If owned
by two or more persons, then all their names will appear on
the title deeds (the documents which are necessary to transfer the property to new owners). Unless the title deeds state
otherwise, each co-owner will have an equal share of the
property. Thus, if one of you contributes more to the purchase
price than the other, and the agreement is that they should
have a larger share of the property, then this should be set
out in the title deeds.

Co-owners may own the property either jointly or in
common. The distinction between these two terms is similar
to the position in England.

Splitting up

If both your names are on the title deeds, then either party
can sell without the other's consent. If one of you wishes to
sell, and the other does not, then s/he can apply to the court
for an order that the property be sold and the proceeds
divided equally. The court has no power to refuse or postpone
such an order.

As in England, if one co-owner fails to pay their share of the
mortgage, the bank or building society could call in the loan,
subject to the other owner taking over responsibility for
paying all the monthly repayments.

PROPERTY IN THE NAME OF ONE PERSON — ENGLAND AND WALES

Set down in writing the details of your living arrangement

If you move into a property belonging to someone else your
position is very vulnerable. To protect the non-owning party
and avoid any lengthy legal wrangles it is vital to consider in
advance what you both intend should happen if things go
wrong — for instance if the relationship ends or the owner
dies or wants to sell.

A crucial question is whether it is intended that the non-owning partner should have a share in the property. If so, how much should this share be — a straightforward half share or a share in proportion to the financial contribution? If it is intended that the non-owner should have a share of the property the legal form for this arrangement will again be a trust. You should go to a solicitor and have a deed drawn up setting out the terms of the trust.

Beware if the non-owning cohabitant is claiming or may wish to claim housing benefit. If they are aware that you are entitled to a share of a property under a trust deed then the Department of Social Security will pay you housing benefit in the same way as if you were an owner of the property (i.e. they will treat your payments as mortgage payments rather than rent). The main difference is that for the first 16 weeks of claiming the DSS will only pay half of your mortgage, whereas your full rent is eligible for payment from the beginning.

If you agree that the non-owning cohabitant is not to acquire a share of the property it is a good idea to write down exactly what each of you expects in terms of contributions to household expenses, "rent" and the notice periods that you both must give. The non-owning cohabitant will not be given security of tenure by the law (see below) so they will only have the degree of security that has been agreed with the owner. If you do not agree in advance to any fixed period of notice then the "tenant" will be legally entitled to a "reasonable" period of notice. After this notice period the "landlord" will always be entitled to evict him/her (see section on Splitting Up).

If you intend the non-owning partner to have continuing rights of occupation in the event of the death of the owner you should draw up a will stating this.

In the absence of any written agreement

A share in the property — Implied trusts:

If the property is in your cohabitant's sole name and you have no written agreement with him/her you will find it very difficult to claim a share of the property, even if you have put a lot of money and work into it. However the courts have been willing in some circumstances to imply the existence of a trust from statements and/or actions of the parties; this is known as an implied trust. The court will then go on to deduce the terms of the trust — that is in what circumstances the trust will come to an end, and the property be sold, and how the sale proceeds should be divided.

The law in this area is not derived from legislation passed by Parliament but is judge-made. This is partly why it is so difficult to give precise guidelines as to how judges will treat individual cases. A quote from the judgement in one of the leading cases, Grant v. Edwards 1986, will illustrate this: "For my part I do not think that the time has yet arrived when it is possible to state the law in a way which will deal with all the practical problems which may arise in this difficult field, consistently with everything that is said in the cases."

The basic legal starting point is that when the property is bought in one person's name but another person contributes towards the purchase price, the law presumes that it is intended that the purchaser will hold the property on trust for both of them. It is possible for the court to be persuaded that this presumption is not correct — for instance if it can be convinced that the contribution to the purchase was intended to be a gift or a loan.

Other situations are less straightforward. It might be possible for the non-owning party to claim an implied trust if s/he did not contribute to the deposit but did pay a share of the mortgage or if s/he made a large enough contribution to household expenses, which could be claimed to have freed the owner's income and enabled him/her to pay a larger mortgage. It might even be possible to claim a trust and a share of the property in a trust if you have not contributed any money but have put in a lot of physical work to the property.

It should be said that the court is very unlikely to imply a trust where a party has not made direct financial contributions to the purchase of the property. It may regard contributions to the mortgage or to household expenses as simply "paying your way". It will also be more difficult to persuade the courts to imply the existence of a trust if you moved into the property after it had already been purchased. Such claims will only succeed if there has been a reasonably clear statement by the owner that s/he regards the property as in some sense belonging to both of you.

The normal starting point is to look at the parties' intentions at the time of purchase but in some cases where there was a major change in the parties' contributions to the property (for instance, if the person claiming the existence of a trust used a substantial redundancy payment to pay off part of the mortgage) courts may recognize an implied trust as arising at a later date. It will all depend on what the court considers to be the intentions of the parties.

The legal concept of an implied trust is not supposed to take into account the details of the relationship but simply to look at the contributions of the parties to the property. However because the doctrine was originally developed to protect firstly wives and then unmarried heterosexual cohabitants, and because its legal basis is the courts' attempts to interpret the original intentions of the parties, judges might well look at the quality and duration of your relationship as well as the degree to which you adopted responsibility for the property.

The courts have tended to assume that the closer a relationship comes to their ideal of marriage (including particularly the presence of children in the household) the more likely the parties were to have had an intention that the property was held in trust. One must assume that the courts are less likely to consider that lesbian or gay relationships approximate marriage and are therefore less likely to imply a trust.

If the court decides that there is an implied trust it will then assess the relative value of the shares of the property. It is most likely to make a mathematical calculation of the relative contributions of money or money's worth. On the other hand, it is possible for the court, once it has agreed that a trust exists, to say that, from the behaviour of the parties, the terms of the trust were that the property should be held in equal shares or in some other proportion not strictly based on the respective financial contributions. Again it is less likely to do so where the relationship does not approximate a marriage.

The next question is whether the court would allow the sale of a property to be postponed by the non-owning party on the basis that the purpose for which the trust was created has not come to an end. On the whole courts tend to conclude that a trust has ended when the relationship breaks down and have only been prepared to conclude that a trust continues beyond this point where a property has been bought as a family home for children. In some cases involving heterosexual families courts have postponed the sale until the children were grown. Whether a court would be prepared to acknowledge a gay or lesbian family in this way remains to be seen.

The property will be valued for the purposes of calculating shares at the time of sale (Turton v. Turton 1987). Some illustrative cases may help to clarify the situation. As far as we are aware there are no recorded cases involving gay or lesbian cohabitants and so we cannot assume that the heterosexist and sexist assumptions of the courts will make them stick to these principles where lesbians and gays are involved.

Eves v. Eves 1975 was a case where the house was in the man's sole name only because he had told the woman that it would not be possible for her name to be on the title deeds as well. The parties acted as though they regarded the house as jointly owned. Ms Eves did not make any financial contributions but did a great deal of work repairing and improving the house. They had two children. The court decided that there was a trust. One of the judges said: "I find it difficult to suppose that she would have been wielding the 14lb sledgehammer, breaking up the large area of concrete, filling the skip and doing the other things which were carried out when they moved in, except in pursuance of some express or implied arrangements and on the understanding that she was helping to improve the house in which she was to all extents and purposes promised that she had an interest." It seems unlikely that a court would reach the same consideration in the case of a gay male cohabitant.

In Burns v. Burns 1984 Ms Burns had been a "housewife" for 19 years and brought up the couple's children. She had worked for a short period but her earnings were used for general domestic purposes and were not crucial in freeing Mr Burns' income to pay the mortgage instalments. She was held to have no rights against her cohabitant because she had made no direct contributions for money or money's worth. The Court of Appeal recognized that the situation was unjust but said that it had no power to invent rights to the property on the basis of injustice, that only Parliament could make new law to correct the injustice.

Ms Richards (Richards v. Dove 1974) lived with Mr Dove for a number of years. At first they lived in rented accommodation. When they bought a house together it was in Mr Dove's sole name. He paid £350 deposit, although she lent him £150 towards it. She continued on the same basis as before to pay the food and gas bills while Mr Dove paid the mortgage. The court held that she was not entitled to a share of the sale proceeds of the house because essentially the couple continued to behave in the same manner as when they lived in rented accommodation, and not as though they intended to buy a house jointly.

SPLITTING UP

Trust deed/Implied trust

If there is a trust deed then the trustee/legal owner must comply with the terms of that trust, or you can take him/her to court. If you feel that you can make out a good argument that an implied trust exists, and your partner is trying to sell the house against your wishes, or s/he is trying to force you to leave the property, you can apply to the court immediately for an injunction to stop this and allow you to remain in the house until the court decides whether there is a trust in your favour and if so what the terms of the trust are. You may also delay the sale if you can convince the court that the purpose of the trust has not been completed. You should consult a solicitor immediately and warn any potential buyers of your interest in the property.

No implied trust — a right to remain in the property?

If you have no legal entitlement to a share of the property you will be living there either under a lease or as licensee (more probably a licence unless you have exclusive occupation of one part of the premises). Although this distinction is crucially important in other situations, where you are living with your "landlord" it is not significant. In either case you will have very little security because the Housing Act 1988 has taken away the protection from eviction by resident landlords in almost all cases. This means that the property owner is entitled to ask you to leave without having to take legal proceedings against you (as landlords must do with virtually every other type of tenant).

The landlord must however give you a reasonable period of notice (equivalent to the length of time between payments of rent) and must not use force or unreasonable threats of force to evict you, otherwise they will have committed a criminal offence. If they simply change the locks while you are out they may be liable to you in civil proceedings (for depriving you of access to your property). This is a very complex area of the law and we would certainly advise occupiers of property who are in the position of having an unwanted "tenant" to seek legal advice before taking the law into their own hands.

A special form called a "Notice to Quit" (easily obtained from legal stationers) will be necessary if the non-owning occupier could be termed a tenant. Otherwise notice in writing is sufficient. Generally at least a month's notice is required. The question of how much notice should be given is a complicated one, unless this detail was specified in a written agreement. If this is not specified the length of notice required may depend on whether the non-owning occupier could legally be termed to have a tenancy or a licence, and the intervals at which rent is due. We do not have the space to go through the complex legal rules concerning notice and so must advise parties in this situation to consult a solicitor or Citizens Advice Bureau.

Generally speaking, the notice period required for the owner is not very long. There is however one very slight legal possibility which would enable the non-owning occupant to prolong his/her stay significantly. Despite the absence of a written agreement the courts have been willing, in some heterosexual cohabitation cases, to imply from the behaviour of the parties the existence of a contractual or an equitable licence.

Normally for a contractual licence to exist you must have paid some money or given something of value such as substantial work on the property. However in some cases where the non-owning cohabitant has not given any "consideration" but has done some act to his/her detriment (e.g. given up a rent-controlled tenancy) the courts have been prepared to imply the existence of "equitable licences". The owner of the property must have encouraged you to "act to your detriment", for instance by assuring you that you will be entitled to remain in the house for the rest of your life or that you will be generally looked after. You will not be able to establish an equitable licence if you simply moved in with your lover because you wanted to live with him/her.

Once the courts have ruled that a contractual or equitable licence exists they then proceed to consider how long the licensee is entitled to live in the property, and upon what terms. This area of law, like the law on implied trusts, is entirely judge-made and even more subject to the whims of judicial discretion. In particular they have been more prone to recognize an equitable or contractual licence where the relationship seemed close to their idea of marriage. In the absence of children we would suggest it is unlikely for the court to recognize the existence of such licences except in exceptional circumstances. Beware also that if you have acted badly towards the owner — for instance abusing them or their visitors — the courts may cancel an equitable license.

(Please note: The above paragraph assumes that the living arrangement commenced after the Housing Act came into force in January 1989. If the arrangement commenced before that date then the non-owning occupant may well have more rights. Again we have to advise you to seek legal assistance.)

Death

In the absence of any agreement to the contrary (i.e. a trust deed or evidence of an implied trust) a non-owning cohabitant will not be entitled to continue occupying the property in the event of the owner's death. The person who inherits the property will probably be entitled to ask you to leave —

unless you can establish that you have an equitable licence, as described above. In this situation a non-owning cohabitant should always seek advice.

PROPERTY IN THE NAME OF ONE PERSON — SCOTLAND

As in England and Wales, if you move into someone else's home, then the terms on which you stay there should be agreed with them. If you are cohabiting with the owner, it is unlikely that you would be regarded in law as a tenant with the partner who owns the property as your landlord. To be a tenant you must pay rent and have exclusive possession of at least part of the property you live in. If you share every part of the property with your partner, then this will not be a tenancy arrangement and basically you are simply staying there by way of an agreement with the owner.

You cannot, in Scotland, become a joint owner simply by virtue of contributing to the mortgage or carrying out improvements. If it is the intention of both parties that you are to acquire a share in the house itself, then the only way of achieving this would be to transfer the property out of the name of the sole owner and into your joint names.

Splitting up

If you are not a joint owner of the property that you live in, then you are in a vulnerable position. None of the legal protection that applies as a matter of law to married couples or heterosexual cohabitants applies to gay or lesbian couples.

Further, the concept of the contractual licence, now fairly well recognized by the English and Welsh courts, has never been developed by the Scottish courts so as to protect the position of a cohabitant who does not own the house that they live in. In this situation, the protection available to you will depend on whether you are a tenant, with your partner who owns the property as your landlord. If you are a tenant, then you have a basic right to notice of the termination of your tenancy. The legal provisions as to minimum notice periods for tenants are complex, but broadly the notice period should be as set out in any tenancy agreement, subject to a basic minimum of four weeks for all residential leases. A Notice to Quit must be in writing. In addition, your partner/landlord will not be able to evict you without a court order.

If you are not a tenant and stay with your partner simply by virtue of his/her agreement, then possibly you are entitled to such notice as is "reasonable" in the circumstances. This could be just a few days to allow you enough time to gather your possessions together. Otherwise you have no other protection.

If you are in the position of wanting your partner to move out, or of being forced to leave against your will, then we recommend that you seek legal advice straightaway to clarify your rights and obligations, since the law in this area is not straightforward.

LIFE, LOVE AND OTHER PROBLEMS

Because laws have been designed exclusively within a heterosexual framework, lesbians and gays will often find it more difficult to know how to respond legally in particular situations. In this chapter we consider various different circumstances of life (relationships, health problems, death, violence and breaches of privacy) in which lesbians and gays may experience particular difficulties.

RELATIONSHIPS

There is no legal equivalent of marriage for gays or lesbians, nor indeed any specific recognition in law of our relationships. This is the result not only of homophobia but also of the law's historical reluctance to recognize any sexual relationship outside marriage. This lack of social recognition can be a source of great stress and also in many cases of legal difficulties.

In some areas, such as joint mortgages and more flexible pension schemes, many major social institutions are changing their policies to adapt to the increasing numbers of people living together outside marriage. Recent years have also seen major developments in the law relating to the rights and duties of unmarried heterosexual couples. In some cases (for instance the Inheritance Provision for Family and Dependants Act) it may be possible for lesbian and gay couples to make use of these legal changes; others, such as the succession rights of heterosexual cohabitants to some tenancies, have been closed to lesbian and gay couples.

Nevertheless the law basically treats lesbian and gay couples in exactly the same way as it treats two individuals who have no emotional ties. Some people are perfectly satisfied with this situation; however where there is inequality in the relationship this legal vacuum can compound the vulnerability of one of the partners. The clearest example is where one partner is being violent; the additional protection brought in for heterosexual cohabitants by the Domestic Violence Act 1976 in England and the Matrimonial Homes (Family Protection) Act 1981 in Scotland, is not available to homosexual cohabitants who must continue to rely on the less adequate measures set out in the section on violence below.

Another situation in which lesbian and gay partners are more vulnerable occurs where one partner has supported the other for years by cooking, cleaning etc., while the other worked. A wife in this same situation would be entitled to make substantial claims on her husband's property. However, since in this country there is no equivalent for cohabitants (even for heterosexuals, never mind gays or lesbians) of the American concept of "palimony", the lesbian or gay partner in this position will not be entitled to claim any share of the property on this basis when the relationship breaks down.

We will also see in the sections dealing with health and death how this lack of legal recognition adversely affects lesbian and gay relationships.

AGREEMENTS

With the absence of a legal framework one sensible solution is to fill in the gaps in the law yourself by drawing up an agreement with your partner setting out your mutual financial obligations. A contract such as this is called a "cohabitation contract". The bad news is that, to date, such contracts have not been accepted as legally enforceable by the courts, even between heterosexual couples. This is because the courts have traditionally viewed such contracts as immoral and contrary to public policy, arguing that they undermine the institution of marriage.

Many legal commentators believe that cohabitation contracts will eventually be recognized by the courts; there has even been a Private Member's Bill attempting to provide for their recognition. Realistically, however, where gay or lesbian relationships are concerned the homophobia of the courts would probably increase further still their resistance to enforcing an agreement.

Nevertheless since most people honour agreements between themselves without resort to the courts it may still be worth setting down the practical terms of your relationship. If you wish to make such a contract it should be in writing so that there is no room for later disagreement about the terms. Ownership of, and rights to live in, a home are best specified in a trust deed (see Housing chapter). Other joint property could also be included in the trust deed or you could simply keep a written record of who owns what and which property is jointly owned. This could save a lot of trouble in the long run. We will discuss below how property is divided in the absence of express agreement. If you want an agreement that one partner should pay the other maintenance or aliment in Scotland on the break-up of the relationship then the agreement should be very specific about the amount to be paid, length of time payable etc.

If you wish the agreement to have any chance of being legally enforceable in England and Wales it should be in the form of a deed. This is a document which uses a special form of words and a seal, available from a legal stationer.

SPLITTING UP

Obviously the best approach to dividing property when a relationship ends is to get together and list all your assets and debts and agree how they should be divided. Remember it will be very expensive to engage in protracted legal disputes. However, some guidelines about how the law regards joint property may be helpful. Broadly speaking all property belongs to the person who paid for it, unless it can be shown that it was a gift. If you have joint bank or building society accounts then both parties will be able to remove all the funds from the account. If you wish to stop this you should put a block on the account.

Provided that you have both contributed substantially (but not necessarily equally) to a joint account then property purchased from that account will belong to the person who actually bought it, unless the court can be persuaded that it was intended that it should be owned jointly. A party can also, in the absence of contrary agreement, withdraw and keep more funds from the account than s/he has paid in. In the absence of proof to the contrary, the courts are likely to conclude that the funds in a joint account belong to both account holders equally. However if all the money in the joint account has been paid in by one party then the court will assume that it, and all property bought with it, belongs to that party.

If the account is in one partner's sole name but, in fact, funds from both partners have been paid into it then the other partner may have a claim to a corresponding share of the fund.

HEALTH

If your close friend or lover falls ill you may all too often find that medical staff exclude everyone who they do not regard as close family. They may also refuse to provide any information about the patient. If the patient is capable of expressing his/her wishes, or if s/he carries a card stating "next of kin" there should not be any problem. Otherwise you may find yourself having a struggle with hospital administrators just when you are least able to cope with it.

You may well have doubts about "coming out" on behalf of the patient, as you may feel it could affect their treatment. There is no simple solution to this problem. You should take someone with you to the hospital. If you have any written documents, such as a power of attorney (see below) these may persuade the medical staff of your status in the patient's life.

Although there is strictly speaking no legal document capable of conferring "next of kin" status for these purposes, it is therefore a wise precaution to draw up a signed statement indicating who you wish to be treated as your next of kin in these situations.

DECISION MAKING

This issue becomes particularly serious when the patient is unable to express his/herself about decisions concerning his/her long-term future (i.e. if they have a permanent mental disability). The case of Sharon Kowalski in the USA illustrates the sort of problems which can occur. Sharon had an extremely committed but closeted relationship with Karen Thompson. She had a car accident which left her with extensive physical and mental difficulties, including severe restrictions on her ability to communicate. Karen was initially refused information by the medical staff because she was not a member of Sharon's family and when she told Sharon's parents the nature of their relationship they attempted to prevent her from seeing Sharon. There followed extensive court battles to determine who should be Sharon's legal guardian with the right to decide where she should live, what treatment she should receive and who should visit her. After a struggle lasting eight years Karen was eventually appointed Sharon's guardian, and they are now living together.

Frightening as this case is, in the United Kingdom there is not even the legal framework for settling disputes of this nature. In England and Wales, under the age of 18 a person can be made a "ward of court" (see Children chapter) and the court will make decisions on the patient's behalf based on what it considers their best interests.

However if the injured person is over 18, apart from the provisions outlined below, no-one is legally entitled to make decisions on behalf of individuals who lack the ability to decide for themselves. The sole legal basis for treatment is that doctors must provide the treatment which they consider is in the person's best interests. In practice, of course, spouses, heterosexual cohabitants, and (in the case of single people) parents are consulted about major decisions. Lesbian or gay lovers (or close friends) will probably have to struggle to have this respect shown to them.

GUARDIANSHIP

Under the provisions of the Mental Health Act 1983 in England and Wales, and the Mental Health (Scotland) Acts 1984 and 1991 in Scotland a guardian can be appointed for someone over the age of 16 if s/he is suffering from a mental disorder (which may be temporary or permanent) and it is necessary in the interests of the welfare of the individual or, in England and Wales, the protection of other people.

Effects of guardianship

A guardian has very limited, narrowly defined powers: to require the person to reside at a particular place; to require the person to attend a certain place for treatment (but not actually to force him/her to have treatment); and to require that the person allow access to a doctor or social worker, or other named person.

Procedure

In England and Wales anyone can apply to the local social services department to be made a guardian. Two doctors must recommend guardianship on the prescribed forms. The nearest relative (for definition see below) must be consulted if practicable. The guardianship does not come into effect until it has been accepted by Social Services and a written statement has been made by the guardian that s/he is willing to act as such. The first two orders last for six months at a time. The subject of the guardianship has the right to apply after each order to the Mental Health Review Tribunal for the discharge of the guardianship.

In Scotland a similar procedure applies, but in addition the application to the local authority must be accompanied by a welfare report prepared by the local authority's Mental Health Officer, and approved by the local sheriff.

If no guardianship order has been made then in England

and Wales no-one has the power legally to make such desisions concerning treatment or place of residence on another person's behalf. This may in effect mean that medical and Social Services staff accept the family's view of what is best for the individual. Of course we would hope that every effort would be made to enable the individual to express his/her views as to important decisions about his/her own life. Sadly this is too seldom the case.

The position is different in Scotland due to the recent revival of the use of tutor datives. Tutors can be appointed by the Court of Session to act as personal guardians for mentally disabled adults. A tutor can have far wider powers than a guardian, and the extent of the powers can be adapted to the needs of the adult in question. They can, for example, include the power to authorize specific medical treatment.

MENTAL ILLNESS

We do not have the space to consider this controversial and complex area in any detail. We will simply go through the regulations concerning compulsory detention as this is an area where gays and lesbians may be particularly vulnerable, and where their partners and close friends are denied the status accorded heterosexuals.

The law in this area is contained in the Mental Health Act 1983 in England and Wales, and in Scotland in the Mental Health Act (Scotland) Acts 1984 and 1991.

Who can be compulsorily detained?

Admission for treatment

A person can be compulsorily detained for treatment on the following grounds:

a) s/he suffers from mental illness, severe mental impairment or psychopathic disorder or mental impairment of a degree where it would be appropriate to receive medical treatment in hospital and

b) in the case of psychopathic disorder or mental impairment such treatment is likely to alleviate or prevent deterioration of the condition and

c) it is necessary in the interests of the health or safety of the patient or for the protection of others that s/he should receive treatment and it cannot be provided except unless s/he is detained.

This order and the first subsequent order last for six months; subsequent ones last for one year.

Admission for assessment

The grounds for compulsory detention for assessment for a 28 day period are that the person is suffering from a mental disorder of a degree which justifies detention for assessment for a limited period and s/he needs to be detained for the protection of his/herself or other people.

Persons in public places

A police constable who finds a person suffering from a mental disorder in a public place can remove him/her to a place of safety where s/he may be detained for up to 72 hours for further assessment. The police should only do this if it appears that the person is in need of immediate "care and control" or if it seems necessary to protect him/her or to protect others. There is evidence that this section has been abused by the police, particularly against black people.

Who can apply for discharge or appeal against these orders?

Application for these orders can be made either by a social worker in England and Wales, or a local authority Mental Health Officer in Scotland, or, in both countries, by "the nearest relative". The application must be supported by their GP and a psychiatrist (or in an emergency with the support of one doctor provided a further doctor's approval is obtained within 72 hours).

In Scotland, in addition, the application must be approved by the sheriff, except in cases of emergency.

If the application is by a social worker or a Mental Health Officer the "nearest relative" should be informed as soon as possible. If the application is for a six month order and the nearest relative objects then the application cannot proceed unless the social worker applies to court to change the nearest relative on the grounds that this opposition is unreasonable.

A person detained can be released at any time by the consultant psychiatrist responsible for his/her care or the managers of the hospital, and they must be released if the grounds for their detention cease to apply. The nearest relative is also entitled to ask for the release of the "patient", but this can be refused if the responsible doctor advises against it.

In England and Wales the person him/herself has the right to appeal against the order to a Mental Health Review Tribunal. This is an independent body who will review the case. Legal aid is available for representation at such a tribunal.

In Scotland the appeal is to the sheriff.

Who is the nearest relative?

The following relatives are considered, in this order, to be the nearest relative: spouse, child, parent, sibling, grandparent, grandchild, uncle/aunt, nephew/niece. The definition of spouse includes a person living with the "patient" for at least six months as his/her spouse, and excludes spouses who are separated, whether by agreement or court order. An unrelated person with whom the individual has been living for not less than five years takes precedent over all these relatives except spouses. The order of priority follows the above list, except that a relative who has been living with the person takes priority of other relatives.

There is no recognition in this legislation of gay/lesbian relationships, nor have there been any cases on the question of whether the definition of cohabitants excludes homosexual partners. If lesbian/gay cohabitants encounter problems the best approach is to explain the situation to the social worker involved and persuade him/her to treat you as the nearest relative.

If there are any conflicts with the nearest relative you can apply to the court to be appointed next relative in his/her place. In order to do this you would have to convince the court that the person currently acting as nearest relative is incapable, or, in England and Wales only, that they are acting unreasonably or without regard to the best interests of the person.

Finances — power of attorney

If a person is unable (for whatever reason) to look after his/her own financial affairs s/he can authorize another person to act on his/her behalf by means of a "power of attorney". It can either be a general power, authorizing the holder to do anything which the donor (maker) of the power could have done, or a power which is explicitly limited to certain items of property or transactions. You can appoint joint attorneys, who must act together. If you appoint attorneys this does not affect your power to conduct your own affairs, unlike the appointment of a receiver or curator bonis (see below).

The document creating the power of attorney must be in the form of a deed, signed by the donor and clearly setting out the limits of the power of attorney (e.g. length of time for which it is valid). In Scotland, if the power extends to dealing with land or property, the document should be signed in front of two witnesses. It is advisable to consult a solicitor, especially if you wish to create a limited power, or land is involved. (One important pitfall is that a simple power of attorney will not be adequate where a property is owned jointly with another.) This document can then be produced as proof to third parties that you are authorised to act on the donor's behalf.

The donor of the power of attorney must have sufficient mental capacity at the time of creating the power to understand the significance of the document and the power which it creates. The power can be specified to take effect at a later date and can be cancelled by the donor at any time.

Enduring power of attorney — England and Wales

Normally a power of attorney is automatically cancelled (revoked) if the donor becomes mentally incapacitated. However, one can use an enduring power of attorney which will not be revoked in this way. Indeed such enduring powers can be expressly stated not to come into effect until the donor becomes mentally incapacitated. Such powers must be in a special form and the potential attorney must sign them in addition to the donor.

When the donor becomes incapacitated the attorney is under a duty to register the power with the Court of Protection (see below). Before registering however, s/he must give notice of his/her intention to do so to the donor and at least three of the donor's relatives. The relatives are placed in classes in order of priority and all relatives in a class must be given notice. The classes are: spouse, children, parents, siblings (half as well as whole blood), wife/widower of a child, grandchildren, nephews and nieces, uncles and aunts. No notice need be given to relatives whose whereabouts the attorney does not know and cannot reasonably find out or to minors or mentally incapable relatives. The notice must be on the prescribed form and the notice to the court should include details of the relatives who have been notified.

The relatives of the donor may object to the power of attorney on the grounds that it was not validly executed, that fraud or undue pressure was used on the donor, that the donor is not actually incapable, or that having regards to the circumstances, the attorney is not a suitable person.

There is no equivalent to an enduring power of attorney in Scotland, though for powers of attorney signed after 31 December 1990, the powers do not lapse on the donor's incapacity.

Where there is no power of attorney

Court of protection — England and Wales:

All other financial affairs of persons who are no longer able to manage their own affairs must be managed through the Court of Protection (see Listings). A friend or relative can apply to the Court of Protection to be made a receiver of the incapacitated person's finances. If the applicant is not the nearest relative s/he should include an explanation of his/her particular connection with the person. S/he should also notify relatives of the application. The application is made on forms provided by the court and must be accompanied by a medical certificate of mental incapacity by the general practitioner or hospital doctor.

Once a receiver is appointed the person who is the subject of the receivership will no longer have the legal power to carry out transactions concerning their own property. Either the subject of the receivership (with proof of mental capacity), or other interested parties can apply to the court for the receivership to be ended or to have the existing receiver replaced.

Curator bonis — Scotland

In Scotland, when a person is not legally capable of managing their own affairs, a curator bonis may be appointed to look after their property. Curator bonis's are usually such people as accountants or solicitors. Application to the court for a curator bonis to be appointed may be made by a friend or a relative, and must be supported by two medical certificates. As with a receiver, once appointed the curator bonis takes over the person's affairs completely and the person him- or herself is legally incapable of carrying out any transaction relating to their own property.

* * *

Both the Court of Protection and its Scottish equivalent charge fees and exercise continuing supervisory functions; they are thus more cumbersome than a power of attorney. However, if someone is already mentally incapacitated without creating such a power, then this will be the only option for dealing with property. If the person does not have substantial assets then it may be possible to get by without any formal mechanisms. With regard to welfare benefits, the Department of Social Security has the discretion to appoint another person to collect and cash a claimant's benefits, if they are incapable of doing this themselves. Ask at the local office how you should apply to be appointed.

DEATH

The trauma of the death of a lover is often made still more painful by the lack of recognition given to lesbian and gay relationships. The lover's family, who may have been estranged for years, will often step back into the picture and be accorded more rights and recognition than the deceased's lover (and friends). This can be particularly painful when making funeral arrangements.

FUNERAL ARRANGEMENTS

A person cannot legally bind anyone to dispose of his/her body after death in a particular way, not even by specifying details in a will. This does not of course prevent you expressing your wishes in a will, and these being obeyed voluntarily. This is certainly advisable if you anticipate any conflicts, for instance between family and friends.

If you make a will (and we shall stress later the vital importance of this for lesbians and gay men) then the people (one or more) that you name in the will as being responsible for putting your wishes into effect (your "executors") have the duty of supervising burial arrangements. In England and Wales, if you have not made a will or have not appointed executors in the will then your nearest relatives are entitled to make the arrangements as well as to arrange your affairs (they would be termed your "administrators"). In Scotland it is the responsibility of the person who occupies the premises in which the body is lying to make the funeral arrangements. If this is a hospital, they will usually ask the nearest relatives to make the arrangements.

A recent English case (In the estate of David Thomas Nickson, deceased; Bunyan and Craig v. Nickson, 1990) has clarified the legal position. The deceased in this case had appointed executors and left directions in his will for a non-religious funeral. His mother challenged the will on the basis that her son had lacked testamentary capacity. She wanted to arrange a religious funeral and so refused to hand over the certificate for disposal of the body, which she had obtained when she registered the death. Without this certificate the executors were unable to make arrangements for the funeral; they therefore issued proceedings to approve the will and applied for an order that the certificate should be given to them. The will was approved and the order directing transfer of the certificate made. The judge accepted that the executors had the primary right to arrange for disposal of the body, and also commented regarding the deceased's wishes for a non-religious funeral: "Although they impose no legally binding obligation, the deceased's wishes impose the strongest moral obligation."

However this case took from May until October to be resolved. In most cases if you are in conflict with your deceased partner's relatives about the funeral arrangements then you are not realistically going to be able to resolve the matter through the law. If the medical authorities have already recognized you as the next of kin (as discussed in the section above) and you are appointed in the will then this should help ensure that you have control over the funeral arrangements. If you are having any difficulties you could seek legal advice and put pressure on the hospital authorities.

The expenses of the funeral are paid out of the deceased's estate.

There are a couple of special legal regulations which apply where someone has died as the result of Aids. The Public Health (Control of Disease) Act 1984 (which applies only to England and Wales) states that where someone has died in hospital from (inter alia) Aids all practicable steps must be taken to prevent anyone coming unnecessarily into contact with the body, and gives doctors or local authority officers the power to certify that the body should not be removed from the hospital except to the mortuary or for immediate burial. Where this has been certified it is an offence to remove the body except for such a purpose. To date, however, this provision has not, to the author's knowledge, been invoked. Similar provisions apply in Scotland in relation to the body of a person who has died of an infectious disease.

PROPERTY

If you die without making a will, in legal terms you are said to be "intestate" and your property will be distributed to your legal next of kin in accordance with the rules of intestacy.

It will only be possible for gay/lesbian lovers to make a claim on your estate in certain circumstances (see below) and this will be costly and very slow. The lesson therefore, if you do not want your "natural" family to inherit your property, is to make a will.

The bad news is that even if you make a will your family may be able to challenge the will and claim against your estate (see below), and in Scotland, in certain circumstances, your spouse and children may have claims on your estate regardless of the contents of the will. The law in this area is extremely biased towards the named heterosexual family.

PROPERTY WHICH IS NOT PASSED BY WILL OR INTESTACY RULES

Tenancies

Most tenancies cannot be passed on to your partner in your will, nor will a lesbian or gay cohabitant have the right to succeed to the tenancy in most situations (see Housing chapter). The principal exception is where there is a joint tenancy, in which case the survivor inherits the whole tenancy.

Joint property

Any joint property will pass automatically to the surviving owner. This means that such property can be utilized immediately without needing to take out special documents for administering the estate. This applies to joint bank or building society accounts, and also to some jointly owned homes. You will need to check the exact legal form in which the co-ownership of the home is framed to determine whether it passes automatically to the surviving owner (see Housing chapter). The survivor will also become solely liable for joint debts.

In England and Wales joint property can be claimed by other relatives under Inheritance Provision for Family and Dependants Act 1975, but if the property is in joint names it will be more difficult for them to persuade the court to make such an order.

MAKING A WILL

If you make a will then you should appoint executors to administer your estate — settling debts and dividing property in accordance with your will. When you die they will need to obtain a formal document called grant of probate in England and Wales, or confirmation in Scotland, to enable them legally to deal with property.

It is easy to make legal errors which invalidate your will and so it is best to have one drawn up by a solicitor. This should not be too expensive and if you are a sole parent and want to appoint a guardian for your child (see Children chapter) you may be able to have this done under the legal advice and assistance scheme.

In England and Wales the will must be signed in front of two adult witnesses who are not beneficiaries of the will. It will not be valid if you have married after making it. In Scotland, the will should be signed on every page in the presence of two witnesses aged 14 or over. If the will is written out and signed in your own handwriting it may be valid, even if it is not correctly witnessed, but it is better to arrange for witnesses. A will is not invalidated by subsequent marriage in Scotland.

Relatives may try to challenge the will on the basis that the beneficiary (the person who will inherit under the will) used undue influence to persuade the person making the will. You should therefore make clear to your lawyer that you are making the will of your own free choice.

If you are ill at the time when you make the will your relatives might also try to challenge the will on the basis that you were not fully mentally capable when you drafted it. If you think there is any danger of this then you could arrange for a doctor to witness the signing of the will.

If you are married or leave children or dependants then, in England and Wales but not in Scotland, they may be able to challenge any will which does not provide for them (see Inheritance Provision for Family and Dependants Act 1975, below). It can help your beneficiaries defeat such a claim if you make a statement accompanying your will explaining why you do not consider that you are obliged to leave a share of your estate to your relatives.

IF YOU DIE INTESTATE — ENGLAND AND WALES

Claims by lovers

If you die intestate your property (apart from jointly owned property which passes to the surviving owner) will go to any surviving members of the "natural" family, who will inherit in the following order of priority: spouse (but not if divorced), children, parents, siblings and grandparents. Where the deceased had children a spouse will inherit £75,000 and any property in excess will be divided between the children. If the deceased had no children but had one or both surviving parents then the spouse inherits £125,000 and any excess goes to the parent(s).

You may be able to make a claim for a share of your partner's property under the Inheritance Provision for Family and Dependants Act 1975 but only if s/he was making a "substantial contribution in money or money's worth to your reasonable needs" immediately before his/her death. In some cases the provision of the rent-free accommodation has been held to be sufficient to justify a claim on this ground.

You must not have given "full valuable consideration" in return for being maintained in this way. "Valuable consideration" can mean that you either paid money or provided them with valuable services. Until the case of Bishop v. Plumley (Court of Appeal, *Times* 18 July 1990) it was thought this meant that providing extensive care for a sick lover might deprive you of the right to claim. In this case Lord Butler Sloss said that the devoted care of Ms Bishop for Mr Plumley could not be assessed in isolation from the mutuality of the relationship, and that the question of whether "full valuable consideration" had been given should exclude actions undertaken through the "mutual love and support" of the couple.

The other situation which might make it difficult to claim is if you lived with your lover, sharing expenses from a joint pool of income. Ironically you are more likely to have a claim under this Act if you contributed substantially less than half to the pooled resources because then you could not be said to have given "full valuable consideration", and you can claim to have been "maintained" by your lover.

If your lover was supporting your children financially prior to his/her death, they will be able to claim under the Act.

If you establish the right to a claim under this Act you will be entitled to receive "such provision as would be reasonable for your maintenance". In deciding what provision is reasonable the court has to take into account not only your needs but also the size of the estate and what other claims there are on it, together with your conduct and "the extent to which and the basis upon which the deceased assumed responsibility for the maintenance of the applicant, and the length of time for which the deceased discharged that responsibility".

Even if you do not have a claim to property under this Act you may be entitled to a share of the property in your own right (e.g. share of a house under an implied trust, as described in the section on Housing) and should consult a solicitor straight away.

Claims by the "natural" family

A spouse does not have to show that s/he was in any way dependent on the deceased in order to make a claim. S/he will just need to convince the court that the will does not make reasonable financial provision for him/her. The standard for assessing "reasonable financial provision" is different from that employed for other claimants. It is based on what the

spouse can reasonably expect (depending on length of marriage, separation period and the needs and legitimate claims
of the other beneficiaries), not on whether s/he actually needs
the money.

Ex-spouses, children and other dependants can also make
a claim on the estate but their claim for provision is based on
what the court decides they actually need for "reasonable
maintenance". If provision has been made in a divorce settlement for an ex-spouse, s/he will not normally have a claim on
the estate. But if s/he is receiving maintenance payments
and there is a reasonable amount of capital in the estate then
s/he may succeed in claiming a share of this.

Time limit

Proceedings must be issued within six months of the grant of
probate, so if you wish to make a claim you should consult a
solicitor as soon as possible after the death.

SCOTLAND

Leaving property by will

In Scotland if you have a spouse and/or children you will not
necessarily be able to freely determine, by will, what should
happen to your property after your death. All of your property, except land and buildings, is subject to the legal rights
of your spouse and/or children (including illegitimate ones),
which take precedence over the provisions of a will. The term
"spouse", in this context, does not include lovers, whether
heterosexual or homosexual, nor divorced spouses.

In outline these legal rights are calculated by taking all
your property (except for land or buildings) and, after payment of debts, dividing it either into two or three shares. If
you leave a spouse and children, then each will have a third
of your estate, with the remaining third being distributed
according to your will. If you die leaving a spouse but no
children, or children but no spouse, then the estate is divided
into two, with half going to the spouse or children as the case
may be, and the other half being distributed according to
your will.

One way of effectively leaving your property in your will to a friend or lover is to invest your estate in land, and so avoid the effect of the above legal rights, which do not apply to land. However, to ensure this is effective you should consult a solicitor.

Intestacy

"Legal rights" will again apply if you die intestate, but, because there is no will, they are subject first of all to the "prior rights" of any surviving spouse. The prior rights of a surviving spouse entitle them, in very general terms, to the house, or lease of the house in which they are living at the date of your death, up to a value of £65,000 together with the furnishings up to a value of £12,000. In addition they are entitled to £35,000 if you die without children, or £21,000 if you die with children. These rights terminate on divorce.

Because of the large sums allowed for these legal rights, they often exhaust the whole of the estate. The only way of avoiding their effect is to obtain a divorce or leave a will, since the rights only come into effect on intestacy.

Once legal rights have been satisfied, any remaining estate is distributed, subject to any prior rights, according to the rules of intestacy (i.e. to any children, failing whom to brothers or sisters, failing whom to parents, and so on through any spouse, grandparents or remoter ancestors in that order).

By way of summary, therefore, if you die intestate without leaving a will, then any gay or lesbian partner, or close friend, will inherit nothing from your estate.

VIOLENCE AND HARASSMENT

One of the most powerful stereotypes of lesbian and gay life is that we live in a sordid, violent underworld. In fact such violence as we experience comes mainly from heterosexual "queerbashers". Whatever the actual incidence of gay/lesbian bashing it has an impact on us all because of the fear it engenders. This insecurity is made worse by the expectation (and all too often the reality) of police indifference or hostility.

In addition, harassment which falls short of violence is all too common. (We consider workplace harassment in the Employment chapter, and harassment by landlords and neighbours in the Housing chapter.)

This section will discuss the civil and criminal remedies which may be used to counter violence generally, starting off with a consideration of the particular problems faced by those experiencing "domestic" violence.

VIOLENT RELATIONSHIPS

Undoubtedly some lesbian and gay relationships involve abuse and violence, although this is far less frequent than male violence within heterosexual relationships. This problem is little recognized in our communities and so the victim can feel isolated. The anguish of trying to disentangle love and violence, shame, disbelief and indecision about whether to leave or to rely on promises to change are intensified by our community's silence on the topic and the belief that you are alone in facing this situation.

The social difficulties faced by "battered women" are compounded for battered lesbians and gays by homophobia. The indifference of police to what they regard as "domestic disputes" will often be mixed with hostility to the victims of the abuse. Women's refuges may sometimes confront a battered lesbian with homophobia just when she is at her most vulnerable.

The legal responses to violence within lesbian and gay relationships are inadequate both in principle and in their mode of operation within homophobic institutions. The first step towards improving the options for lesbians and gays trapped in abusive and violent relationships is a greater awareness of the problem within our own communities.

Sometimes simply knowing the legal options, telling your lover that you are prepared to take them to court (possibly by a letter from a lawyer) may put an end to the violence.

Courts have the power to order your partner to stop assaulting you or damaging your property, or to prevent them from entering your house/flat. Even if your home is in joint names you may be able to obtain an order preventing your partner from entering the property for a limited period of time while you organize a permanent separation. (See page 94 for more details.)

These court orders are only intended to act as temporary measures. If they do not make your lover alter his/her behaviour within the relationship you will have to separate. Lesbians may consider the option of staying in a women's refuge. Some councils will provide accommodation for lesbians or gays who are unable to continue occupying their former accommodation because of domestic violence, and some also have a policy of rehousing couples after the break-up of their relationships. It is only fair to add that at the moment, because of the homelessness crisis, such councils are few and far between. Unfortunately this is just part of the neglect of the needs of lesbians and gays in housing provision.

If you are homeless as the result of domestic violence and have children living with you (or are "vulnerable" in some other way — see Housing chapter) then the local authority is under a legal obligation to rehouse you. However even in this situation many councils are adept at evading their legal obligations. They may well insist that you attempt to remedy the situation with injunctions first. If you are in this position consult a law centre or solicitor.

GENERAL RESPONSES TO VIOLENCE

Police

The widespread bigotry towards lesbians and gays by the police force leads to a trivialization of incidents where lesbians and gays are the victims of crimes: no proper investigations, only minor charges being bought against the perpetrators, and sometimes even intimidation or direct abuse of the lesbian and gay witnesses. They are even less likely to respond positively to requests for help in dealing with a violent relationship.

If you go to the police station to report an incident it is best to take someone else with you, if possible write down what happened and go as soon as possible after the event. The police have a great discretion in how they respond to requests for assistance for the public. They have no duty to arrest or prosecute. If you do not feel that they have responded appropriately you may wish to consider a formal complaint against them (see Crime chapter).

If the police decide to prosecute for assault the process is then taken out of your hands. You cannot later decide to withdraw the case. If you do not appear at the trial as a witness then you can be imprisoned for contempt of court. This is rare in practice but has happened to some heterosexual women who felt unable to give evidence against male partners who have been violent towards them.

Another way in which the process can backfire against the victim is that even if the court finds the assailant guilty it can at the same time "bind-over" the victim to keep the peace. This means that if the victim commits an offence or the police are called to a disturbance which they could term "breach of the peace" within a set period of time (generally six months or a year), s/he will have to forfeit a sum of money (usually £100). Bind-overs are most likely to be imposed in domestic or neighbour disputes.

Bail

Generally criminal proceedings are concerned to punish the perpetrator rather than protect the victim. However, if the court considers it appropriate, it can impose bail conditions on the perpetrator which remain in force from the initial until the final hearing. These conditions may include staying away from the victim or a certain area in which the victim lives. If the accused does not obey these bail conditions s/he may be kept in custody until the final hearing of the case. Unfortunately the victim has no direct say in whether these conditions are imposed, but can only ask the police to request the prosecution to apply for them.

PRIVATE PROSECUTIONS

In England and Wales, if the police refuse to bring a prosecution then you can bring a private prosecution yourself. You do this by applying for a summons from a magistrate. You will have to prove to the magistrate that on the face of it an offence has been committed. The summons will then be issued, giving a date for a full hearing in a few weeks or months time.

Such proceedings are expensive and legal aid is not available. If s/he is found guilty the assailant may be ordered to pay your legal costs, and possibly compensation. On the other hand if s/he is found not guilty you may be ordered to pay his/her legal costs. The courts are less likely to make a guilty finding where the prosecution is a private one.

In Scotland, private prosecutions may only be brought with the permission of the Lord Advocate, and are extremely rare.

CRIMINAL INJURIES COMPENSATION BOARD

If you report a crime of violence to the police, even if they do not prosecute, you are entitled to claim compensation from the Criminal Injuries Compensation Board, provided that you have fully co-operated with the police. In cases of "domestic violence" there must be good reason why the offender was not prosecuted.

The Board scrutinizes carefully claims arising from sexual relationships. Compensation will not be paid unless it is clear that the offender will not benefit from the award. Hence no award will be made if you are still part of the same household as the offender.

If the Board consider that you have used "provocative words and behaviour" this may lead to a reduced sum of compensation. This provision might be used against lesbians and gays who are the objects of queerbashing attacks. A further danger may lie in the requirement that you show that "having regard to your conduct . . . your character and your way of life" it is appropriate that you receive a full award. This could also lead to a reduced amount of compensation.

You need to apply on forms that can be obtained direct from the C.I.C.B.(see Listings). They are quite simple to fill in, so you may not need legal help unless the application is particularly complicated. You must apply within three years of the incident. The compensation will be for your physical injuries, as well as damage to personal property such as clothes or glasses. You can also claim loss of earnings due to injuries.

CIVIL ACTION

Civil action is useful as a means not so much of punishing the abuser but of protecting the abused party. It is likely to be more appropriate than criminal proceedings where the person who is harassing or being violent is known to you.

What effect does an injunction have?

An injunction is a court order specifically forbidding an individual from particular actions. The equivalent order in Scotland is termed an interdict. If s/he does not obey the order there is no immediate remedy. For example, you cannot simply ask the police to arrest the person for breach of the injunction (as you can with injunctions under the Domestic Violence Act 1976, which only applies to heterosexual cohabitants). Instead you must apply to the court for him or her to be committed to prison for contempt of court.

This application must be delivered personally (by someone other than yourself) at least two clear days before the hearing date.

Frequently the court will not order committal to prison on the first breach. It might, for instance, make an order suspending committal for as long as the person continues to respect the order. You may well therefore have to make several applications before you receive an effective remedy. Clearly this is not only expensive but enormously stressful.

Can I obtain one?

In order to apply for an injunction you must first commence a suit for damages, and as part of these proceedings apply for an injunction. You must therefore establish that the abuser has committed a legally actionable wrong against you. We set out below the different actions which may allow you to take legal proceedings. In addition, you must convince the court that an injunction is necessary to prevent the abuser inflicting further harm upon you. Judges differ in the extent of threats, violence or abuse that must have occurred before they are prepared to order an injunction. The grounds upon which you can obtain an interdict in Scotland are very similar though not identical.

Battery

A battery is the intentional infliction, with hostile intent, of physical contact without the "victim's" consent. From this definition it is apparent that it is not necessary for the abuser to have inflicted a serious injury before you can start proceedings, however a court may not be willing to order an injunction on the basis of a "slight" assault — one slap or punch. Medical evidence of any injuries inflicted is always helpful in persuading a court of the necessity for an injunction. Battery in not a separate legal course of action in Scotland, but is included in a broarder definition of assault.

Assault

An assault is legally defined as an act which causes a person to fear the infliction of immediate, unlawful force. Thus you can commence proceedings before any physical violence has occurred, solely on the basis of threats. However most courts will be reluctant to issue an injunction on this basis and legal advice on your particular circumstances is essential.

Trespass

A person's right to peaceful enjoyment of their property (which includes not only land which you own but also land which you lawfully rent) is considered very important in the British courts. You can sue someone for trespass on your land (i.e. if you are the sole owner or tenant and you have not given them a licence to live there, or if you have effectively terminated the licence — see Housing chapter). In England and Wales, but not in Scotland, you will have a legal action even where no damage has been done. Trespass can also be to goods, for instance if someone has deliberately destroyed your possessions. However, once again, this does not apply to Scotland.

Even if the person who is being violent is the joint owner of your home it may still be possible to obtain an injunction excluding them (on a temporary basis) from the home if this is the only way in which you can exercise your right to peaceful enjoyment of your share of the property (Davis v. Johnstone 1978). If the abuser is the sole owner of the home and you have been living there with their permission ("a licence" in legal terms) then, in England and Wales, you will generally be entitled to reasonable notice of at least a month before you have to leave. If they are making it impossible for you to live there during that time then you might be able to get a court order excluding them during the period of your notice.

In Scotland if you are living in someone's home, with their permission you will also be entitled to "reasonable" notice, but this may be no more than a day or two, depending on the circumstances. An interdict excluding the person from their home would not be possible in this situation.

Nuisance

In legal terms a private nuisance is the "unlawful interference with a person's use or enjoyment of their land". An action for nuisance may be your only option if you are suffering harassment which falls short of violence, threats of violence or trespass. In legal terms this sort of harassment is known as "molestation", and an injunction restraining some-one from doing it is known as a "non-molestation injunction".

How can I obtain an order?

In England and Wales you start proceedings in the local County court and can apply for an injunction at the same time. Unless you can convince the court that the violence is very severe you will have to give your opponent two clear days notice of any application for an injunction. Again the papers must be personally handed to him/her by someone other than yourself.

In Scotland, application may be made either to the local Sheriff court or the Court of Session.

At the final hearing of your application the court can order your assailant to pay damages to you to compensate for your injury. They can also order him/her to pay your legal expenses. If you fail in your application the court can order you to pay your opponent's legal costs.

Legal aid

In practice you will need a solicitor to take such proceedings and, since few people will be able to afford the full legal costs involved (hundreds or possibly even thousands of pounds), you will need to apply for legal aid. To obtain this the legal aid board must be convinced that not only do you come within their financial limits but also the matter is serious enough to justify legal action.

CONFIDENTIALITY

For all too many lesbians and gays the social cost of being open about their sexuality forces them to keep their private life concealed. What rights do we have to keeping such information private?

The short answer is that there is no specific right to privacy in British law. If someone is spreading lies about you then you can sue them for defamation, slander or libel. As the 1992 case involving singer Jason Donovan demonstrated, in the right circumstances juries will award substantial damages to heterosexuals falsely "accused" of being gay. However, courts are less ready to protect the privacy of lesbians and gays. If the information which is being spread about you is true then only under certain circumstances will other people be legally bound to keep it confidential. If the circumstances outlined below apply then you will be able to take proceedings to enforce confidentiality. A fundamental obstacle to legal action in this area is that legal aid is not available for slander or libel actions, and would be very difficult to obtain for breach of confidentiality.

If you have suffered a loss which you can prove stemmed directly from a breach of confidence (for instance if you have been sacked because someone told your employer that you were gay or lesbian) you will be entitled to apply to the court for financial compensation ("damages"). Once you have started proceedings you can apply for an injunction or interdict restraining the person from communicating the information which is the subject of the proceedings.

In order to sue for breach of confidentiality the other person must owe you a duty of confidence. This may arise from the relationship between you (e.g. a doctor/patient, solicitor/client or employer/employee relationship) or it may be a duty which you have specifically imposed (for example, if you stress to someone that you wish what you do or tell them to remain confidential).

The information must be of a confidential nature, that is it must not be widely known. In some cases where part of the claimant's life is already in the public domain this has been held to be a basis for refusing to protect other aspects of it. Finally the information must be "worth protecting."

A recent English case clarified the attitude of the courts to some extent, but case law on this area remains very undeveloped. In Stephens v. Avery (1988) the plaintiff and first defendant were close friends who discussed personal matters on the express basis that the confidences were to remain secret. The first defendant passed on to the second and third defendants, who were the editor and publishers of a newspaper, details of the plaintiff's sexual conduct, including details of the plaintiff's lesbian relationship with a woman who had been killed by her husband. The plaintiff brought an action for breach of confidence. The defendant argued that she could not bring the action because: a) information about a person's sexual behaviour outside marriage is not protected by law because the information is immoral and the discussion itself "mere tittle tattle" and b) the relationship between the plaintiff and the defendant was not such as to give rise to a duty of confidentiality, being a mere friendship.

The defendants lost the action. The judge stated with regard to ground a): "I very much doubt whether the wholesale revelation of the sexual conduct of an individual can properly be described as trivial tittle tattle. . . . There is no common view that sexual conduct of any kind between consenting adults is grossly immoral. The sexual conduct of the plaintiff was not so morally shocking in this case as to prevent the third defendant, a major Sunday newspaper, from spreading the story all over its front and inside pages."

With regard to ground b) the judge said: "the express statement that the information is confidential is the clearest possible example of the imposition of a duty of confidence."

This is a new, and very uncertain area of law, and because of the expense involved is not able to offer protection to the many lesbians and gays who are made vulnerable to exposure by society's homophobia. It is certainly an area in which law reform and the extension of legal aid is needed.

PRESS/ADVERTISING

Even if you yourself do not have the misfortune to be caught up in a vindictive press campaign, the way that the media in general represent lesbians and gays still has a powerful, if indirect, impact. In the majority of cases it stirs up homophobia and undermines our self image. It was only in June 1990 that the Press Complaints Commission (the self-regulation organization of the press) recognized that words such as "poof" were offensive and should not be used.

However the Press Complaints Commission appeared to subsequently backtrack on this decision (which was greeted with scorn by the "popular" press) when it refused to accept further complaints concerning the use of the word. In any event, the Commission has no powers to enforce its decisions.

There is substantial public support for effective legal sanctions on press reporting. Whether or not this will be of assistance to lesbians and gays remains to be seen.

Advertising also frequently contains powerful negative images of lesbians and gays. The organization to whom complaints should be addressed is the Advertising Standards Authority. A 1989 campaign organized against the Whitbread adverts for Flowers beer ("Not all flowers are pansies") scored an encouraging success with press and even Parliamentary support forcing the company to withdraw the offending posters.

* * *

This chapter has indicated some of the ways in which homophobia impinges on the legal options of lesbians and gays in their everyday lives. The wide range of issues involved cannot be addressed by one easy option, in particular lesbian and gay marriages would only solve some of the problems, even for those of us who would take such a step. The real solution is far more ambitious: for the institutions and practices of society to equally reflect the lives of all of those who live in it including the ten per cent of us who are lesbian or gay.

CARING FOR CHILDREN

Many lesbians and gay men have children — whether these have been conceived in heterosexual relationships prior to "coming out" or, as increasingly is the case, are the product of conscious choices to parent by lesbians or gays. There are no specific laws regarding lesbian or gay parenting. This lack of acknowledgement, however, reflects deep social prejudices against the possibility of non-heterosexual parenting, and the law as applied through the courts has been particularly punitive to lesbian and gay parents.

In recent years, as more parents have refused to conceal their sexuality as the price for gaining custody of, or access to, their children, the attitude of some judges does seem to be moderating. At the same time hard-pressed social services have been prepared to cast their nets wider when looking for foster and adoptive parents, and, in some areas of the country at least, this has become a parenting option for lesbians and gays.

Nevertheless the reality persists that lesbian and gay parents live under constant threat of losing their parental rights — usually to the other biological parent, but occasionally to other relatives or by having their children "taken into care". This sense of being constantly embattled has been sharpened in recent years by explicit, political assaults on the rights of gays and lesbians to parent, accompanied by virulent media campaigns. In 1990/91 there were two such deliberate attacks in Parliament. During the passage of the Human Reproduction and Embryology Bill there were concerted attempts by the right-wingers to restrict access to donor insemination solely to women in heterosexual relationships. These achieved a degree of success, despite heated lobbying and the objections of the major clinics providing these services. Shortly after these debates the government sought to make political capital by restricting the abilities of local authorities to place children for fostering and adoption with gays or lesbians. Lesbian and gay campaigners, with the support of many fostering and adoption agencies successfully removed explicit references to lesbians and gays, but considerable media and political hostility persists.

This chapter will be divided into three parts: firstly we consider the legal position of lesbians and gays who have been bringing up children in a heterosexual context — how can your desired contact with these children best be maintained? Secondly, we examine the legal implications of the alternative means by which lesbians or gays may become parents: donor insemination, co-parenting, fostering and adoption. Finally, we will consider the means by which the state has the power to intervene — that is when Social Services seek to remove children from the home, or to obtain powers to supervise their upbringing.

CHILDREN OF HETEROSEXUAL RELATIONSHIPS

Many, if not most, lesbians and gay men form heterosexual relationships prior to coming out. When there are children, the break-up of these relationships may lead to disputes about who should bring them up, and the degree of contact which the parent who is not living with the child should have. Such disputes can, of course, arise where both parents remain heterosexual but the animosity which frequently results from a heterosexual's discovery that their ex-partner is lesbian or gay increases the risk that children will be used by them as mean of punishment.

In addition, the hostile attitude of the law towards lesbians and gays as parents means that they face a range of obstacles not encountered by most heterosexual parents. If they are also black and/or working class the prejudice of the judges is likely to be increased. For this reason, we would advise, where possible, that you seek to resolve disputes outside the courts. Court battles over children are inevitably very stressful, particularly if you are lesbian or gay when you are made to feel that you and your lifestyle are on trial. In addition such legal disputes can be enormously expensive.

Despite this advice it is useful to have an awareness from the beginning of the factors which will be considered if the worst happens and you are forced to go to court. By preparing for this you can strengthen your bargaining position and increase the likelihood of a favourable resolution without going to court, as well as improving your chances in that eventuality.

If you are in dispute with the other parent about the children it is important to know your legal options, how the courts are likely to act and how to improve your chances of getting the parenting arrangements which you want. We set these out below. After reading them it is wise also to talk to someone knowledgeable about your particular circumstances. For lesbians we would suggest that you contact the ROW Lesbian Custody Group, and for gay men we recommend Gay Legal Advice (see Listings). They can give you some preliminary support and advice. They should also be able to suggest sympathetic local solicitors with the relevant expertise.

If you are lucky they may also know of appropriate support groups in your area. If you do end up in a protracted legal struggle you will certainly need support. Alternatively the local lesbian line or gay switchboard may have suggestions. Obviously friends and family may also be good sources of support. Do not underestimate the amount of stress under which you will be placed and your need for emotional support which may well be more than even the most wonderful lover can provide.

The factors which we discuss below apply broadly to legal decisions, whether or not the parents are married and regardless of sex — where these factors make a difference we will comment. We will then outline the different procedures which can be used to resolve disputes over children, finance and housing for married couples and unmarried couples.

One final point, always to be remembered, is that where children are concerned the courts' orders (with the one exception of adoption) are never final. Either parent is always able to return to court and ask for the living arrangements of the child to be altered, even where these have already been resolved through a lengthy legal battle. Of course, the court will need to be convinced that some important changes have occurred since any previous orders were made, and the longer the children remain with one parent the harder it becomes to persuade the court that they should be moved. While parents who have lost custody of their child will find that this rule presents some hope, for lesbian and gay parents who have their children with them, it can feel like a constant threat.

KEY LEGAL CONCEPTS

The law in England and Wales concerning children was completely reorganized by the Children's Act 1989, which came into force in October 1991. The Act does not, on the whole, apply to Scotland. We shall therefore briefly explain the main areas where Scottish law differs. The general advice about tactics in custody disputes will apply in both jurisdictions.

With regard to private family law in England and Wales, the terms "custody" and "access" are no longer employed by the law. This shift in terminology is intended to represent a corresponding shift in the reality of arrangements for children whose parents have separated, and to discourage lengthy legal disputes.

It is important to note that parental disputes can now only be resolved through the law if the child is under the age of 16. None of the orders set out below can be made with respect to young people over that age, and any existing orders cease to have legal effect when the children reach that age — save in "exceptional circumstances". Under the old law custody and other orders could be made up to the age of 18. This reduction in the age limit appears to be a recognition that orders relating the young people of 16 and over are in effect unenforceable, unless they are prepared to co-operate. At the same time parental responsibility for maintenance continues to apply past this age (see below).

PARENTAL RESPONSIBILITY/CUSTODY

The new Act talks about "parental responsibility" rather than custody in an attempt to focus on the duties of parenthood rather than the view of children as possessions to be fought over by parents.

Where parents are married (or become married to each other)

Both have parental responsibility for their children and this continues automatically after divorce, regardless of any court orders specifying with whom the child should live. Indeed, parental responsibility continues regardless of the wishes of the parents themselves, and regardless of any subsequent living arrangements for the child or whether the local authority has obtained compulsory care orders. The only legal method of ending parental responsibility is by an adoption order which transfers all responsibility to the adoptive parents. All other orders conferring parental responsibility are additional to, not a substitute for, the parental responsibility of the biological parents.

Where parents are not married

In this case only the mother will have parental responsibility automatically, the father has to apply to the court for a parental responsibility order or draw up a formal agreement with the mother. Biological fathers who have not acquired parental responsibility still have a financial responsibility for the child and count as related for the purposes of inheritance.

What does parental responsibility mean?

It does not mean that the child lives jointly with all those having parental responsibility, nor is the continuing responsibility of both parents after a divorce the equivalent of joint custody orders in the old system. Although both parents have the right to make decisions concerning the child, there is no duty on them to consult each other in advance about decisions, no matter how serious, nor can one parent veto the decision of the other, except by going to court. (The position was unclear in previous law but there was thought to be a right of veto by the parent not involved in a decision.) Now, in practice, most decisions will be taken by the parent with whom the child is living and the other parent would need to go to court if s/he objects.

RESIDENCE ORDERS

These are orders which specify with whom the child should live — the equivalent of the pre-existing legal concept of "care and control". It is possible for the court to make an order that the child should reside in more than one place, or with more than one person, and indeed it could specify in some detail how the child should spend its time (i.e. Monday to Wednesday with the mother and from 5pm Wednesday to 10pm Sunday with the father etc.). However, courts have in the past discouraged such orders as too disruptive for the children.

CONTACT ORDERS

These, broadly speaking, replace access orders: "requiring the person with whom the child lives . . . to allow the child to visit or stay with the person named in that order, or for that person and the child otherwise to have contact with each other" (for example, telephone calls and letters are allowed to be exchanged).

SPECIFIC ISSUES ORDERS

Where interested parties disagree about what decisions should be made for the child (for instance which school s/he should attend) either parent can apply to the court for a binding decision on this issue.

PROHIBITED STEP ORDERS

These orders restrain in some way the actions of another person in relation to the child for example by preventing a child from being taken out of the country.

CONDITIONS

In the past, conditions have mainly been attached to access (contact) orders, for example, access is granted on condition that the child will not be brought into contact with any gay or lesbian lovers. The Court of Appeal ruled in M v. M 1977 that it was not appropriate to impose as a condition of staying access that the mother's lover who jointly owned the house should be absent.

HOW COURTS DECIDE DISPUTES ABOUT WHICH PARENT SHOULD LIVE WITH THE CHILD

A major objective in changing the law to a situation where both parents will invariably retain parental responsibility after the divorce, is to "lower the stakes" in cases of separation and divorce. This same desire (as well as the less admirable desire to reduce the escalating costs of family litigation) is behind the specification that the courts should not make any of the above orders unless they feel that this would be better for the child than making none. This increases the pressure to resolve matters amicably and without court order. Most significantly it means that upon divorce there will not automatically be any orders relating to the children. (Under the previous system an order specifying the arrangements for custody, care and control and access to the child would always have to be made by the court.)

Best interests of the child

The dominant consideration which the court is supposed to employ in deciding issues is the "best interests of the child". This is a notoriously vague concept. For the first time the Children's Act introduced a "checklist" of factors which courts are required to consider: the wishes and feelings of the child (considered in the light of his/her age and understanding); his/her physical, emotional and educational needs; the likely effects on him/her of any change of circumstances; his/her age, sex and background; any harm which s/he has suffered or is at risk of suffering; how capable the parent or other person is of meeting his/her needs.

These represent the range of factors which judges had previously considered in their decisions and as such will not effect any marked change in the basis of decision making. There is no guidance as to what weight should be given to these different factors, nor do they prohibit the court from taking into account factors which are not included on this list. The existence of a checklist may make it easier to challenge a decision through an appeal where undue weight has been given to a factor not included in this list at the expense of factors which are on the list. We consider below the significance of some of these factors.

The judge (or magistrates depending on which type of court is hearing the case) will base their decision on the evidence presented by the parents, and any witnesses which they may call on their behalf. In addition a social worker attached to the court (called the Court Welfare Officer) will prepare a report based on visiting the parents, speaking to the children and possibly making other enquiries — for instance talking to staff at their schools. This report will usually have a lot of influence on the judge. It is very difficult to change welfare officers; an application would have to be made to the court, which would need very convincing reasons to authorize a change.

Sex of the parent

Despite a clear ruling by the Court of Appeal (In re H, a minor 1990) that there should be no presumption that children, particularly young children are most appropriately cared for by their mothers, this attitude is still strong.

Sexuality

You will notice that nowhere in the list of factors to be considered is sexuality mentioned, nor indeed is conduct mentioned. Courts are not supposed to make orders to punish or reward parents for their conduct, but they will consider the conduct of the parents in so far as it relates to the upbringing of the child. The homosexuality and lifestyle of parents has in all too many cases been considered by judges a reason for not allowing children to live with that parent and even, on rare occasions, forbidding that parent visitation rights. In recent years some progress has been made in reversing this judicial trend, partly through the successes of the lesbian mothers custody campaign. However these prejudices still run strong. It will be useful to look more closely at some of these preconceptions so that you can try to counter them.

Many courts have used the fact that society is prejudiced against lesbians and gays to suggest that the child will be stigmatized and teased at school. Another common concern is that children will lack proper, heterosexual role models and may grow up gay themselves or have problems with their "gender roles" (i.e. without a father boys will not learn to behave like men). Some judges voice prejudices concerning the stereotypically predatory nature of lesbians and gay men, such as that your friends or lover will seduce the child. Perhaps most powerful, and because of their vagueness very difficult to counter, are fears that the children will be in moral danger (the lingering taint of sin attached to homosexuality) and the presumption that given the option between a heterosexual and a homosexual home the former is simply and incontestably to be preferred.

Wishes of the child

The practice prior to the new Act was that children's wishes were considered, but would not necessarily be given much weight unless the children were considered old enough to be resistant to parental pressures and bribes — usually about aged nine or ten. Even then, their wishes were not necessarily determinant as courts sometimes acted out of a paternalistic belief that they know better what is in children's long-term interests. It may be that courts will give more weight to children's wishes under the new Act, since the checklist makes this the first requirement for judges to consider.

It will, of course, still be possible for courts to decide that a child is too young for his/her wishes properly to be taken into account or that other factors outweigh the importance that should be attached to them. Nevertheless, the whole tenor of the new Act reflects an increased respect for the autonomy of children and, in turn, follows judicial trends in recent years. For example in one case (M v. M Transfer of Custody: Appeal 1987) the Court of Appeal held that the trial judge was plainly wrong to transfer the custody of a 12-year-old girl from her father to her mother against the girl's clearly stated and strong wishes.

Children are not generally allowed to give direct evidence in the court hearing, as it is felt that this imposes too much stress on them. Their views should be asked by the court welfare officer and recorded in his/her report. On rare occasions a judge may ask older children (over about aged ten) to talk to him or her in private.

Stability

Courts are reluctant to impose upon children any more changes to their lives than are inevitable. Thus, there is a very strong presumption in favour of leaving the child with the parent with whom s/he is living at the time of the court hearing. The longer this arrangement has lasted, the less likely the court is to disrupt it. In practice, this means that if you have left the children in the care of their other parent it is important to you that the case should be heard as soon as possible. On the other hand, if you are living with the children, it will be to your tactical advantage to have the case heard as late as possible.

Siblings should be kept together

Another strong assumption of the courts is that, where possible, brothers and sisters should be kept together.

Material circumstances

Courts will obviously consider the practical arrangements which the parents can make for the child such as housing, schooling and financial security. This is why in the procedural sections below we give quite a bit of detail about the financial and housing arrangements that can be made by the courts.

Contact with the children

The above discussion relates mainly to considerations about which parent should have the day-to-day care of the child. The overriding principle in connection with contact by the parent who is not living with the children is, once again, consideration of the best interests of the children. Contact is the children's right, not the parents'. In practice, courts overwhelmingly believe that it is in the interest of children to have continuing contact with both parents. In some circumstances, where it is felt that the child is unsafe for some reason, or possibly as an interim measure to assess the quality of the contact, an order for contact may be made conditional on other people being present — for example a social worker, or on it taking place at a family centre specifically set up for this purpose. The court may be concerned that the child should not be exposed to a gay lifestyle and therefore may attempt to impose such conditions or other more unusual (and outrageous) conditions.

WHAT YOU CAN DO TO IMPROVE YOUR POSITION IF YOU ARE IN DISPUTE ABOUT WHERE YOUR CHILD SHOULD LIVE

Try to avoid legal disputes

Whenever possible always try to strike a bargain rather than get involved in legal disputes. What you use to bargain with will obviously depend on your ex-partner. Perhaps they will be prepared to settle for extensive visiting. Perhaps they will be prepared to agree to your proposals for the care of the children in exchange for your agreeing to a less favourable financial settlement. You might even consider sharing the care of the children. Agreements can be reached at any time, even if court proceedings have begun, indeed many cases are settled at "the door of the court".

Don't trust him/her

In this process it will almost certainly be to your advantage
to conceal your sexual orientation from your ex-partner. Bear
in mind however that this will mean either concealing it from
the children or putting the strain of secrecy onto them, if they
are having continuing contact with their other parent. If you
are involved in a legal dispute, and your partner is making
allegations about your sexual orientation, you should think
very carefully before lying to the court. If you are discovered
to have been lying this will strongly prejudice the court
against you. If you decide to conceal your sexuality from the
court, you will not be able to discuss this with your lawyer, as
they are not allowed to help to conceal the truth from the
court.

Wherever possible keep the child with you
— try and remain in the family home

Both of these points are crucial because of the emphasis that
the courts place on providing children with stability. Except
in the unlikely event that you persuade your ex-partner to
leave the home, you may suffer considerable strain in sharing the home until your disputes have been resolved. See the
section below on the legal position concerning interim arrangements in shared housing.

If your partner is being violent then consult the section on
Violence (page 89). You may be able to obtain an emergency
court order forcing your ex-partner to leave the home. If this
fails, and you do not feel able to tolerate the threat of violence
any more, take the children with you to a refuge.

If you try to leave before a residence order has been made,
you will find that the council will not provide you with
permanent housing, as they will first wish to see where the
court orders the children to live. If you can find somewhere
adequate and preferably near enough so as not to disrupt the
children's schooling it may be acceptable to move, however it
would be wise to consult a solicitor before doing so.

Even if you have a residence order for the children to live
with you, be aware that if the council considers you have

voluntarily left a home in which you were entitled to remain they are unlikely to agree to rehouse you, unless the reason you have left is your partner's violence (see Housing chapter, page 42).

If you've already left without the children

This does not necessarily mean that you will not succeed in obtaining custody, but it is urgent that you take action. Consult a solicitor as soon as possible. If you have not been seeing the children you should start regular contact as soon as possible. It is vital that you convince the court of your continuing care for the children. Be regular and keep to arrangements. Any problems will almost certainly be used by your partner's lawyers to try and imply that you are an inadequate or uncaring parent.

Plan for the future

The court will obviously want to know how and where you plan to live with the children. If a residence order for the children is made in your favour the court will try and ensure that you have somewhere to live with the children. As we will see there are various different orders which enable you to stay in the family home on an extended basis. Would you be able to keep up the necessary payments — with financial support from your partner if necessary? If not, can you show that the council would be prepared to house you (see pages 42–44). If you will be working, what childcare arrangements will you make?

COURT TACTICS

Lovers

If you have a long-term lover consider whether or not to involve him/her in the case. If the court is aware of their existence it may well be considered suspicious if they are not called as a witness, particularly if you intend living with them, or involving them in the care of the children. It is difficult to predict how the court will react and it is unfortunately rather a case of "damned if you do, and damned if you don't". The court may be disturbed at the idea that you will be "flaunting" your relationship in front of the children — concerned that you might be physically affectionate in front of them. On the other hand it might approve of a "marriage-like" relationship.

Respectability

It is a fact which you will have to take into account that the more you approximate to conventional middle-class respectability the more the judge will like you. This might mean for example showing that you have what they would regard as an integrated social life — with friends of the opposite sex who can provide the "role models" that the court finds so important. Certainly if your family are prepared to offer you support this is likely to favourably impress the judge. Probably the less active you are politically, particularly within the women's or lesbian and gay movements, the better. Obviously the clothes which you and your witnesses wear to court will be important for creating a good impression.

Only you, with advice from your lawyer, can decide how you wish to present yourself to the court.

Stressing your ex-partner's unsuitability

This is a particularly unpleasant aspect of what used to be termed "custody disputes". Your ex-partner will be doing this about you, and using homophobia as well. This is not the time to be noble — think of any criticisms of his or her parenting, criminal record, mental instability or alcoholism.

Welfare report

As we explained above, a social worker will be appointed to prepare a report for the court. This will contain his or her impressions of you and your ex-partner, your homes and your parenting abilities. The court welfare officer will probably want to visit you in your home and talk to the children separately. This is a very influential factor in the final decision. It is vital that you make the best impression.

Beware, court welfare officers may be very traditional. Even if they appear liberal and friendly it is wisest to be careful about what you say to them. Present a clean home. If you have decided to play down your politics then look around for tell-tale posters or books. You should consider carefully, in advance, your attitude towards telling the children about your sexuality, and how you will deal with the sort of problems they may encounter.

Psychological evidence?

Where the issue of your sexuality has been raised think about how to deal with it. You might want to tackle the myths head on by presenting psychological evidence that it is not detrimental to bringing up the children.

WHAT TO DO IF YOU LOSE THE CASE?

You should consider appealing, although the grounds for appealing are very difficult to satisfy. You will not be entitled to a re-hearing on the facts of the case, but you will have to convince the appeal court that the original court interpreted the law wrongly.

You can make a new application at a later date. Remember no order on children's cases is ever final. If your children are obviously unhappy with their other parent then you can apply to the court again on this basis.

You may want to take the children out of the country. You will be entitled to take the children out of the country for a period not exceeding one month, provided that you give notice to the person who has a residence order for the children (it is a criminal offence under the Child Abduction Act 1984 to take them without providing such a warning). The person who has a residence order in their favour can then apply to the court for an order preventing you from removing the children if s/he suspects that you intend to remove them permanently.

If you are intending to abscond with the children in this way, be warned that many countries now enforce each other's "custody" orders and will deport the children if you are located.

SCOTLAND

The framework of parental rights in Scotland, as in England and Wales, centres on the married, heterosexual couple. If the child's parents are married, then they will both automatically have parental rights. If they are not married, then only the mother will automatically have parental rights, although as we explain below it is possible for the unmarried father, or indeed anyone, including a lesbian or gay partner, to apply to the courts for sole or joint parental rights over a child.

Parental rights include the actual care and custody of the child, and also the right to make decisions about their upbringing such as their education, medical treatment, name and property. The older the child is, the more parental rights diminish in favour of the child making up his/her own mind about such matters.

The law in this area has recently been altered by the Age of Legal Capacity (Scotland) 1991. Broadly the position under this Act is that parental rights are exercised by a child's parents or guardians up until the age of 16. Where both parents have parental rights, then the rights may be exercised jointly by both parents, and each may make a decision about the child without the consent of the other. In the event of dispute, either party may apply to the court to have the matter decided.

If the parents have been married but later separate or divorce, then, in practice, only one party will retain custody. Despite this, the parent without custody retains all the other parental rights that they had previously, including a right of access to the child. If there is a dispute about any of these parental rights then either party may apply to the court for a decision. The court will then rule on the dispute. The factors that are taken into account are very similar to the considerations in England and Wales described above. Likewise the discussion of tactics to follow in custody disputes is equally relevant to Scotland.

Quite separate from the question of parental rights is the issue of the child's right to financial support (known as "aliment" in Scotland), which s/he can exercise against either or both parents, or the partner of a parent who has taken over a parental role in the household. The fact that a parent does or does not have custody is irrelevant. The obligation to aliment continues until a child is aged 18, or 25 if in full-time education or training.

OTHER ASPECTS OF SEPARATION

DIVORCE: APPLIES EQUALLY TO SCOTLAND

Advantages

You may want this psychological severing of the ties. The more practical advantage of taking divorce proceedings is to resolve financial disputes. You can resolve disputes about financial support for you and your children without getting divorced, but if you or your partner own the property in which you are living divorce provides the most favourable forum for determining the ownership of your home. Similarly, there are limits on the amount of money that can be awarded as a lump sum in other proceedings, but no limits on the amounts that can be ordered in divorce proceedings (see below).

Disadvantages

Your immigration status may be adversely affected, you risk antagonising you partner, perhaps leading to a contest over the children, and finally the procedure for divorce/judicial separation is likely to be more long drawn-out, and possibly more expensive than if you merely apply to the court to resolve the issues of finances and childcare.

JUDICIAL SEPARATION?

For those who cannot get divorced (e.g. if you have not been married for at least one year), or if you do not want to (for religious reasons for example) you may be able to be legally (or in lawyer's jargon "judicially") separated. The grounds which you will need to establish are identical to the grounds for divorce (see below), and judicial separation provides the

same financial remedies as divorce. The one practical difference is that neither of you can remarry.

Divorce procedure

Divorce is still not available in England, Scotland or Wales
simply on the request of one party. You must first have been
married for a year. You must prove to the court's satisfaction
that your marriage has irretrievably broken down. You must
show that one of these circumstances applies:

a) Your spouse has committed adultery. (Unless s/he is prepared to sign a statement admitting to it this can be the most
difficult ground to get courts to accept.) Adultery is defined as
heterosexual, penetrative intercourse, thus lesbian/gay affairs do not qualify!

b) Your spouse has behaved in such a way that you cannot
reasonably be expected to live with him/her. Gay or lesbian
affairs come under this heading, along with violence, alcoholism, and a host of other behaviours. However, boredom is not
enough to satisfy this ground!

c) Your spouse has deserted (that is left without your consent) for at least two years.

d) You have lived apart for at least two years and your spouse
consents.

e) You have lived apart for at least five years.

Thus, unless your spouse has behaved badly or consents, you
will not be able to get a divorce for five years.

Nowadays there is little practical relevance as to which
spouse initiates the divorce, since conduct does not have a
significant effect on financial or child orders. If you do not
have the legal grounds required to divorce your spouse, they
may be able to divorce you.

GENERAL PRINCIPLES OF FINANCIAL SETTLEMENTS ON SEPARATION

Financial support for children

The Child Support Act 1991 will revolutionize the practice and principles of claiming financial support for children. It applies to Scotland as well as England and Wales, and will start to come into force in 1993, being phased in over a three year period. At present it is necessary to claim financial support for children through a court, and there are no fixed rules about how much should be paid. The Child Support Act introduces a fixed formula for assessing the payment level (taking into account the income and outgoings of the parent who is not caring for the child). It also establishes an agency within the Department of Social Security which will be responsible for the assessment and enforcement of almost all claims for child maintenance, regardless of whether or not the family is claiming any social security benefits. It is to this agency which you will need to apply if you are seeking maintenance.

A parent is liable to pay maintenance in all circumstances, regardless of whether or not s/he is currently seeing the child, has ever lived with him/her, or was ever married to the other parent.

There are provisions for annual reviews of the maintenance, and either parent can apply for a review if there has been a change of circumstances which would make the amount of maintenance paid substantially different.

Financial support for yourself

The Child Support Act's formula for calculating the maintenance payable for children includes an amount intended to represent payment to "the parent as carer". This is not intended to act as spousal maintenance, and any claim for this must be brought separately through the courts. It is only if you are, or have been married to your ex-partner that you can apply for such periodic payments (i.e. money to be paid on a regular basis generally, weekly or monthly) for yourself.

You can apply for such payments either when you are taking divorce/judicial separation proceedings, or in quicker proceedings in the magistrates' court. (To use these quicker proceedings you will need to show either that your partner does not provide enough money to keep you and the children; or that s/he has behaved in such a way that you cannot reasonably be expected to live with him/her; or that s/he has deserted you or that you and your spouse have been separated for at least three months and s/he has been paying voluntary maintenance during this period).

How much maintenance is awarded will depend on the financial resources and requirements of you and your partner. There is no fixed formula as there is for children. The first concern of the court will be to make sure that the children are provided with a home (see below) and that the person who is caring for them has adequate income to maintain this. It is only once this goal has been achieved that the court will consider the question of what is a "fair" distribution of joint property and incomes. The court will consider all relevant present and potential resources. Thus, if either of you are cohabiting, the court will take into account at least a part of the financial resources of these cohabitants.

A further principle, which the court attempts to promote, is that spouses should, to the maximum extent possible, become financially independent of each other. This means that the court may look at your future earning capacity, and consider whether it is reasonable to expect you to go back to work in the future. Courts in this situation have increasingly chosen to order only a short period of income payments to an unemployed wife, sufficient in their view to allow time for her to find employment.

On the other hand, if the working partner has sufficient financial resources for the court to move on from considering how to maintain reasonable lifestyles for both parties and the children to considerations of fairness, it may order extended financial support for a woman who has forsaken a career to bring up children for many years and who is, as a consequence, realistically unable to find suitable employment.

In some cases where an owner of the family home has lost his/her right to live there this might be compensated by reducing the amount of income that s/he would otherwise be expected to pay to maintain his/her ex-partner.

You can go back to court at a later date and ask for more maintenance for yourself provided that you have not re-married. Similarly your ex-partner is able to go back to court and argue that his/her payments should be reduced if their circumstances change.

If you are on income support

The basic principle is that the DSS will reduce your income support by the amount of maintenance which you receive, apart from a small weekly sum which you will be allowed to keep. If you do not claim any maintenance, the DSS will do so on your behalf. The Child Support Act 1991 allows the DSS to assess, collect and enforce maintenance payments from parents whose children are not in their care. Mainte-nance can be collected not only for children, but also for persons on income support who are looking after the children for whom maintenance is being claimed, provided that they are under 16.

If you refuse to co-operate with the Department of Social Security in tracking down your ex-partner, they will with-hold some, or all of your income support, unless you can persuade them that providing the information will create "a risk" that you, or any child living with you will "suffer" harm or undue distress.

The family home

If you have not been married to your partner then the basic principles set out in the section on "splitting up" in the Housing chapter will apply. The only distinction being that in England and Wales, if you have children and are living in rented property then, whether or not you are married, courts have the power to transfer the tenancy from your partner's name into your name if you will be looking after the children. If such an order is made then you will be able to force your partner to leave. Unless they are violent you will probably not be able to force them to leave until an order is made. If you are in this position you should take legal advice.

Looked at from the other perspective, this means that if you have the sole tenancy of a flat you will normally be able to force your ex-partner to leave, but if s/he will be looking after the children you may find yourself evicted.

In Scotland, the situation differs depending on whether or not you are married. If you are not married and you are a council tenant or if the tenancy was in joint names, then the court will transfer the tenancy. Otherwise the court will only allow the transfer if you have already been granted occupancy rights. Occupancy rights are only available to heterosexual cohabiting couples, not homosexual ones.

Owner-occupation and divorce

The comments below apply whether the property is in joint names, or in the sole name of either party. If you are married and taking divorce or judicial separation proceedings then you can apply for the transfer of the property or its sale and the division of the sale price in those proceedings. Until an order is made both spouses have the right to remain in the matrimonial home, regardless of who legally owns the property. The only exception is where one party is being violent to the other, in which case it is possible to apply for an injunction.

It is far more advantageous for the party who will be looking after the children to apply for a transfer in divorce or judicial separation proceedings, rather than seeking to establish a trust as unmarried couples must do. This is because the court will not primarily focus on the relative financial contributions to the property but on the question of who will be looking after the children and how they can be provided with a home. Its next concern will be how to provide the other party with a home. Only after that will it consider the question of what would be a fair division of the value of the home in the light of unequal financial contributions. The court may order that the house be placed or remain in joint names on the condition that it should not be sold until the children are grown up, and specifying how the sale proceeds should be divided at that later date. The court may alternatively order that it be transferred or remain in your sole name upon condition that you pay your ex-partner a lump sum, perhaps to be raised by extending the mortgage. You will need to consider whether you can afford to remain in the family home with the children or need to find a cheaper property. In this case the court will order the sale and division of the proceeds, again seeking to ensure that you have enough money to provide a home for the children.

Capital

In divorce/judicial separation proceedings the court can order unlimited amounts of money to be transferred from one spouse to another, or to the children. In other family proceedings the sums of money which can be transferred in this way are limited.

It is not possible to go back to court at a later date and ask for more money. A lump sum order will typically be made to compensate a spouse who loses their share of the matrimonial home, or where one partner deserves a share of the other's accumulated assets or perhaps even compensation for the loss of future assets.

Legal aid

The basic principles of the legal aid system are set out in the Legal Aid section of the Legal System chapter (page 285). If you have used legal aid to reach a financial settlement your legal costs will be deducted from any capital received by you over a certain amount, or added as a charge to your home (i.e. a loan secured against the property) if it is not sold. Any maintenance which you receive will be unaffected.

DONOR INSEMINATION

What is donor insemination?

Donor insemination is a means by which a woman can become pregnant without having sexual contact with a man. It can be arranged through clinics or by individuals through self-insemination. Many women find that using a clinic is an alienating experience (there is also a charge for the service); however this method does assure anonymity which will be important if you wish to ensure that the donor has no contact with the child, and also provides screening for health risks, such as HIV.

Legal restrictions on donor insemination

Prior to 1990 there was no legal regulation of donor insemination. The Human Fertilization and Embryology Act 1990 (applying to Scotland as well as England and Wales) sought to control some of the new developments in reproductive technology. Although donor insemination itself is not particularly new, or indeed particularly technological, clinics supplying this service found themselves regulated for the first time.

The Act does not apply to all donor insemination, merely to those which are defined as "treatment services", that is when it is provided "to the public or a section of the public for the purpose of assisting women to carry children." Thus private arrangements are not affected. However, clinics providing this service can now only do so if they receive a licence from the Human Fertilization and Embryology Authority.

There was considerable outrage from the pro-family traditionalists' lobby about the possibility of lesbians (and indeed other single women) being able to conceive through this means without the encumbrance of a man — thus undermining the "sanctity of family life". They sought to explicitly ban lesbians and single women from using these services. As the result of a political compromise, the Act makes it a condition of any licence that "a woman shall not be provided with treatment services unless account has been taken of the welfare of any child who may be born as a result of the treatment (including the need of that child for a father)."

At the same time, the Code of Guidance issued under the Act states that "Centres should avoid adopting any policy or criteria which may appear arbitrary or discriminatory." Nevertheless, where single women are asking for donor insemination, the Code specifically directs that the centres should consider the child's need for a father and "should pay particular attention to the prospective mother's ability to meet the child's needs throughout his or her childhood."

There are various procedural requirements which may help to promote a fair application of these somewhat contradictory principles. The decision should be made quickly, the applicant's views must be taken into account, and she should be given an opportunity to meet any objections raised by the centre. If a centre refuses treatment, it must explain the reason and give the applicant a chance to reapply.

Undoubtedly the licensing provisions are dangerously vague and normative, perpetuating the ideology that the presence of a father is vital to a child's welfare. Although the present Code of Guidance attempts a balanced approach to the implementation of the Act there is a danger that the guidelines may be revised in a more discriminatory fashion.

It is too early yet to say how this statute has affected the provision of donor insemination by clinics. Obviously it provides reinforcement for the existing discrimination against lesbians that is practised in some clinics. The Pregnancy Advisory Service and British Pregnancy Advisory Service are non-profit making organizations, both of which formerly offered donor insemination services to lesbians and opposed the restrictions on availability contained in the Act. The PAS's practises under its equal opportunity policy will presumably be unaffected, unless the licensing authority chooses to threaten the withdrawal of its licence under the provisions of the Act. However the British Pregnancy Advisory Service has now stopped providing donor insemination altogether stating that it is uneconomical.

The sperm donor's legal relationship to the child

The other impact of the Act is to regulate the relationship between the donor and the child. Once again these provisions only apply if the insemination has taken place through a licensed clinic; private arrangements remain unaffected. Donors who provide sperm to a clinic will have their anonymity preserved. A child resulting from the insemination is only entitled to know certain medical details about the donor, not his identity. While the relevant regulations may be changed, the Act explicitly provides that such alterations will not take effect retrospectively.

The Act also specifies that a sperm donor to a clinic will not be treated as the legal father of any resulting child. However this provision applies only to sperm donated through licensed clinics. Private donors will therefore be liable to be treated as the father. The same basic framework applies as with the father of any illegitimate child; thus the donor is entitled to apply through the courts for contact, or even orders for parental responsibility and residence. The court will decide whether to make such orders according to what it considers to be in the child's best interest, regardless of the relationship (or lack of it) between the "parents".

The lack of any pre-existing relationship between the donor and the child might prevent a court from ordering contact, for instance if the child was five and the donor had not had any previous contact with him/her. The general approach of the courts however is that a child should have a "father-figure" (preferably the biological father) wherever possible. The growing emphasis of case law and statutes in recent years has been on the importance of fathers. Given this tendency we think it likely that a court would order contact with the donor, particular where the child is being brought up by lesbians. The consequence for a woman seeking to become pregnant by donor insemination is that, if she does not wish the donor to have contact with the child, the only guaranteed way of achieving this is by making all arrangements through a third party to retain anonymity.

Maintenance from the donor?

The other aspect of the conventional father/child relationship is the "father's" duty to accept financial responsibility for the child. The mother of a child can sue the father for maintenance for that child, at any time up to his/her sixteenth birthday, even if she has previously signed an agreement to the contrary. Again we can only deduce the courts' attitude in this situation. Their decision will be based on "the child's interests", rather than any agreement between the "parents". However, where there has been no contact between the donor and the child, and particularly where the mother has agreed not to claim maintenance, it is unlikely that a court would order maintenance.

The Department of Social Security has the power to claim maintenance from the father of children receiving income support. The amount of maintenance is assessed under a fixed formula. It will not, however, benefit the children themselves since any such maintenance will be deducted from the amount of income support paid by the DSS. This potential problem has become a serious threat since the Child Support Act 1991. This provides that mothers can now be penalized by the DSS by withholding income support if they fail to disclose the identity of the father and co-operate in locating them. There is now a real risk for sperm donors that they might be forced to pay maintenance for children if the mothers at some point claim income support.

Agreements

A woman may decide that she wishes the donor to be involved with the child. It is possible to draw up an agreement setting out the terms of the future relationship with regards to both contact with th child and maintenance. The Family Law Reform Act 1987 (applying to England and Wales) legally recognized such arrangements for the first time. The courts retain the power to overturn the arrangements if they consider that they are contrary to the interests of the child. The situation in which they are most likely to do this is where an agreement has been made that the donor will not have contact with the child (this will not affect the DSS's power to claim maintenance for children receiving income support).

The Children's Act 1989 specifies that such "parental responsibility agreements" must be in the form laid down by the regulations and, when further regulations are made, will have to be officially recorded in the prescribed manner. The agreements are legally binding on the parties, unless varied by court order. Such agreements have not yet been formally recognized by the Scottish courts.

CO-PARENTING

The legal framework for bringing up children has tradition-ally applied exclusively to married couples. Unmarried hetero-sexual couples with children have only recently gained any substantial recognition in law. Alternative parenting ar-rangements have had even less legal protection and recogni-tion. The major problem was that parents could not legally surrender, transfer or share their parental rights and duties with regards to children except by going to court. Outside of wardship (see below), only certain categories of people were even able to apply for such orders. As we shall see below the Children's Act 1991 has fundamentally altered this.

How important is the legal recognition of a co-parent's relationship with the child?

Apart from the increased social recognition which legal status brings to co-parents, there are more concrete benefits. From the child's point of view, if the natural parent becomes unable to look after him/her, having a legally recognized co-parent can provide continuity and security. Without this, there is a danger that someone with little connection with the child or possibly the local authority may intervene and assume responsibility for the child.

From the co-parent's point of view it can be difficult to maintain a relationship with the child if the relationship with the biological parent breaks down, and legal recognition may be some protection. Having said this, legal recognition of a co-parent requires court approval unless it is in the form of guardianship, which only takes effect on the biological parent's death (see below). Court proceedings are generally very expensive, although legal aid may be available. Even more significant is the homophobia of the legal system. It is generally possible for other members of the biological family or the local authority social services to intervene in family proceedings, and thus there will always be a risk that a court might order the child to live with a distant relative, or impose an order that Social Services should supervise parenting arrangements. Whether or not to seek legal recognition as a co-parent is a difficult choice, and we merely set out the legal alternatives.

LEGAL APPLICATION BY CO-PARENTS

The Children' Act, in a potentially radical departure from previous legislation, provides that, with the prior permission of the court, anyone can apply for a residence or contact order. Permission must be granted by the court if it decides that it is in the children's best interests to do so. Because the Act does not, on the whole, apply to Scotland, we shall deal with the position in Scotland separately.

If the child has lived with you for at least three years out of the past five years (this period need not have been continuous but must not have ended more than three months prior to the application), then you can apply for a residence or contact order without prior approval by the court. You can also apply without prior court consent, provided that you have the consent of the people who have parental responsibility for the child, or, where the child is the subject of a residence order, the consent of each of those in whose favour the residence order is made.

Potentially, therefore, a co-parent who has split up with the biological parent of a child could apply for a contact or residence order. S/he would be able to do this without the prior leave of the court, where the child had been living with him/her for the requisite period of time.

It is too soon to say whether the theoretically progressive effect of this legislation will be blocked in practice by the prejudiced attitudes of the courts.

CO-PARENTING — SCOTLAND

In Scotland, it is only the married parents or unmarried mother who automatically have parental rights, the most important being care and custody of the child. However, under the Law Reform (Parent and Child) (Scotland) Act 1986, anyone, be they a relative or not and including the child him- or herself, may apply to the court for all or any of the parental rights to be exercised jointly with another or alone. This can include an application to have the parental rights removed from a parent or other person who already has them.

Gay or lesbian partners who are not parents, however long they may have been living with or even looking after the child, do not, therefore, automatically have any rights. This is the case even though they may have acquired an obligation to aliment the child. However, they are entitled to apply to the court under the 1986 Act for an order conferring parental rights, either solely or jointly with another, and even to the exclusion of a parent who previously had such rights.

The apparently unlimited breadth of such applications for parental rights is in practice limited. The courts will only make orders regarding parental rights if they consider it is in the child's best interests. This operates in a similar way to the situation in England and Wales (described above). As in England and Wales, where the applicant or applicants are gay or lesbian, for example the gay or lesbian partner of one of the parents, then the courts have shown themselves reluctant to grant such applications. This is particularly so if the application would have the effect of depriving a natural parent of their parental rights. Further, the fact that a parent is gay or lesbian can be used against them in an application for parental rights brought by someone else, in particular in an application for custody.

GUARDIANSHIP

A guardian is appointed by a biological parent to exercise all his/her parental rights and duties upon his/her death. When the appointment takes effect depends on whether or not parental responsibility or residence orders have been made by the courts.

If the child is legitimate, or if the father of an illegitimate child has been to court and obtained an order of parental responsibility, then this surviving biological parent will have sole legal responsibility for the child and the appointment of a guardian by the deceased parent does not take effect until the death of the surviving biological parent. If the parent who appointed a guardian has a residence order in his/her favour at the time of his/her death then the appointment of a guardian takes place immediately.

How to appoint a guardian

Both parents of a legitimate child can appoint guardians, regardless of who has an order of residence. The father of an illegitimate child can appoint a guardian only if he has been to court and been awarded parental responsibility.

Anyone can be chosen to be guardian of a child, and it is possible to appoint more than one. The appointment does not need to be in a particular form, as long as it is in writing, signed and dated (probably it is wise to have the signature witnessed). You can include a clause in your will appointing a guardian.

The courts, therefore, do not have any control over who is appointed as a guardian. However, anyone with a connection to the child can apply to the court to be appointed guardian or have the guardian removed. If there is any disagreement between joint guardians (for instance about where the child will live) the court will decide. As always the basis for their decision will be the best interests of the child. In the absence of anyone with parental responsibility or guardianship, the death of the biological parent leaves the child without a legal carer. The correct procedure for an adult caring for, or wishing to care for, a child in this position is to apply for a residence order or perhaps adoption (see below). Legal advice is essential in this situation.

FOSTERING AND ADOPTION

In the past it was almost impossible for "out" lesbians and gay men to adopt or foster children, because any long term arrangement requires the approval of Social Services and/or the courts, and the homophobia in these institutions meant that this approval would be withheld. However the attitudes of some Social Services Departments (mainly in London) have changed and this has now become a real option.

Unfortunately fostering and adoption by lesbians or gays has come under persistent attack by the homophobic press. Partly in response to this, the government attempted to include in the Statutory Guidance to the Children's Act a paragraph limiting the use of lesbian and gay foster and adoptive parents. Paragraph 16 originally stated: "It would be wrong arbitrarily to exclude any particular groups for consideration. But the chosen way of life of some adults may mean that they would not be able to provide a suitable environment for the care and nurture of a child. No-one has a 'right' to be a foster parent. 'Equal rights' and 'gay rights' have no place in fostering services."

Intensive lobbying, not only by gay and lesbian groups but by professional and voluntary bodies working in this area, resulted in the line specifically referring to gay rights being dropped from the Guidance. The emphasis is now exclusively on the best interests of the child, rather than singling out a particular group of potential foster-parents for punishment. Indeed Paragraph 9 of the statutory Guidance and Regulations explicitly addresses the needs of young lesbians and gay men: "Gay young men and women may require very sympathetic carers to enable them to accept their sexuality and to develop their own self-esteem."

These changes marked a clear vindication of the principle of lesbian and gay involvement in this area and had the fortunate side-effect of focusing more agencies on the possibility of recruiting lesbian and gay foster parents (the National Foster Care Association, for instance, started a recruitment campaign specifically addressing these groups). However, lesbian and gay fostering and adoption continues to be the subject of media furore, thus placing political pressure on local authorities which may lead to restrictive practices.

What do fostering and adoption mean?

Fostering a child gives the foster parents no legal rights to make decisions for the child or to keep the child if the natural parents wish him/her to be returned, or the local authority wishes to move him/her. An adoption order, on the other hand, transfers all the rights and duties of biological parents to the adoptive parent(s).

HOW DO YOU FOSTER?

Precisely because fostering is in principle a temporary arrangement the process is simpler than for adoption and does not require court approval. Generally you apply to the local authority or to a voluntary fostering agency to be placed on their list of prospective foster parents, and, if you are accepted, they will ask you to provide fostering for a specific child or children. This may be for a specified period of time — for instance while their parents are in hospital — or more open ended — perhaps until a permanent adoptive placement can be arranged. Fostering placements may in fact last a number of years and indeed foster parents do sometimes apply to adopt the child in their care.

You may arrange privately to foster a child, but any fostering arrangement which lasts more than 27 days must be notified to the local Social Services Department, who will then investigate your personal circumstances and indicate whether or not they approve the placement. If they do not, either because they find you or your living situation unsuitable, you can appeal this decision to a juvenile court.

If the agency which has placed the child with you wishes to remove them, it will almost certainly be impossible for you to legally prevent this. However, if the child has been with you for a long time, you may be able to apply to the court for an order that the child remain with you. If you are in this situation you should consult a solicitor immediately.

ADOPTION

If you want to adopt a child you should approach either a voluntary agency, such as the British Association of Fostering and Adoption, or your local authority. Even if you arrange for a private adoption, you must always notify the local Social Services Department of the placement. All prospective adoptive parents are subjected to a lengthy process of scrutiny by a social worker as to their emotional and material ability to parent. If you are accepted as a potential adoptive parent you may still have a very lengthy wait before you are "matched" with a particular child. If you agree to offer the child a home then s/he must be placed with you for a period of at least three months before adoption proceedings can be commenced.

The final stage of the process is that a court must also approve the adoption. The adoption process can take a long time, generally at least a year. The consent of the parent(s) of the child is normally necessary before s/he can be adopted. The court does however frequently use its power to dispense with the necessity for this consent where it considers that consent is being withheld unreasonably. It is possible that if the prospective adoptive parent were lesbian or gay then the court would not consider that the parent was acting unreasonably by withholding his or her consent. Or the court might simply refuse to make the adoption order because it did not feel that it was in the interests of the child.

There has, as far as we know, been no case where this has been given as justification for refusing an adoption order, but it is likely to influence the courts' general attitudes. In January 1991 a judge refused to allow a lesbian to adopt a two-year-old boy who had been placed with her by Newcastle-upon-Tyne City Council, but on the basis that the bond with his original foster mother was too strong to be broken, rather than because the lesbian applicant was inherently unsuitable. However, it is extremely likely that the judge was indeed influenced by the press outrage over the case.

A gay man would be doubly disadvantaged by the courts' assumption that young children need to be with female carers wherever possible.

Only a married couple or a single person can apply to adopt a child. While there is nothing to stop one member of a lesbian or gay couple applying this would mean that the non-adoptive parent had no legal connection to the child.

In Scotland, a child over 12 has to consent to the adoption before the order can be made.

Can your child be adopted without your consent?

Looking at the process from the point of view of the biological parent it is possible to lose parental rights over your child through adoption simply because of your sexuality. In one case (Re D; 1977) the House of Lords granted the application of the mother and stepfather to adopt, specifically in order to stop all contact between the child and his gay father. It is very unusual to cut off a biological parent's contact in this situation, and we would hope that other courts would not follow this precedent.

CARE AND WARDSHIP

Local authorities have a legal duty to make sure that children are properly cared for. If they consider that a child is at risk of harm, or being neglected, they can use care proceedings or wardship to take over parental rights. We do not know of any cases where children have been removed from parents simply because of their sexuality, but it may be a factor which will prejudice the courts against you if the local authority have started care or wardship proceedings.

If the young person is lesbian or gay this might be a factor which would encourage the court to conclude that s/he was dangerously beyond his/her parent's control (see page 136). You should always consult a solicitor immediately if care proceedings are threatened.

Again the law in this area has been changed in England and Wales by the Children's Act 1989 and so we cannot be sure how it will be applied in practice.

CARE PROCEEDINGS

If the local authority wants to take your child away without your consent (to place him/her "in care") they must first of all satisfy a court that such an action is necessary in the interests of the child. The local authority must specifically prove to the court that the child is suffering, or is likely to suffer, significant harm and that the harm, or likelihood of harm, is attributable to the care given to the child, or likely to be given, not being that which it would be reasonable to expect a parent to give him/her or that the child is beyond the parents' control. Normally a full court hearing is required before the child is removed. You will have a chance to answer the local authority's arguments. Both parents should receive notice of the local authority's intention to take the child into care, regardless of whether or not they are married. If you receive such a notice you should consult a solicitor immediately.

In exceptional circumstances the local authority may apply to the court to remove a child without first giving notice to the parents. They will have to satisfy the court that either they are attempting to investigate the welfare of the child and that such investigations are being frustrated by access being unreasonably refused and that access is urgently required or that they have reasonable cause to suspect that a child is suffering, or is likely to suffer, significant harm if s/he is not removed. These emergency protection orders last eight days, with the possibility of an extension of a further eight days. Parents can apply to the court to have the order discharged and the child returned. Once again, if you are in this position you should consult a solicitor immediately.

WARDSHIP

Anyone can apply to the court in England and Wales to make a child the ward of the court. Once the child is a ward the court has all parental rights; as long as the wardship lasts it will decide where the child lives.

The Children's Act 1989 is designed to make wardship proceedings largely unnecessary, since in most situation third parties can apply for residence, contact or other orders. Local authorities used to sometimes use this as alternative means of removing a child from his/her parents. It will now be very difficult to do so since it is necessary to have the court's permission before starting wardship proceedings, and this will be very difficult to obtain.

In any event, there is little advantage now in taking wardship proceedings. They are likely to be more expensive than simple applications for residence orders under the Children's Act and the continuing involvement of the court is another significant disadvantage.

Once wardship has started both parents (whether or not married) will receive court papers and a date for the initial court hearing. The court decides whether or not to continue wardship and where the child should live according to what it thinks are the best interests of the child. There are no particular grounds which need to be fulfilled before the court can remove the child.

Wardship is not recognized in Scotland.

AIDS

"Aids is a medical condition but it is also a social problem. It can mean the loss of jobs, and incomes, as well as friends, lovers and families. Some people with Aids literally do not have enough money to live" — Michael Howard, Chair of Frontliners

"HIV works like a barium meal. It goes right through a system and shows up all the faults" — Ros Pendlebury, Aids and Housing Project

Acquired Immune Deficiency Syndrome (AIDS) is not a "gay illness" but in this country gay men have, up to the present time, been the group most affected by the disease. For this reason homophobia has been mixed with the widespread phobia of the able-bodied towards those who have physical or mental disabilities, producing a particularly lethal brand of public prejudice. We shall discuss in this chapter some of the mechanisms for dealing with the disabling illness and the social prejudices attached to it.

Strictly speaking Aids is not an illness, it is a condition in which the body's natural defence mechanism against illness (the immune system) has broken down ("immune deficiency") leaving the individual vulnerable to a wide variety of infections. Aids can therefore be associated with a wide variety of symptoms, the most common include sweats, diarrhoea, loss of vision, nausea, dementia, oral thrush, and loss of weight.

Human Immunodeficiency Virus (HIV) is the virus which can cause Aids. People with HIV (referred to as HIV-positive)

do not have any symptoms of illness unless they have developed Aids. Most remain well for several years (it is calculated only one third develop Aids within seven years). It is not yet clear whether all people who are HIV-positive will go on to develop Aids. HIV infection is not highly contagious. It can only be passed in bodily fluids such as sperm, blood or vaginal fluids. It is spread by unsafe sex, shared needles and by transfusions of contaminated blood.

In the space available we can only touch on some of the issues involved and refer you to the organizations listed at the back of the book (see Listings). Naturally the other chapters of the book may also be relevant.

TESTING FOR HIV

It is possible to test blood in order to detect whether it is infected with the HIV. The test measures whether antibodies have been developed in the blood as a result of exposure to the infection. These antibodies take about three months to develop and therefore a negative result to the test does not necessarily mean that someone is free of infection. Similarly, it follows from what we have said in the introduction to this chapter that a positive test result is not an indication of the current health of the individual. The question of whether to take the test is a complicated one and you should receive counselling before you make the decision. The Department of Health has stated that counselling before having a test is essential — but in many situations this is not offered. You should demand it.

Can you be tested without your consent?

As with many areas of the law concerning medicine the precise legal position regarding testing for HIV without the patient's consent is vague: it is not defined by any statute and so the position remains unclear until a case has been decided by the courts.

There appears to be agreement that the consequences of a positive finding to an HIV test are so significant that express consent to this particular test is required before it is performed; it should not be made simply as a part of a regular check-up.

Two courses of legal action are potentially open to a patient who has been tested without prior consent. Although it might be possible to sue for battery (the application of unlawful physical force) for technical legal reasons which we do not have the scope to consider, the consensus of legal opinion is that an action for negligence is more appropriate. A health worker owes a duty of care to patients, and if a patient suffers loss because a worker fails to comply with this duty s/he is entitled to sue for negligence. The nature of the care which a health worker is expected to give to patients is that which is considered acceptable by a substantial body of professional medical opinion.

The question of whether testing without consent is permissible therefore hinges upon the views of the medical profession. The British Medical Association (the leading professional organization of doctors) has passed a resolution stating that express consent to the test is necessary. However the BMA qualified its statement by adding that a test could be performed where the doctor believed it was in the best interests of the patient. Since knowing that s/he has the virus does not help a patient to prevent deterioration in his or her health it is difficult to envisage when such a situation would arise.

Guidelines issued by Edinburgh's Royal College of Surgeons, the Royal College of Surgeons and the British Orthopedic Association state that surgeons can test without consent if they, or a member of their team, have been injured, and possibly contaminated with the patient's blood, in the course of the operation. If you refuse to have a test health workers are entitled to assume that you are HIV-positive, and to take extra precautions. These guidelines suggest that doctors can enquire into the lifestyle of patients and ask those who they perceive to be in "high risk" groups to take an HIV antibody test in advance of the operation. But they still cannot insist on your having a test merely on the basis that they consider you to be a member of a "high risk" group. Nevertheless, these guidelines represent a worrying

development, which could lead to hospital assessment procedures discriminating against "high risk" groups.

Given the overwhelming medical opinion that testing
should only take place with specific consent, a health worker
who tests without this would almost certainly be considered
by the courts to have failed in their duty of care, and be liable
for negligence. If the individual concerned can convince the
court that s/he has suffered a legally quantifiable loss as a
result of negligent testing then the court would order financial compensation for this loss.

CONFIDENTIALITY

The doctor-patient relationship (and indeed the relationship
between any health worker and a patient) is one which, by its
very nature, binds the doctor to strict confidentiality. The
only exceptions to this rule of confidentiality are where the
patient consents to disclosure of the information; where
disclosure is in the best interests of the patient; where a
doctor is complying with a court order or where the public
interest requires disclosure — for instance to avoid a health
risk to other people. This last exception might apply if a
doctor could not obtain an infected person's consent to inform
their sexual partner.

In a recent case (X v. Y 1988 2AER 479) a Health Authority
obtained an injunction restraining a national newspaper
from publishing information about two doctors who had Aids.
The judge stressed the importance of confidentiality in order
to encourage people to have tests performed.

If you are tested in a venereal clinic the absolute confidentiality of this information is guaranteed, because the National Health Service (Venereal Diseases) Regulations 1974,
which apply to such clinics, require Health Authorities to
ensure that the identity of those examined or treated for any
sexually transmitted disease (including HIV) is not disclosed
except for the purposes of treating persons with the disease
or preventing its spread. These regulations do not apply to
general practitioners or private hospitals, and they do not
apply at all in Scotland.

In practice there are various situations (applying for

employment or life insurance are the most common) where you have no choice but to authorise disclosure of your health records. You cannot insist on partial disclosure. If you think this might cause problems in the future you should consider being tested at a VD clinic or somewhere else which will not automatically inform your GP so that the fact that you have been tested is not included in your medical records. An unjustified breach of confidence by a doctor would entitle you to sue for breach of confidence and would undoubtedly also be serious professional misconduct. We consider below the channels of complaint against various medical staff.

OBTAINING MEDICAL TREATMENT

The law governing the provision of medical treatment within the NHS provides little protection to people with Aids (PWAs). A GP or a dentist can strike a patient off his/her list or refuse to accept them as patients in the first place. Neither the law nor professional rules prevent this, except that a doctor should not remove a patient from his/her list in the middle of an acute illness.

People with Aids may well find that they are better informed about potential treatments than their general practitioner. If you want to be placed on a particular treatment and your doctor refuses, whether through lack of knowledge or because of lack of resources, you have no legal right to demand a particular sort of medical treatment under the National Health Service. The courts have refused to intervene even where there was an undisputed need for an immediate operation, on the basis that the District Health Authority was unable to provide one because of scarce resources. However, if you are in this position you should ask your doctor for a second opinion, and if s/he continues to refuse treatment you should complain to the local Family Health Service Authority.

On the other hand, you are legally entitled to refuse treatment. Problems may nevertheless develop in this area if you lose the mental capacity to make or communicate your decisions. In the earlier section concerning Health (page 73) we explain that there is no legal mechanism within Britain by which you can delegate the power to make decisions about medical treatment to another person. The medical staff are entitled to assume the patient's consent to any treatment which is medically necessary. Consulting the "next of kin" is not legally required.

In anticipation of a point at which treatment can only painfully prolong the act of dying increasing numbers of people are attempting to make "living wills". These are documents which direct medical staff not to have the document-maker's life artificially prolonged beyond the point where recovery is impossible. The instructions are supposed to come into effect where the maker is no longer capable of making his/her own decisions about medical treatment. Such documents are not at present legally binding in Britain, although in USA they are, and around ten million Americans have made them.

Although doctors are entitled to act solely on the basis of their judgement about the medical requirements of treatment, in practice if you leave clear instructions about what you wish to be done in particular circumstances these will often be obeyed. These instructions need not be in any particular form, but the more formal the document the more weight it is likely to be given. They may also include instructions about who should be treated as the next of kin.

COMPLAINING ABOUT MEDICAL TREATMENT

Capital Gay reported in March 1990 that a gay man who named his lover as next of kin when admitted to Luton Hospital for routine observation was isolated from other patients, refused clean sheets and a bath, fed on paper plates and offered an "Aids test" over a ten day period. The hospital later apologized and promised a full investigation. Such stories about mistreatment of those who are HIV-positive, or are regarded as being members of "high risk" groups, are all too common.

The fundamental response to such developments must ultimately be a political one. On an individual level there is unlikely to be any legal remedy and you will have to rely on the inadequate medical complaints procedures. Each hospital has its own complaints procedure which you should follow. If you are dissatisfied with the response to your complaint you can contact the Health Services Commissioner. They will not investigate questions of clinical judgement, and will only investigate those complaints for which there is a legal remedy if they consider that it is not reasonable to expect the complainant to invoke such a remedy. The Commissioner has complete discretion as to whether to pursue a complaint. If they do so, a successful inquiry may lead to an apology and possibly a change in practices.

If you wish to complain about a general practitioner you should write to the local Family Health Service Authority. You should do this promptly, as they will refuse to investigate if you delay too long without good cause. If your complaint involves serious professional misconduct it may be investigated by the General Medical Council (the national body with responsibility for regulating the medical profession), which has stronger powers for punishing malpractice.

EMPLOYMENT

TESTING

A prospective employer is legally entitled to make such enquiries as s/he thinks appropriate before offering a job to someone (provided s/he does not act in a way which is discriminatory on the grounds of sex or race as defined by the Race Relations Act 1976 and Sex Discrimination Act 1975). We discuss the general question of medical records in the chapter on Employment, and you should consult that chapter for details, in particular, of the Access to Medical Records Act 1988 (which entitles you to see a medical report before it is submitted to the employer).

As the law currently stands an employer can ask you to have an HIV test before offering you employment. Measures proposed in Parliament to make this illegal have not, so far, been successful. You would therefore be faced with a difficult choice unless you could persuade the union to intervene on your behalf. We would suggest that anyone faced with this decision should contact the Terrence Higgins Trust. They can offer advice and may be able to intervene on your behalf.

The legal situation with regard to testing within your current employment is very different. If your employers ask you to undergo an HIV test you would almost certainly be entitled to refuse. If they then dismissed you for this refusal you would be entitled to claim unfair or wrongful dismissal.

As we discuss in the Employment chapter you must have been employed for two years before you are entitled to claim for unfair dismissal and the remedies for wrongful dismissal are very restricted.

It may be worth considering whether a claim for racial or sexual discrimination might succeed, as there is no qualifying period of employment before you can make such a claim. The law in this area is particularly complicated, so make sure that you are referred to specialist legal advice by consulting one of the agencies at the back of the book (see Listings).

If you do not have a satisfactory legal remedy these agencies may be able to use informal pressure on the employer. It will also be worth consulting your union.

MEDICALS FOR EMPLOYMENT INSURANCE SCHEMES

We will examine in the insurance section the problems that can arise with HIV testing, particularly for gay men who are seen by the insurance companies as a "high risk" group. This can become a problem in the employment context because many larger employers run group insurance schemes. These will usually involve periodic medicals, as part of which you may be required to have your blood tested for HIV. If you refuse to have the required medical or refuse the blood test you will forfeit your right to insurance under that scheme. The doctor examining you will have your implied consent to disclose the results to the insurance company (the whole purpose of the medical). They will probably also have your implied consent to disclose the results to your employer.

DISCRIMINATION

Because employers have been affected by the panic and prejudice about Aids, employees who are known to be gay may be asked to take the test for HIV. Fellow employees may object to working with them because of ill-informed fears about "catching Aids". The measures which we discussed in the Employment chapter to protect your job will all apply equally here.

In short, if you are HIV-positive this in itself would not constitute a fair reason under the employment legislation for dismissing you, as long as your health was not affected (we consider below the situation where your health is affected). If you qualify for protection under the unfair dismissal legislation then the section in the Employment chapter concerning prejudice from fellow workers and the employer's duty to act fairly towards employees suffering harassment will apply. The requirement that employers follow the correct consultation procedures is likely to be important in determining whether or not they have acted reasonably in dismissing you.

The Department of Employment's guide for employers suggests that they should have "Aids policies" to counter fears and prejudices which may arise. It also states that "It should be made clear that any threats of industrial action or refusal to work with someone with, or suspected to have, HIV will be dealt with firmly."

A House of Commons Committee set up specifically to look at problems associated with Aids stated "Terminating employment on the grounds that a person is infected with HIV is likely to be regarded as unfair dismissal unless a valid reason can be given. Pressure exerted on an employer by other employees or by customers is not a valid reason" (House of Commons Report 182 HMSO).

Even if you are not protected against unfair dismissal LAGER or Terrence Higgins Trust may be able to advise you and negotiate a settlement.

ILL HEALTH

Because their immune system is damaged people with Aids are prone to periods of infection by diseases of different natures, lengths and severity. The pattern of the illness is varied and unpredictable, although as a rule many people with Aids remain fit for work long after they have contracted the disease.

Having Aids will not in itself justify dismissal unless the employer can provide a reason which qualifies as fair under the Act. The law provides that if you are physically unfit to carry out the work for which you have been employed for a sufficiently long period your employer will be entitled to dismiss you. S/he is not necessarily obliged to seek alternative employment within the organization for you, but if it is readily available then s/he should consider you for it. S/he should consult you before dismissal.

How long your employer must wait before s/he will be entitled to dismiss you depends on a lot of factors in the specific situation. The law primarily regards the employers as entitled to protect their businesses rather than seeking to protect the sick employee. Factors which are taken into account in assessing the fairness of a dismissal include: the size of the employer's business, the nature of the job, how long you have worked there and whether the illness can be regarded as long term. Generally you will be regarded as being entitled to a period of sickness which is at least as long as the period for which you are entitled to receive sick pay under the contract of employment.

Employers should always obtain medical evidence before sacking workers for ill health. However if you refuse to allow your employer access to your health records s/he will be justified in assuming incapacity.

If you have had a series of intermittent illnesses your employer may warn you that continued absences will lead to dismissal. If you do not explain that the underlying cause of the illnesses is Aids, and continue to have intermittent illnesses, s/he may be able to convince a tribunal that s/he was justified in dismissing you on the basis of the knowledge which s/he possessed at the time. Explaining that you have

Aids may help, or may make the situation worse. You would be wise to consult an expert organization such as the Terrence Higgins Trust or LAGER before taking such a step.

You will be paid sickness allowance from your employer either for the period of time stipulated in your contract, or if no mention is made in the contract, the law would regard it as payable for a "reasonable period".

If you are not entitled to sickness allowance you will be entitled to statutory sick pay. It is paid by the employer at three different rates depending on your usual level of wages. It is not paid for the first three days but thereafter is paid for 28 weeks.

WELFARE BENEFITS AND AIDS

There are many very comprehensive sources of information about welfare benefits. CABs and advice agencies are usually well versed in this field. For those points of particular relevance to people with Aids the Terrence Higgins Trust provides free advice and assistance.

We will confine ourselves here to outlining the state benefits which are available, stating the basic requirements to qualify for them and mentioning specific points which may be of particular relevance to people with Aids.

There is no standard payment for people with disabilities or long term illnesses. Instead there are a variety of benefits, some related to how you became disabled, some to your specific mobility or attendance needs, some depend on whether you have paid enough national insurance and some are related to the level of your other income (means-tested).

For a person with Aids this confusion can be added to because many of the disability related benefits require a qualifying period of illness before they will be paid. The fluctuating nature of the illness may make this difficult to fulfil.

Two alternative types of benefits provide for basic living costs if you become long-term sick. If you have paid enough national insurance then you may be entitled to sickness benefit, and after a certain amount of time, to invalidity benefit. This is usually paid at a higher rate than the alternative source of income (income support) and it is not means tested.

Income support is means-tested, which means that you must have used up almost all your capital, and have only minimal alternative sources of income before you can claim it (we explain how this works in the next section). It is intended to provide a basic income for those not in full-time employment. The emphasis is on basic, as the rates are very low.

Income support replaces the old supplementary benefit system. This system, for all its faults, could produce significant (though still inadequate) increases in income to reflect the higher costs of long-term illness or disability. However new claimants from April 1988 onwards have had to claim under the income support scheme, often getting substantially less than their previous entitlements under supplementary benefit. The new scheme is disgracefully inadequate to meet the additional needs and expenses of the long-term sick and disabled.

In exceptional circumstances, where you have been eligible for supplementary benefit continuously from April 1988 onwards, and have what the law accepts as a good cause for late claim, you are able to backdate your claim to your original date of eligibility, and be paid under the old regulations. This might be very advantageous and if you think it might apply in your case you should consult your local Citizens Advice Bureau or welfare rights centre.

In addition to these benefits aimed at providing a basic income, we will discuss below the main disability related benefits — disability working allowance, disability living allowance, severe disablement allowance (for disabled people) and invalid care allowance (for carers).

INCOME SUPPORT

Broadly speaking the major requirements for income support are that you:
- Live in Great Britain.

- Are over 16.
- Do not have capital over £8,000; (if you have capital over £3,000 but under £8,000 your entitlement will be reduced).
- Are not in full-time education.
- Do not work more than 16 hours per week unless you have a mental or physical disability which is accepted as reducing your earnings by at least 25 per cent from what you would otherwise have earned. Or you are caring for someone with disability living allowance. Voluntary work does not count either, provided the only payment you receive is for your expenses.
- Finally you must be available for work. This means that you must "sign on" at the UBO unless you are aged 60 or over, incapable of work, registered blind, a lone parent, caring for someone with disability living allowance or your disability has reduced your earning capacity by 25 per cent.

In practice, most people with Aids will be able to claim on the grounds of incapacity with medical evidence in support.

How much do you get?

Your income support is calculated by adding a personal allowance, and any premiums to which you are entitled, to your eligible housing costs, and deducting your income from other sources. We explain these elements in more detail below.

Personal allowance

If you qualify for income support you are assigned a personal allowance in the regulations which depends on your age, whether you are single and/or have children and whether you qualify for one of the premiums.

If you are having a sexual relationship with someone you are living with this will be ignored for income support purposes provided that it is a homosexual relationship (one of the rare advantages!). However, beware the non-dependant deduction from your housing costs (see below).

Premiums

An additional weekly fixed amount will be paid to you if you qualify for one of the premiums. There are lone parent and old age premiums and, most relevant for these purposes, carer's, disability and severe disability premiums.

Disability premium

To qualify you must be:
- under aged 60
- receiving disability living allowance, disability working allowance, severe disablement allowance or invalidity benefit; be registered blind or have been treated as incapable for work for a continuous period of 28 weeks (once you have got the premium a gap of up to eight weeks is ignored).

Severe disability premium

This can be added to a disability premium or higher pension premium. You must be:
- single parent or live alone. (The exceptions to the requirement that you live alone are: if the other person with whom you are living also receives disability living allowance; or is under 18, a joint occupier, a sub-tenant or boarder or someone employed by a voluntary body to look after you and for whom you are paying a charge.)
- receive disability living allowance (higher and middle rates only).
- no-one must receive invalid care allowance for looking after you.

Deductible income

Your income, as calculated by income support regulations, is then deducted from the personal allowance to calculate your actual benefit payment. All income earned and unearned, with a few exceptions, is taken into account for these purposes. Disability living allowance is not deducted. Generally the first £5 per week of earned income is ignored. If you receive one of the disability premiums or you are a lone parent then you will have £15 per week disregarded.

Housing costs

Some housing costs are paid by income support — notably mortgage interest payments but not repayments of capital off the mortgage or the cost of life insurance premiums attached to some mortgage policies. However for the first 16 weeks when you are receiving income support only 50 per cent of your mortgage interest payments will be paid through income support; you should try and negotiate a rescheduling of the mortgage to take account of this. Any extra interest that this generates will be paid by income support. Otherwise you will have to pay out of your own funds.

All other eligible housing costs (e.g. rent) are paid through a separate benefit called housing benefit. This is also income related. The rules are complex and we do not have room to discuss them here apart from one provision that is likely to particularly affect lesbians, gays and people who need a carer to live with them.

Non-dependant deduction

Generally if you have someone living with you who does not legally count as your dependant (i.e. is not a child) then the regulations assume they are contributing to the housing costs, whether or not they are in fact doing so, and deduct a set amount from your allowance for housing costs. The exceptions are if they are tenants (in which case, broadly speaking, the rent will be treated as your income and therefore your allowance reduced accordingly); a joint occupier (i.e. jointly liable for the rent or mortgage in which case only half the housing costs will be paid) or a person engaged by a charity or voluntary body to care for the claimant and who is paid by the claimant. In addition, if you are receiving disability living allowance or are registered blind no deduction should be made.

STATUTORY SICK PAY

Most employees will receive statutory sick pay from their employer after the first three days absence from work. A doctor's certificate may be required. The amount you receive will be related to the level of your earnings. Statutory sick pay lasts for 28 weeks after which you can go on to invalidity benefit.

Although this money is paid by employers, it is separate from any sick pay which your employer may be obliged to pay to you by your contract of employment. You may receive this on top of statutory sick pay. If the amount of sick pay to which you are entitled is low, you may be able to "top it up" with income support.

SICKNESS BENEFIT

Sickness benefit is a contributory benefit for people who are incapable of work because they are sick or disabled, but are not eligible for statutory sick pay. Before receiving this you must have paid enough national insurance contributions. You will, once again, receive sickness benefit after the first three days of illness and during the first 28 weeks of illness/ incapacity.

Sickness benefit is paid at a fixed amount per individual (plus a dependant's allowance for spouse or children). You may be able to earn a certain amount of money without having it deducted from your benefit provided your doctor agrees that the object of the work is primarily therapeutic (the therapeutic earnings rule). If your earnings exceed the limit (currently about £40 per week) then you will lose your entitlement to sickness benefit entirely. For this reason, and because you may otherwise have to repay benefit it is essential to get skilled advice before earning. You will always need medical support and DSS permission prior to commencing work.

Disability living allowance and unearned income do not effect payment level. You may also be eligible for some income support, but other state benefits are not payable at the same time.

INVALIDITY BENEFIT

After you have been incapable of work for 28 weeks (and provided you have paid sufficient national insurance contributions), you will receive invalidity benefit. There are two different components of invalidity benefit: invalidity pension (a flat amount plus additions for dependants); invalidity allowance (an additional age-related amount provided you are at least five years beneath the state pension age). The additional earning-related pension has been phased out since April 1991. The same rules as for sickness benefit apply with regard to income, including a therapeutic earning limit.

SEVERE DISABLEMENT ALLOWANCE

This is a fixed rate basic income payment which is not means-tested nor based on insurance contributions. It is paid at a lower amount than income support but could be useful if capital or income resources make you ineligible for income support. If you are claiming income support as well as severe disablement allowance you will automatically qualify for a disability premium.

To claim you must be between 16 and 60/65 and incapable of work — and be assessed as 80 per cent disabled for 196 days or have become incapable of work before you were 20 and been so ever since. You will automatically count as 80 per cent disabled if you are in receipt of the middle and higher care components offered or the higher mobility component of disability living allowance.

DISABILITY LIVING ALLOWANCE

This non-means-tested benefit was introduced in April 1992, and represents an amalgam of two previous allowances — the mobility and attendance allowances. It consists of a care component payable at three different rates, and a mobility component payable at two different rates.

Care component — higher/middle rates

The highest rate of the care component is payable to those who satisfy both the daytime and one of the night-time rules. The middle care rate is payable to those who satisfy either a day or night-time rule.

Day

You must require frequent attention throughout the day in connection with your bodily functions or continual supervision during the day in order to avoid substantial danger to yourself or others.

Night

You must require prolonged or frequent attention during the night in connection with a bodily function or another person must need to be awake for a prolonged period or at frequent intervals for the purpose of watching over you. The attention must be in connection with bodily functions, and must not be of the type normally provided for healthy adults (e.g. not shopping or cooking but it might include help with cutting food, eating, using the toilet, dressing or washing). Supervision must be continual and be necessary to avoid a substantial danger.

Lowest rate

The lowest rate can be claimed by a person under 65 who either requires in connection with their bodily functions attention from another person for a significant portion of the day or cannot prepare a cooked main meal for themselves, when provided with the ingredients. A "significant portion of the day" is likely to be interpreted as at least 40 minutes.

If you are receiving income support and receive the top two rates of the care component this will also entitle you to severe disability premium. All levels of th care component entitle you to a disability premium for income support.

Mobility component

Higher rate

You must be unable or virtually unable to walk, taking into account the speed, distance and manner of your walking. Only your ability to walk without severe discomfort should be taken into account. You will also be eligible if the exertion required to walk would constitute a danger to your life or lead to serious deterioration in your health.

People who are both deaf and blind will be automatically deemed "virtually unable to walk".

People who are "severely mentally impaired" or have "severe behavioural problems" will also automatically qualify, provided that they get the higher rate of the care component.

One point to bear in mind for people with Aids is that the exertion required to walk a significant distance (roughly 100 yards) may well constitute a danger to your health. Many PWAs have successfully claimed mobility allowance on this ground. Dizziness is a common side-effect of the AZT drugs supplied to PWAs. This, and the debilitating fatigue which is a common feature of Aids, may both affect your ability to walk.

Lower rate

This rate is payable if you are so severely disabled physically or mentally that, disregarding any ability to use familiar routes, most of the time you cannot walk out of doors without guidance or supervision from another person.

For both rates of the mobility component your personal circumstance (e.g. remoteness of your house, inability to use available public transport) will not be taken into account.

Qualifying period

The criteria set out above must have been satisfied for three months, and must be likely to continue to be satisfied for the next six months, before you can qualify.

The exception to this rule is if you are suffering from a

progressive disease which can reasonably be expected to be fatal within the next six months. If you satisfy this condition you will automatically be entitled to receive the highest rate of care component.

DISABILITY WORKING ALLOWANCE

This new allowance is designed to pay for some of the additional expenses of people with disabilities who are working. However, the benefit is means-tested: you must have less than £16,000 capital and must earn under a certain figure per week, otherwise your benefit will be reduced, or possibly even withdrawn (the maximum that you can earn and still be entitled to a disability working allowance is about £85 if you have no dependants).

To qualify for this allowance you must work for more that 16 hours per week, have recently been getting a qualifying benefit (such as invalidity benefit, severe disablement allowance, disability living allowance or a disability premium) and be considered to be at a disadvantage in getting a job. You should get advice before applying, as some people are worse off on this benefit.

Disability benefits in general

The vital factor in applying for all these benefits is good medical supporting letters and probably also a detailed account of your physical condition, explaining how it creates the particular needs for which the different allowances are given. Unless you feel confident that you are eligible for these allowances it is probably wise to go to a Citizens Advice Bureau and ask for their assistance in making the application.

CARERS

Invalid care allowance

This is a benefit for people of working age who are unable to work because they are caring for a severely disabled person. They do not necessarily have to live with the person but must provide at least 35 hours per week caring for the disabled person. The disabled person must be receiving the two higher rates of the care component of the disability living allowance. ICA is not means tested, so any other sources of income will not affect it.

Income support

If you have no other sources of income you may be entitled to claim income support and/or housing benefit. If you claim income support, and receive invalid care allowance (or if you would be if not for overlapping benefits) you will be entitled to an additional amount of income support, the "carer's premium".

You should consult pages 148–150 for the general rules regarding income support and housing benefit. Note in particular that whilst claimants of income support must generally not work more than 16 hours a week, this will not apply if you are caring for someone who receives either of the top two bands of disability living allowance. In addition, if you are living with the person who you are caring for, this will lead to a reduction in their housing benefit, unless one of the exceptions applies.

SOCIAL FUND

The income generated by these benefits is not adequate to meet the regular needs of a long-term ill or disabled person, never mind the occasional larger items which are required. A variety of grants and loans are available from the DSS for items such as furniture and exceptional travel costs.

With the exception of funeral and maternity grants, the social fund payments are at the discretion of the individual DSS official (although within a framework of directions set out below). There is no right of appeal, you can only ask (within 28 days) for a review of the decision at a higher level. The payments also come from a fixed local budget, so that if all the money has been spent, you will be less likely to get a grant, however great your need.

WHAT PAYMENTS ARE AVAILABLE?

Budgeting loans

You must be getting income support for 26 weeks. Savings above £500 must be exhausted first. The sort of items for which you might claim are: essential furniture, bedclothes, essential home repairs. The social fund can only loan an amount that you are likely able to repay. There is no interest charged on the loan and the terms of repayment should be determined by your financial circumstances, but within a maximum repayment period of 78 weeks (104 very exceptionally).

Crisis loans

These are given only if they are "the only means of avoiding serious damage or serious risk to the health of" the applicant or his/her family. Some items and some people are excluded from eligibility. Again the loans are limited to your ability to repay. Assistance to meet the need must not be available from family, friends or charities.

Community Care grants

These are not repayable and so are clearly a far more helpful resource. To be eligible you must receive income support. If you have any capital in excess of £500 the excess must be set off against the amount of grant you would otherwise have got. Some items are specifically excluded.

Grants are made where they will:

- Help the person (or member of family) re-establish him/herself after a stay in residential care.
- Help the person (or member of family) to remain in the community rather than enter residential care.
- Ease exceptional pressure on a person (or family).
- Assist with travel (within UK) to visit someone who is ill, attend a funeral, ease a domestic crisis or move to suitable accommodation.

The list of people who are considered in priority need and therefore have a stronger chance of a grant includes people who are terminally ill, and this includes people with Aids.

Items for which grants might be awarded include the need for a washing machine and/or tumble drier to cope with the extra laundry produced by incontinence or heavy night sweats. The grants are only supposed to pay for one-off items, rather than regular expenses, such as high protein diets. So, if you need money for such items you will have to get advice about how to obtain these.

Funeral grants

These are paid where the claimant is taking responsibility for a funeral. The claimant must be receiving income support, family credit or housing benefit. The grant only covers the very basic expenses, and you must claim within three months of the funeral. The payment will be reduced by the amount of the deceased's estate which is readily available. It will also be reduced by any capital which the claimant has over £500.

LOCAL AUTHORITY ASSISTANCE

Community care grants are not available for items which are provided by the local authority. The Chronically Sick and Disabled Persons Act 1970, the substance of which applies only in England and Wales, makes it the duty of local authorities to provide certain items to people who are substantially and permanently handicapped and can establish a need for them. Increasingly there is a means-tested charge for some of these services. Home helps, meals-on-wheels, holidays, telephone rental, radio or television and adaptations to the home may be provided in suitable situations. Some local authorities provide incontinence pads, or a laundry service for people who are incontinent (sometimes these are provided by the local health authority, and so your GP may know about these services).

In practice, the provision of many of these items and services is limited in availability because the authorities do not have sufficient funds. You should contact the local

Social Services Department to ask for them. If you are refused, there is no appeal procedure but you can write to the Secretary of State and ask him/her to investigate and "use his default powers", which means order the local authority to provide the item or service. Better still, get your local CAB or one of the organizations at the back of the book to write on your behalf. It can take months to get a response but does sometimes produce results. It can also be very helpful to contact your local councillor/member of parliament, or possibly the local press.

INDEPENDENT LIVING FUND

This is a fund set up by the government to make payments to severely disabled people who need help with personal tasks/personal care in order to live independently in the community. It is not a state benefit, and there is no appeals procedure. The applicant must need to pay for personal care or domestic help. S/he must also live alone or with someone who is unable — through illness or disability, other responsibilities or the amount of care needed — to provide the total amount of assistance needed.

The applicant must either receive the higher rates of the care component of the disability living allowance or satisfy the criteria for these apart from the qualifying period. S/he must be receiving income support or if their net income exceeds the income support level the excess must be less than the amount needed to pay for essential personal care and domestic assistance.

If you qualify, assistance may be given with the cost of personal care. If you do not quite satisfy the criteria it is still worth applying because the fund is administered more flexibly than DSS benefits. This fund has been chronically underfinanced since it was set up, and so may not be able to give you any assistance, but it is worth a try.

After April 1993 it will no longer be possible to claim money from the Independent Living Fund, although it will continue to pay existing awards. Instead you will need to approach your local authority for help under the Community Care Scheme.

SPECIFIC AIDS LEGISLATION

The initial media panic around Aids led to the introduction of some legislation which although potentially very threatening to the civil liberties of PWAs (and incidentally providing fuel for misinformed bigotry), has very little relevance to the spread of the disease and hence has hardly been used — the Public Health (Infectious Diseases) Regulations 1985. We set out below sections which relate to Aids. The provisions are all enforced by the same procedure: by an authorized officer applying to a magistrate, with no requirement that the person against whom the order is sought should have prior notice of the application. There are penalties in the Regulations for refusing to comply with an order. Appeals against orders must be made to the Crown court.

Medical examination (Section 35)

Application can be made by a doctor nominated by the local authority for a compulsory examination of an individual on the basis that it is expedient to examine the person medically in the person's own interests, or those of his/her family, or the public generally. Either the person's doctor must consent or s/he must not have a doctor.

It is debatable whether this section could ever be invoked. Since neither HIV infection nor Aids is treatable it cannot be in someone's own interest to be compulsorily tested. The only possible situation where it could be of use would be if the results were passed on to the person's sexual partner. However nothing in this legislation permits the disclosure of the result without the consent of the person concerned, and so even in this situation it would not be of use.

Removal to hospital (Section 37)

An order compulsorily removing someone to hospital can be made where an individual has Aids (not just HIV) and their circumstances are such that proper precautions to prevent the spread of disease cannot or are not being taken and this creates a serious risk of infection to other people.

There must also be sufficient National Health Service hospital accommodation available and the District Health Authority must consent to the person's admission.

Detention in hospital (Section 38)

Where a person with Aids is currently in hospital and, if s/he were to leave hospital and would not have suitable accommodation to allow precautions to prevent the spread of the disease, or if proper precautions will not be taken in other places where the person might be expected to go, an order can be made under this section compelling him/her to remain in hospital.

The methods by which Aids is spread mean that the usefulness of this section is very limited. However, it could conceivably be used against someone who abuses drugs by injection.

This is in fact the only section under which an order has been made. The patient subsequently appealed and the case was settled by consent, with the patient agreeing voluntarily to stay in hospital.

Scotland

The Public Health (Infectious Diseases) Regulations 1985 apply only to England and Wales, but similar provisions for Scotland are contained in the Public Health (Scotland) Act 1897 and the Health Services (Public Health) Act 1968.

INSURANCE

The insurance industry is very worried about the effect of the spread of Aids upon their finances. You will not get insurance if you are HIV-positive or have Aids. The insurance companies have gone further than this however. They have responded by panicking, and in particular by discriminating against groups which they regard as "high risk", such as gay men. The most common situation when you will want to apply for life insurance is in connection with a mortgage (see

Mortgage section). Insurance companies now will often insist that two male co-buyers or single men over a certain age take an HIV test before they grant insurance. They may also ask lifestyle questions on the form or from your general practitioner. This might be a reason for being very guarded about the information which you pass on to your GP.

If they know or suspect that you are gay you may be turned down outright or may be asked to take a test. If you decide to do so and are negative you may still be charged higher premiums to reflect what the insurance companies see as a higher risk.

Another common method by which insurance companies attempt to screen out "bad risks" is to ask if you have ever had an HIV test (or even had counselling about one). Even if you have had a negative result from the test your application will often be turned down.

Once you have had an application rejected you will find it almost impossible to obtain insurance in future because application forms almost invariably ask if you have ever been rejected for insurance. So if you are in a situation where you seem to be likely to be refused (e.g. the company is demanding an HIV test and you plan to refuse) it is advisable to withdraw your application first.

A House of Commons Social Services Committee report in August 1989 recommended that the government should seek the agreement of insurance companies not to ask questions about HIV testing as it deterred people from tests. At present, however, insurance companies are entitled to ask whatever questions they like and to reject applications on whatever grounds they consider fit, although you could try complaining to the Insurance Ombudsman if you feel you have been unfairly treated.

Even if you cannot get normal insurance cover you may be able to get a policy which excludes payments for death from Aids, but most lenders will not accept such a policy in connection with the mortgage.

HOUSING

In the first ever survey of the housing needs of people with Aids, "Housing and HIV in South London", 83 per cent of the respondents felt that there was a problem with the quality of their housing and 54 per cent wanted to move. A large proportion of the sample were living in damp, unhealthy conditions with poor mobility standards, insecurity, a lack of space for carers and/or were experiencing harassment from their neighbours.

Aids or an HIV diagnosis can affect your housing situation in many ways. It may cause you to lose your employment and become reliant upon inadequate state benefits. This in turn can lead to rent or mortgage arrears and the loss of your home through possession proceedings. It may lead to homelessness because of rejection by your partner or housemates or through an illegal eviction. Alternatively, you may have a home but it may be intolerable, or even dangerous, to live in because of poor living conditions or harassment from neighbours.

Other sections of this book may be relevant, for instance the section on harassment from neighbours or landlords in the Housing chapter. If it is possible for you to stay in your present accommodation with special adaptations or repairs see the above sections on local authority assistance and applications to the social fund. Advice on benefits or debt counselling from the Citizen Advice Bureau may be also helpful.

We will concentrate in this section on local authority provision of accommodation for people with Aids. If you are homeless this will be your major resource for housing. Various housing associations do accept referrals from Aids agencies and we suggest that you contact the ones listed in this section at the back of the book.

HOMELESSNESS AND LOCAL AUTHORITIES

We discussed in the Housing chapter the circumstances in which local authorities are under a duty to provide housing. In summary, they will only be legally obliged to provide you with permanent accommodation if you are homeless, in "priority need" and not intentionally homeless. You must fulfil all three criteria to be rehoused by local authorities and even then they may still argue that it is the responsibility of some other local authority to house you unless you convince them that you have strong local connections. We consider the particular implications of these factors for PWAs and those who are HIV-positive below.

On a practical level getting good advice on local procedural and policy guidelines before you make your application can make a traumatic process easier and increase your chances of success. You should either contact one of the specialist Aids agencies at the back of the book or the local Housing Advice Centre.

Homeless

You are legally homeless even if you have a roof over your head if you do not have a right to be occupying your present accommodation (e.g. you are squatting), if it is accepted that it is not reasonable to expect you to continue living there or if you are likely to be made homeless within 28 days.

You may be able to argue that the physical conditions of the property are such that it would not be reasonable for a person with Aids (or HIV) to continue living in them. You might also be able to argue that it is not reasonable for you to continue living in your present accommodation because you can no longer afford it. A third ground for arguing that you can no longer reasonably be expected to live in a property is that you face harassment of such a level that the stress is a serious threat to your health. In these circumstances the local authority will often want to be satisfied that you have exhausted all other remedies against the harassers (see pages 48–49). Domestic violence should also be accepted as a basis for being unable to continue living in a property, but again local authorities are likely to insist that you attempt legal remedies for the violence first.

Medical support for all these arguments is invaluable, and may even convince the local authority that the stress of civil proceedings against harassers is an intolerable and dangerous burden, particularly if you are already ill.

Priority need

People with a disability or a medical condition which makes finding adequate housing more difficult and more essential are classed as "vulnerable", and in priority need of housing. Most local authorities accept without further argument that people with Aids or ARC have a priority need; however many will not regard people who are HIV-positive and asymptomatic as coming within this category.

The Association of London Authorities guidelines on local authorities' responsibilities for the homeless specify that asymptomatic HIV-positive people should be regarded as vulnerable and in priority need.

Intentionally homeless

The question of whether you are intentionally homeless may be linked to the question of what constitutes "reasonable accommodation", considered above. If you voluntarily leave accommodation which the local authority considers it reasonable for you to occupy then they will not be legally obliged to rehouse you, however great your priority need, because you will be "intentionally homeless". If you are in this situation therefore you should try to persuade the local authority in advance that it is unreasonable for you to continue occupying a property.

Local connection

Many PWAs choose to move closer to medical facilities and support networks. If you move to London you may find, because of the housing crisis, that local authorities will refuse to house you on the basis that you do not have a "local connection". If you have had your "normal residence by choice" in the area for six months out of the last year or three out of the last five years you should be accepted as having a "local connection". Otherwise a family connection or "other special circumstances" can be used to establish a "local connection".

For many gay or lesbian PWAs friendship networks are likely to be more important than family. This factor, and the importance of proximity to medical and other social facilities, should be used to establish a "local connection".

If the local authority accepts that you are in priority need but denies that you have a local connection they are still obliged to provide you with temporary accommodation.

Rehousing through the local authority housing list

Anyone is entitled to place their name on the local authority housing list. However stocks are now so rare that it is effectively only those with priority need who will be housed. A PWA can apply for rehousing through this route as a "category A" medical priority. Needless to say, good medical evidence is essential to support your application. This may enable you to avoid temporary housing while waiting for housing.

What you will be offered

In London immediate rehousing into permanent accommodation is rare. Most local authorities provide only bed and breakfast accommodation for an initial period, which may last a number of months. The shared and unhygienic facilities in bed and breakfasts make these totally inappropriate for PWAs and some local authorities instead provide temporary accommodation in short-term leasing schemes.

Aside from the need for the accommodation to be appropriate to your present, and likely future medical condition (which sounds obvious but is unfortunately a common problem) you may wish to be rehoused with your lover or a carer. If the local authority provides you with accommodation they are also obliged to rehouse "anyone who can be reasonably expected to live with" you. This means that a heterosexual cohabiting partner would also normally be rehoused, but local authorities may not be prepared to treat homosexual couples equally. There are no court cases on this point but it is certainly worth fighting for.

Even if a local authority refuses to rehouse you with your lover on the basis of your relationship the state of your health (or your future prognosis) may make it reasonable to have a carer living with you.

If you are offered accommodation for yourself and your partner or a carer it will most likely be a tenancy in your sole name. This will leave the other person more vulnerable than if you had a tenancy in joint names and it would be worth raising this point with the local authority.

COUNCIL TENANTS — TRANSFERS TO MORE SUITABLE ACCOMMODATION

If you are already a council tenant you may need to transfer to other accommodation for a number of reasons — for instance your present accommodation may be damp or without adequate heating and therefore leave you more vulnerable to opportunistic chest infections or you may have mobility difficulties which require easy access accommodation. Alternatively you might need to move to an accommodation which is large enough for a live-in carer. You will need to apply for a transfer through your neighbourhood housing officer and ask specifically for a priority transfer as ordinary transfers take a very long time. Again medical evidence supporting your application will be very important. The crisis in council stock can mean that such transfers are difficult to obtain in some areas, particularly in London. If you are having problems seek assistance from a local Citizens Advice Bureau or law centre.

YOUNG PEOPLE

One of the most powerful homophobic myths depicts "predatory homosexuals" preying on innocent youth and thereby replenishing their ranks (since they are unable to do this through the "natural" means of heterosexual reproduction). To date British laws and social policy have been constructed on the basis of this nonsense, criminalizing young gay men and threatening those who seek to help young lesbians and gays, rather than providing protection for them against a hostile society.

The results are devastating for those "innocent youths" who are themselves lesbian or gay. A research project by the London Gay Teenage Group (*Something to Tell You*, 1984, Lorraine Trenchard and Hugh Warren) found that 19 per cent of the group of lesbian and gay youth surveyed had attempted suicide because of their sexuality. Negative self-images; problems at home, at school and possibly with the police; isolation and a lack of accessible support services are just some of the pressures confronting young lesbians and gays. These pressures are compounded by the relative powerlessness of young people in our society, trapping them within families which are all too often hostile and homophobic. This lack of autonomy has been increased in recent years by the Tory policies of cutting welfare benefits and drastically restricting the housing options of young people — presenting some with the stark option of staying in an abusive home or facing life on the streets.

Some lack even this "choice". Eleven per cent of those surveyed by the London Gay Teenage Group had been thrown out of their home. The scores of homeless, destitute youngsters on the streets of London are themselves testimony to the effects of Tory policies on young people.

Social Services involvement, whether as the result of family breakdown or of direct attempts to control young people's sexual behaviour, can all too often merely exacerbate the situation because of the homophobic and authoritarian attitudes and modes of operating within Social Services Departments. The Guidance issued by the government to accompany the Children's Act 1989 placed a new emphasis on the responsibility of local authorities (in the context of arranging family placements) to be sensitive to the needs of young lesbians and gays: "The needs and concerns of gay young men and women must be recognized and approached sympathetically." However, this Guidance does not have direct legal force, and since it may be in conflict with the notorious Section 28 it remains to be seen how much effect this requirement will have in practice. The continuing political controversy over the use of lesbians and gays as foster parents suggests that any positive new measures adopted by local authorities will be the subject of struggle.

In this chapter we cover a range of situations in which young lesbians and gays may face difficulties because of their sexuality, and attempt to discuss some of their options.

CRIMINAL LAW

A long-standing difficulty for gay teenagers, and one which can constrain those organizations seeking to help them, is the ludicrously high age of consent for gay sex.

In 1987, 35 young men between ages 16 and 21 received criminal convictions for having sex with consenting male lovers. While in 1989, 23 teenagers were jailed for gay offences. The way that figures are kept makes it difficult to disentangle those who had committed sexual assault in the true sense of sex with an unwilling partner, as against those who were being punished for consensual sex.

Although we would stress that young gay men are more likely to become involved with Social Services, the mere possibility that such charges can be brought exposes the paradox that the laws which allegedly exist to protect young people actually contribute to their isolation and lack of self-respect. The fear of criminal charges is used to pressurize gay teenagers into giving evidence against their older lovers, in situations where they themselves do no wish to bring such charges. These laws increase the stress which gay teenagers experience, provide a tool for police harassment and can hamper the work of sorely needed organizations which befriend and counsel young lesbians and gays.

We will briefly outline here the legal position regarding young lesbians and gays having sex. (For further information see Crime chapter.)

SEX FOR GAY MEN IS ONLY LEGAL IF BOTH PARTNERS ARE OVER 21, IT TAKES PLACE IN PRIVATE AND IS CONSENSUAL. For further details of "legal" gay sex see pages 217–220.

ANY SEX UNDER 16 — ENGLAND AND WALES

The law regards young people under 16 as being incapable of legally consenting to sex. This means that anyone who has sex with such a young person is committing the crime of "indecent assault" (see page 229), whether or not the young person agreed to or even initiated sex. This applies equally to lesbian, gay and heterosexual sex, although in practice gay or lesbian sex is far more likely to be punished.

In a situation where both partners are under 16, the absurd position in the criminal law is that both young partners are committing indecent assault on each other. In practice, criminal charges in such a situation are extremely unlikely to be brought.

Two legal exceptions

The general rule is that people under 16 are committing a crime but: young people under the age of ten are not held to be criminally liable for their actions, so that no charge can be brought; and, curiously, it is believed that young boys under 14 are regarded as legally incapable of penetrative intercourse and thus a charge of buggery could not be brought against such boys, regardless of the true facts.

Lesbian sex over 16 is legal

In broad terms the same criminal laws apply as for heterosexuals (although the Crime chapter gives some indications of situations where young lesbians might, nevertheless, have trouble with the law).

YOUNG GAYS IN SCOTLAND

As in England, sex between men under 21 is a crime, and may be charged as one of a range of offences (see pages 242–248). Once again young people who are supposedly protected by this legislation can themselves face charges, although they are, in practice, more likely to be referred to local authority supervision or a Children's Hearing. A child under eight is deemed incapable of committing a crime.

The one exception to this situation is where the older party is under 24, has never previously been charged with such a crime and had no reason to believe that the other party was under 21.

YOUNG LESBIANS IN SCOTLAND

Lesbian sex, though not itself explicitly a crime, may be charged under Section 5 of the Sexual Offences (Scotland) Act 1976 where one or both parties are under 16. The Act makes it an offence punishable by up to two years imprisonment, to use lewd, libidinous or indecent practices on a girl aged between 12 and 16. Her consent to sex does not make any difference, and the crime applies equally to heterosexual and lesbian activity. Under 12 the more general crime of lewd practices would be charged.

As with under-age gay sex, for the younger party Social Services involvement is more likely than criminal charges, and lesbian charges are in any event very rare.

GENERAL ADVICE

British law, in general, reflects an inadequate emphasis on rights and is particularly weak in the area of young people's rights. Such issues have traditionally been viewed through the twin blinkers of respect for the privacy of the family and paternalistic concern with the best interests of the child, at the expense of a consideration of their autonomy. In practice there is likely to be a great deal of difference in how you will be treated by agencies and regarded by law if you are 15 or 16 rather than 13 or 14.

If you are having difficulties at home or in care, the best advice is, if possible, to find a sympathetic, respectable adult, preferably straight and definitely not your lover, to speak on your behalf.

TROUBLES AT HOME

The degree of control over your person and behaviour which your parents can legitimately exercise is a particularly unclear area of law. Parents have a legal right to punish you — and this can include physically. However if such punishment is too severe or frequent you could consider involving the police or Social Services. Obviously what people will regard as acceptable varies, but Social Services will usually regard physical punishment which leaves a bruise and happens more than once as excessive. Involving Social Services is a fairly drastic step and you might try talking to Childline first.

We discuss in the section below the level of mistreatment or neglect by your parents which will provide grounds for Social Services to remove you from their care. Social Services may become involved and attempt to mediate between you and your parents even where your parents are not mistreating you to this extent, but there are no other legal constraints on the way your parents look after you. You are obliged to follow their rules. If you do not, they could themselves involve Social Services, perhaps even to the extent of asking the local authority to look after you.

What if they throw me out, or ask the local Social Services department to look after me?

Although by law your parents have a responsibility for caring for you while you are under 16, you do not have a right to live in their home and if they want to throw you out it will be difficult to stop them. Alternatively, your parents may approach Social Services and ask them to look after you for a while.

If they do either of these things your options are limited. Provided that you are old enough to have "sufficient understanding" of the proceedings, in England and Wales you are entitled to apply to the court for a residence order (under Section 8 of the Children's Act) on your own behalf, either with a sympathetic relative or any respectable, preferably straight, adult who would be prepared to have you living with them. Realistically, if Social Services are opposing this move, the courts are unlikely to approve. But if you are in this situation it would be worth seeing a solicitor to discuss the situation.

If you do not know such an adult, then you should consult a local advice agency and see if there is a local advocacy group for young people so that they can help you sort out a solution, either with Social Services or your parents. Alternatively you may wish to try living independently, in which case see below.

Can they stop me leaving?

In England and Wales, young people under 18 need their parents' consent to leave home unless they are married. In Scotland, parental consent is required until the age of 16. However the police and Social Services have a great deal of discretion about whether to become involved. Generally if you are over 16 and living independently and opposed to returning home the police and Social Services are unlikely to step in — although they may be more likely to do so where your parents suggest that you are at risk through involvement in a gay lifestyle. The younger you are, the more likely they are to intervene. While in general they are likely to be more paternalistic towards young women, assuming that the potential risk is greater, there is a particular danger for gay men since the police could pursue a criminal investigation concerning under-age sex.

The police have the legal power to detain anyone under 17 if they have reasonable cause to believe that the young person would be likely to suffer "significant harm" unless they are removed to suitable accommodation (Section 46, Children's Act). Although they are under a duty to ascertain and consider your feelings they are unlikely to allow this to change their minds about removing you from somewhere that they consider unsafe. This ground for intervention is very vague.

Once the police have discovered your whereabouts, the Social Services may become involved, checking on the circumstances and background of any other people with whom you are staying. If the police detain you under the above provision they will either return you directly to your parents or pass you on to Social Services.

If the police and Social Services in England and Wales refuse to become involved, your parents may attempt to take legal proceedings. They can ask that you be made "a ward of the court", which means that the High Court takes over parental responsibilities and can tell you what to do. The Children's Act attempts to restrict the use of wardship so that it will be more difficult for your parents to take this action now.

In practice the most difficult thing about leaving home is likely to be getting an income and housing. It will not be easy and the more advanced preparations you make and the more advice you get from agencies, such as the local Gay Switchboard or Lesbian Line, the better. We list some other helpful agencies at the back of the book. We examine the problems of living independently below, but first a warning about the sort of trouble that older friends, lovers or indeed voluntary agencies can get into if they help you leave home.

Helping young people who have run away

No-one is legally obliged to return young people on the run to the police or their parents, nor to answer questions about their whereabouts — although if you provide false or misleading information to the police they could charge you with obstruction. If there is a court order for the return of a child/young person refusing to obey, this could be contempt of court. It is also possible in England and Wales to be charged with child stealing under Section 56 Offences Against the Person Act 1861 if the young person is under 14; or Section 2 Child Abduction Act 1984 if they are under 16. The first offence is committed if someone takes away, receives or harbours the child "with intent to deprive" a parent or other person who has lawful custody of him/her. The second offence is committed if someone "takes or detains" the young person "without reasonable excuse" from the person with legal custody of them. This definition includes inducing the young person to leave or to stay away.

The definitions of these offences therefore depend on a subtle distinction between responding to a young person's independent actions and actively encouraging them to leave or stay. This can obviously be a very difficult distinction to draw, and adults helping young people who have left home are clearly placed in a difficult position.

The equivalent Scottish provision is the crime of "plagium", applying to the taking of young girls under 12 and boys under 14. The child's consent is irrelevant. If the young person is over 12 or 14, but under 16, then there is no criminal offence committed but the parents or guardians can seek a court order for delivery. This is unlikely to be successful if the young person is unwilling to return. What usually happens in these situations is that the local authority become involved and they can place a supervision order on the young person to check that they are being properly looked after. If the young person runs away and stays with people who are not relatives, then effectively these people become foster parents and must notify the local authority.

None of these offences is committed by anyone who has a "reasonable excuse" for taking or detaining a child. It would be possible for any third party assisting an adolescent to put forward their consent as providing such a reasonable excuse, although courts might not accept this defence, if they considered that the young person was too young to live

178 TROUBLE WITH THE LAW?

independently.

As far as young lesbians are concerned Section 20 Sexual Offences Act 1956 applicable to England and Wales makes it an offence to take "without lawful authority or excuse" a girl under 16 from the possession of her parent/guardian without their consent. Although there is nothing in the wording of the offence to this effect, proceedings are only usually taken if there is a sexual element involved. Unlike the offences outlined above, the case of R v. Olifier (10 Cox 402) makes it clear that if the girl leaves home on her own it is not an offence under this section merely to refrain from returning her to her parents.

Probably a much more real threat is the possibility of being charged under Section 50 of the Children's Act in England and Wales, and Sections 69–71 of the Social Work (Scotland) Act 1968 in Scotland if you help someone running away from care. This section makes it an offence to remove a young person who is in care, or assist or incite them to run away or remain away.

If such a runaway comes to you, you will clearly be placed in a very difficult position. It might be most helpful to try and liaise through a third party with Social Services to try and correct the situation which caused the young person to run away from care.

The Children's Act provides an exemption from criminal prosecution where safe houses run by voluntary organizations have been registered by the Secretary of State. Otherwise such homes might be liable to prosecution, as offering an inducement to leave home or care.

LEAVING HOME — YOUR OPTIONS

Social Services

If you are having serious difficulties at home you may want to contact the Social Services Department. It is now possible for a 16-year-old to place him/herself in the care of the local authority. If you are under 16 the local authority cannot voluntarily receive you into care if your parents object. If your parents do not object, then the local authority has a duty to provide you with accommodation.

Once you are 16 the local authority has a duty to provide you with accommodation if you are "in need" and if your welfare is likely to be seriously prejudiced if no accommodation is provided. They have a general discretion (which means that if they do not want to, you cannot force them) to provide accommodation for "children" (including young people up to 21) if this will safeguard and promote their welfare.

Although the law speaks about a duty to provide "accommodation", this expression should not mislead you. You will very rarely be provided with independent accommodation — more likely a place in a community home or hostel or possibly with foster parents. Social Services generally see their duty as reconciling families, and in any event once you are "being accommodated by" the local authority you may not like the decisions that are made for you, any more than the rules that your parents laid down. So this option should be viewed with caution. It is probably best, if possible, to clarify in advance where you would like to live and then, perhaps through a third party, explore how likely it is that this can be provided by Social Services. If the local Social Services Department is prepared to co-operate and, for example, help you get an independent council flat or place in a hostel, then this might be a good option.

If you are desperate to leave, you could find out from a local advice agency if there are any safe houses for runaways in your area. Such houses provide temporary accommodation and will help you try and sort out your situation.

If you are "accommodated" by the local authority in this way you are free to leave at any time but if the Social Services believe that you will be at risk they can apply for an order to prevent you from leaving.

Living independently/housing

The housing options for young people generally are very restricted. The central problems are lack of available, cheap accommodation and of a source of income with which to pay the rent. In England and Wales there are in addition some technical legal problems for young people. You are not legally entitled to own property if you are under 18 and landlords may be reluctant to rent to you if they know you are under 18 because they believe that they will not be able to sue you if you do not pay the rent. Actually contracts with young people under 18 are enforceable if they are for the "necessities" of life and therefore landlords would be entitled to sue you for rent. In practice of course if you look old enough private landlords will not request a birth certificate.

In Scotland you can own property from any age, but under the age of 16 your parents or guardians will have to deal with any transactions on your behalf, unless they are what are known as "common transactions" for someone of your age. Whether a deal regarding property would fall into this category will depend entirely on the circumstances. Over the age of 16 you have complete capacity to make any contract without parental consent. However there is a rule which provides that if you enter into a contract when you are under the age of 18, and it is in some way prejudicial to you, then until the age of 21 you can apply to the courts to have the contract set aside. This rule of law is unlikely to affect landlords, but a person selling a property could ask for the deal to be ratified by a court.

The practical problem of raising the money is likely to be a far more real hindrance. If you are on a low income you may be able to claim housing benefit to pay the rent on your accommodation, and should consult a Citizens Advice Bureau. You will probably need money for a deposit. You may be able to obtain exceptional housing benefit to pay for this; although this will only be paid in "exceptional circumstances" you can apply to the Social Fund for a crisis loan (see page 156), but generally only for rent in advance, rather than a deposit. Local authority housing is the largest source of cheap accommodation but most councils nowadays will not house you unless you are accepted by them as being "vulnerable" as well as unintentionally homeless (see Housing chapter). Generally they do not accept that young homeless people are vulnerable unless they fall within a particular group — such as being pregnant, disabled or coming out of care. Some have a more helpful approach to the problem of teenage homelessness, accepting that all homeless people between 16 and 18 are vulnerable, and therefore rehousing them.

This situation may be improved because the Children's Act, at least in England and Wales, imposes a new duty on local authorities to provide accommodation for any 16- or 17-year-olds in need, whose welfare they consider will be seriously prejudiced if no accommodation is provided. Authorities also now have the discretionary power to provide accommodation for young people even where they are not "in need" if this will safeguard and promote their welfare. It is too early yet to be able to assess the practical impact of these provisions.

In practice, bed and breakfast hotels may be your most immediately available option but be warned that income support (if you are "lucky" enough to be able to claim this) will only pay for such accommodation for a very short period (eight weeks in London, Birmingham, Glasgow and Manchester and four weeks elsewhere) unless you are under 19 and have left home because of threats or other difficulties; are pregnant or have a child; have recently left care; are a student or chronically sick.

Such accommodation is usually pretty bad. Hostels are often preferable, but most long-term hostels have waiting lists and are difficult to get into. Squatting may actually be your best immediate option. The Advisory Service for Squatters can sometimes put you in touch with squats which have spaces or hostel accommodation.

EMPLOYMENT

Under 13 you are not legally entitled to work. Between 13 and 16 you may get a job but there will be restrictions on the number of hours and times which you are allowed to work and on the type of work — most notably you are not allowed to work for more then two hours on any school day or on Sunday. There may also be restrictions imposed by local bye-laws. Once you are 16 there will still be some legal restrictions on the type and extent of your employment — for instance you cannot legally work in a bar or betting shop.

YOUTH TRAINING SCHEMES

If you cannot find yourself a job, do not wish, or are unable, to continue education and are aged 16 or 17 you will be able to join a youth training scheme. In fact you will have little choice, since you will not be able to claim welfare benefits if you are this age, except in exceptional circumstances (see below).

These schemes last two years if you leave school at 16 and one year if you leave at 17. They are supposed to provide job training and some will lead to a job at the end, but they vary widely so look around first.

You will be paid an allowance roughly the equivalent or slightly more than income support. If you live away from home because, for instance, there are no suitable schemes in your area, you can get a lodging allowance.

EDUCATION

If you leave school at 16 but want to continue in education, whether you receive income from the state in the form of either income support or an education grant will depend upon the type of course which you are doing and the number of hours which you are working. The rules are complicated and you should check with a CAB or student welfare officer. There is very little support for people from ages 16 to 18 who want to study but cannot get financial support from their parents. If you are under 19 and receiving education up to and including A levels for more than 12 hours a week, you will only be entitled to receive income support if: you have a child which you are caring for, you have a disability which means that you are unlikely to get a job in the next 12 months or you have to live away from your parents because you are in physical/moral danger, or there is a serious risk to your physical/mental health, or you are "estranged" from them. This last expression means that you are living apart with no desire for prolonged emotional or physical contact. The stress is on your emotional relationship with them so that even if your parents have been providing you with some money to live on you may be able to qualify under this exception. The DSS may want this confirmed by your parents or a respectable third party.

WELFARE BENEFITS

If you are under 16 you cannot get benefit in your own right. Since September 1988, most 16- and 17-year-olds have not been entitled to claim income support. The government claims to have provided Youth Training places for all young people in this age-group and will therefore only pay income support to particular groups who are not obliged to take a YT place: single parents; pregnant women 11 weeks before the baby is due; registered blind people; people whose physical and mental disability means that they are unlikely to find work within 12 months; carers for people receiving disability living allowance and some asylum seekers. Otherwise you will only get income support for a short period (three to four months) between leaving school and taking up a YT place, and may receive a "bridging allowance" if you are changing jobs or YT schemes.

If you do not fit into any of these circumstances you will only be able to get money from the DSS if you can show that you would otherwise suffer unavoidable severe hardship.

If you are receiving income support you will also receive some allowance for your housing costs, and may be able to claim additional payments for specific items (for instance, essential furniture) from the social fund.

BEING TAKEN INTO CARE

The Social Services Department of the local authority can take court proceedings to remove you from your parents and assume parental responsibility for you — "take you into care" — if they believe that you are at risk while living at home. They may do this either because of your parents' actions or your own behaviour. If you or your parents disagree with this decision there will be a court hearing and the magistrates will decide.

The court will only make an order placing you in care if you have suffered or are likely to suffer "significant harm". This means ill treatment (including sexual abuse and non-physical ill treatment); impairment of physical or mental health, or your physical, intellectual, social or behavioural development. The court must also be convinced that this harm is due either to your parents' not providing you with a standard of care which they could reasonably be expected to give you or because you are "beyond parental control". Even if these two grounds are proved the court must only make an order if it is satisfied that doing so would be better than making no order at all. You will be represented by a guardian ad litem — a social worker who will report on your best interests — and, to the extent that this is compatible with your welfare, your wishes, and you will have your own lawyer in the proceedings.

If the court decides that these grounds are not made out, and/or that it is not appropriate to make a care order, it may decide to make a supervision order which gives Social Services increased powers to intervene and supervise the way your parents treat you at home.

Social Services also have the power to apply for an emergency order removing you to their care for eight days (which can be renewed for a further seven days) if they believe that you will suffer significant harm without this protection.

While these orders cannot be made if you are 17 or over, they remain in force until you are 19.

BEING TAKEN INTO CARE — SCOTLAND

The procedure in Scotland is different. In Scotland you can be taken into care if Social Services have taken over parental rights (for example if your parents are unable to look after you properly), or when an order to this effect has been made by the Panel of the Children's Hearing. The Panel at the Hearing can make a variety of orders, but the situations which are most likely to lead to you being taken into local authority care include neglect or assault at home, having committed a criminal offence, being "in moral danger" or beyond your parents' control. These last two categories are particularly vague and there is a danger that courts may, for instance, conclude that having an actively lesbian or gay sex life in itself means that a young person is in moral danger and/or out of their parents' control.

WHILE YOU'RE IN CARE

If you are in care the local authority has the power to make decisions about your life, although they have a legal duty to consult you and your parents about decisions. You will have your own social worker who will consult with you and explain the local authority plans. You will probably live either in a community home or a foster family. If you have been in care for some time and are relatively young they may try and arrange for you to be adopted, but this can only happen if you agree. If you are 16 or over you could try to persuade Social Services to help you live independently, and either sponsor an application for you to be housed by the council, or arrange for you to stay in a hostel.

Both foster parents and community homes can lay down rules and punish you for breaking them, but the staff of community homes are not allowed to use corporal punishment and should never lock you in your room.

If you do not like your foster parents or the community home you should tell your social worker or your parents. If you want to complain about a particular rule or something that someone has done you should use the local authority's complaints procedure. Local authorities are legally obliged to establish and tell you about complaints procedures, and must give you written notice of their conclusions about your complaint.

If you are getting no satisfaction through these complaints procedures, you are entitled to apply to court for an order about where you should live, and should consult a solicitor. The Children's Legal Centre can provide you with initial advice and perhaps also suggest a good local solicitor.

If you want outside advice about how to cope with the system you could contact the National Association of Young

People In Care (see Listings).

You have the right to have continuing contact with your parents. The local authority will regulate how often you see them, but again they should take your wishes into account. If you do not wish to see your parents you should not be made to do so. If the local authority stops your parents from seeing you, even at your own request, your parents will have the right to go to court (although in practice a judge is unlikely to force you to see them in this situation). The new Children's Act creates a new duty for local authorities in England and Wales to promote contact with not only parents but other relatives, carers and friends. How wide this definition is, and how it will work in practice, remains to be seen.

Leaving care

Young people in care can now, with the leave of the court, apply for the care or supervision order to be legally ended ("discharged"). Once again, in England and Wales, you will be represented by a guardian ad litem and lawyer. Alternatively your parents may apply for the care order to be discharged or indeed Social Services may ask the court to approve this. You are again entitled to separate representation at court.

The new Children's Act gives local authorities in England and Wales a duty to "advise and befriend" young people (up to the age of 21) who have been "in care". Unfortunately, although local authorities have the power to provide maintenance for young people when in employment, education or training, and to provide grants to them, generally this assistance is at their discretion. That means that you cannot take the local authority to court if they fail to provide such help. It will depend on the policy, and ultimately financial resources, of your local authority. A 1991 survey, completed just before the Children's Act came into effect, showed that nearly half Social Services Departments did not have a policy for helping young people leaving care, and 56 per cent were unable to provide the accommodation that they themselves believed care-leavers needed.

Running away from care?

The police have the power to arrest you and return you to the local authority. If you are caught there is a danger that you will be placed in a "secure unit" — that is a home with special security measures. Section 21a of the Child Care Act allows them to place you in such a unit if you "have a history of absconding and are likely to abscond again" and if your physical, mental or moral welfare will be at risk.

LEGAL AID

If you are considering applying for any of the court orders that we have mentioned above, or want some further legal advice, your first stop should be your local Citizens Advice Bureau to see what advice they can give you (this is free) and, if necessary get a referral to a solicitor who specializes in this area of law.

Special rules apply for assessing the financial resources of young people to see whether they will be eligible for legal aid. Once you are 16 you are assessed on your own income and capital. If you are under 16, an adult should apply for legal aid on your behalf and their financial resources will be assessed. If your parents refuse to be assessed, or if the assistance which you are seeking is contrary to their wishes, then you can be assessed on your own income and savings instead.

In care proceedings the usual means test has been waived for all parties.

YOUR PARENTS ARE SPLITTING UP

We explain in the chapter on Caring for Children the different legal process by which disputes between your parents about who you should live with, how often you should see the other parent and other important decisions such as schooling and religion, can be resolved. Your views will always have to be considered by the judge when making a decision. You will not generally be allowed into court during the case as this is felt to be too upsetting. You can apply to be represented. Indeed, you can yourself apply for any of the orders which the court can make, although in England and Wales you will first have to ask the court for permission to do so. This will only be granted if the court considers that you have sufficient understanding to make the application.

TROUBLE AT SCHOOL

School for young people who are lesbian or gay, or think they might be, is often an alienating and isolating place. Most keep quiet about their feelings for fear of victimization because of their sexuality. Little information, support or positive role models are provided for those questioning their sexuality. A few Labour education authorities and individual schools have attempted to address these problems, educating against ignorance and bigotry. The Tories attempted to ban such positive policies through Section 28, and other measures (see Section 28 chapter). Here we will simply provide broad guidelines about the complaints procedures which you as an individual pupil can follow if you are unhappy at school, and the disciplinary measures which schools can take if they are unsatisfied with you.

In broad terms, your first line of complaint is to the school Head. Your next level of complaint is to the governing body of the school, then the local education authority and finally the Secretary of State. Your school may have a formal complaints procedure which the school secretary should tell you about.

It may well be worth recruiting outside adult help on your behalf; if you cannot rely on your parents, check to see if there are any local groups for young lesbians and gays who may be able to help. Alternatively you could contact the Childrens Legal Centre or the Advisory Centre for Education or the Scottish Child Law Centre (see Listings).

If you are not attending school, the local authority can apply for a supervision order. This gives them the duty and power to assist you and your parents in securing proper education. Once again the supervisor is under a duty to take your wishes (as well as those of your parents) into account when making decisions. In Scotland it is the local education authority that refers the matter to the Reporter to the Children's Panel, which can lead to a supervision requirement being made, to be implemented by the local authority Social Work Department.

WORKING WITH YOUNG GAYS AND LESBIANS

If you are working with young lesbians and gays and receiving grants from the local authority you will be concerned about the impact of Section 28. You should turn to the chapter specifically on this subject. If you are not local authority funded then Section 28 will have no effect upon you whatsoever.

For all groups working with young lesbians and gays the criminalization of gay sex under 21 has potential implications. It is theoretically possible for charges of conspiracy to corrupt public morals, and conspiracy to outrage public decency, to be brought against workers with young lesbians and gays. Conspiracy charges can normally only be brought where there is an agreement to commit a crime. However these two charges can be brought where the behaviour involved is not itself a crime. In addition, both charges are dangerously vague. Youth workers are very unlikely to be in a situation when the second offence could even theoretically be brought, because it relates to public acts of an "obscene or disgusting" nature. The second offence, conspiracy to corrupt public morals, is, in theory at any rate, more of a threat. It was used a few years ago to convict a magazine publishing contact ads for gays over 21, and, although it has not been used since, as long as the offence exists there is a danger that its use could be revived.

It might also be theoretically possible, in some circumstances, for workers to be charged with procuring an act of gross indecency — sex between men (see page 218). This would only be possible if sex took place between two young men as the result of an introduction in the group. In addition, since young people under 16 are held to be unable to consent to sex and therefore any sexual contact (even between two girls/boys both of whom are under 16) is criminal, it could be an offence for anyone to encourage or assist in the commission of such a "crime" (the offence of "incitement"). We would stress that it is extremely unlikely that such charges would ever be brought. The prosecution would have to show that a worker had taken some deliberate and active step, with the specific intention of helping the unlawful sex to occur.

The probability of such charges is not very high but it means that consideration should be given to the running of such groups. Young people should leave the group when they reach 21 and only be allowed to join when they reach 16.

CONCLUSION

As we will also see in the Crime chapter, young gays and lesbians are effectively penalized by the law under the guise of protection. Young people are trapped in families by their inability to obtain housing, employment or welfare benefits. Criminal sanctions can be brought against those helping young people leave their families. On the other hand parents are given the power to raise their children in whatever way they think fit, within only the broadest legal constraints. They can place their children "in care" at will.

What is required is access by young lesbians and gays at school to information which will help them come to terms with their sexuality, and indeed develop a positive self-image. More funding is needed for counselling services, hostels, emergency housing and recreation facilities specifically serving young lesbians and gays.

IMMIGRATION

by Sue Shutter

Immigration law exists in order to define who can be kept out of a country, who can be allowed in under certain circumstances and after satisfying certain conditions, who is free of control altogether, and what penalties can be inflicted on people who break the law. It exists in order to help to define the state that enacts it, not in order to help people to travel there. British immigration law has developed from Britain's colonial history; there are still some advantages to being a Commonwealth citizen (a citizen of a country which used to be ruled by the British and which decided to join the Commonwealth after independence) but these are being eroded as the UK looks more towards Europe. EC citizens are in general in a better position. British immigration law does not mention lesbians and gay men at all.

RIGHT OF ABODE

People who are not subject to immigration control are stated to have the "right of abode" in the UK. They are free to come and go as they like, their passports are not stamped as they travel in and out of the country and no restrictions can be put on them. People who have the right of abode are:

British citizens

The definition of British citizens is complex. The present law, the British Nationality Act 1981, came into force on 1 January 1983, so the situation is different for people born before or after that date.

People born in the UK before 1 January 1983 are British citizens automatically, unless their father was a foreign diplomat working here at the time of the birth. People born here from 1 January 1983 are British citizens only if either of their parents was a British citizen or was settled (allowed to stay permanently) in Britain at the time of the birth. If the parents are not married, only the mother's status counts. People may also become British citizens, by applying to the Home Office for this through a process called registration or naturalization; anyone who was registered or naturalized in the UK is automatically a British citizen. British citizenship can be inherited from a parent who was British in any of these ways at the time of the child's birth; before 1 January 1983, only a father who was married to the mother of the child could pass on citizenship, but since that date, both parents can do so.

Some Commonwealth citizens

A Commonwealth citizen who had a parent born in the UK has the right of abode and is not subject to British immigration control — again, a father only counts if he was married to the mother. Also a Commonwealth citizen woman who was married before 1 January 1983 to a man who had the right of abode in any of these ways automatically gained the right of abode herself.

European Community

After joining the European Community (EC) on 1 January 1973, Britain is also bound by the Treaty of Rome, which covers the movement of EC citizens between EC countries. At the time of writing (July 1992) the EC consisted of Belgium, Denmark, Germany, France, Greece, Ireland, Italy, Luxembourg, the Netherlands, Portugal, Spain and the UK. The EC encourages such migration and the Treaty makes it illegal to put any barriers in the way of people migrating for an economic purpose. Thus EC citizens are not subject to British immigration control.

EC citizens are free to travel to any other EC country, including the UK, in order to take or seek work, to set up in business or self-employment, and to provide or receive services. An EC citizen doing any of these things is entitled to bring in, or to be joined by, his/her family: a spouse, children up to the age of 21 or older if still financially dependent and dependent parents, grandparents and great-grandparents. The checks and regulations explained below which apply to families under British immigration rules do not apply to the families of EC citizens; it is easier for another EC citizen to be joined by family than it is for a British citizen. Although the EC definition of family is wide, it does not mention a gay or lesbian partner, or any other partnership which does not entail marriage. The interpretation of "family" differs from country to country; the Netherlands, for example, may allow a lesbian or gay partner to join an EC citizen working there under this provision, but the UK does not.

EC citizens rarely have problems with British immigration control. The only time that this is likely is if people have been claiming benefits here. EC citizens are entitled to do this on the same basis as other people settled here, but the DSS is supposed to tell the Home Office about an EC citizen's claim, and the Home Office may send out threatening letters. There is nothing that it can do to make EC citizens leave the UK just because they are claiming. If they leave the UK voluntarily and then try to return, they can be refused re-entry unless they can satisfy an immigration officer that they can support themselves now without claiming.

Republic of Ireland

Ireland is an EC country so all the rights of EC citizens also apply to Irish citizens in the UK. Also, the UK and Ireland form a "Common Travel Area", meaning that there are no internal immigration checks within it for people travelling between the countries. Thus there are no immigration officers checking people who travel across the Irish Sea (people may well be checked but this is under the Prevention of Terrorism Act provisions, not immigration law) and passports are not stamped. However, anyone who is not a British or Irish citizen who enters the UK from Ireland is deemed to have been allowed to enter for three months as a visitor, even though nothing has been stamped on his/her passport and no information has been given. People who have had previous immigration problems in the UK and who then re-enter through Ireland may have done so illegally; they should obtain specialist advice.

Irish citizens are not subject to immigration control when coming in through Ireland; they are automatically allowed to remain here permanently and there are no restrictions of any kind put on their stay. Sometimes people from countries where there was large Irish immigration in the past, for example the United States, may be able to qualify for Irish citizenship through descent from an emigrant parent or grandparent and may then qualify to remain in the UK as an Irish citizen. An Irish citizen working in the UK has the right for his/her spouse to live here too; the Home Office will normally allow a person from abroad, of whatever national-ity, who marries an Irish citizen, to stay permanently.

BRITISH IMMIGRATION LAWS AND RULES

Anyone else is subject to immigration control and in order to come to Britain has to fit in to some part of the immigration law and rules. The immigration laws are the Immigration Act 1971 and the Immigration Act 1988, which set out the broad framework of the law and go into detail about immigration offences and penalties. The detail of how people can qualify to get into Britain is in immigration rules which are ancillary to the law. Rules can be changed very quickly and easily; they do not have to be debated three times in each House of Parliament but can just be written by the Home Office and come into force immediately; they will only be debated if an MP asks for this and then can only be accepted or rejected in their entirety, not altered after debate. Thus things can change very quickly and it is not safe to rely on reference books for an up-to-date view of the law; it is worth checking with one of the organizations listed at the end of this book to be sure that information is still up-to-date.

The immigration rules often state that in order to qualify to enter or remain in the UK people have to "satisfy an immigration officer" of particular things. This means that immigration officers have a vast amount of discretion, in deciding what information or evidence will "satisfy" them and what will not. This discretion of officials and the wording of the rules explains why the results of the rules are very different for people from different countries, of different sexes and of different colours.

Another common phrase used in the immigration rules is that people must show they can be supported and accommodated "without recourse to public funds". Public funds for immigration purposes means income support, housing benefit, family credit and being rehoused as homeless persons only. No other benefits count as public funds and no other benefits can have any immigration law consequences. Being admitted to the country subject to this public funds requirement does not always mean that the person is ineligible to claim benefits. It may do; for example, a visitor is not entitled to claim anything. But an elderly mother who has come to join her children here is able to claim income support if she needs to do so, for example if her children's financial circumstances have changed by being made redundant or by the birth of a grandchild. If the person here signed a special form, known as an "undertaking" promising to support the person from abroad, this gives the DSS the power to attempt to recover any income support (not any other benefits) from the sponsor. Although the DSS has written threatening letters, in the 11 years that this provision has been in effect, it has taken only one case to court.

Another element of immigration control is carried out through visas. When a country is made into a visa country this means that all citizens of that country, for whatever purpose they are coming, must get permission in advance of travelling to the UK, from the British Embassy or British High Commission in the country of origin. People who are visa nationals and who come here without getting a visa can be refused entry and sent straight back just for this reason. Visa countries are (1 July 1992) Afghanistan, Albania, Algeria, Angola, Armenia, Azerbaijan, Bangladesh, Belarus, Benin,

Bhutan, Bulgaria, Burkina Faso, Burma, Burundi, Cambodia, Cameroon, Cape Verde, Central African Republic, Chad, China, Comoros, Congo, Cuba, Djibouti, Egypt, Equatorial Guinea, Ethiopia, Gabon, Georgia, Ghana, Guinea, Guinea-Bissau, Haiti, India, Indonesia, Iran, Iraq, Jordan, Kazakhstan, Kirgizstan, North Korea, Laos, Lebanon, Liberia, Libya, Madagascar, Mali, Mauritania, Moldöva, Mongolia, Morocco, Mozambique, Nepal, Nigeria, Oman, Pakistan, Philippines, Romania, Russia, Rwanda, Sao Tome e Principe, Saudi Arabia, Senegal, Somalia, Sri Lanka, Sudan, Syria, Taiwan, Tajikistan, Thailand, Togo, Tunisia, Turkey, Turkmenistan, Uganda, Ukraine, Uzbekistan, Vietnam, Yemen, Zaire.

Visitors

The immigration rules state that in order to come in as visitors people must satisfy an immigration officer that they are just coming for a visit, for a definite length of time which cannot be more than six months, that they intend to leave the UK at the end of the time they requested and that there is the money available to support them here for that time, without the visitor needing to work or to claim benefits. Visa nationals need to satisfy immigration officials at the British post in their country before travelling here; others can arrive here and apply to the immigration officers at the air or sea port for permission to enter. The subjective nature of the rule means that the refusal rates for different countries are very different, usually because immigration officers are not satisfied about their intention to leave; in 1990 one in 53 Jamaicans were refused entry but only one in 3,386 Norwegians and one in 5,544 Canadians.

In order to show that just a visit is intended, immigration officers may ask for proof of what the visitors do in their country of origin, so a letter from an employer, stating that people are on leave and when they are expected back, or from a college, stating that the people are students and when the next term begins, can be useful. It is more difficult for a person who is not working, or whose job is working on a family farm, to satisfy the immigration officer in this way. It is also always more difficult for black people from Third World countries to satisfy an officer that they intend to return, because of immigration officers' stereotyped preconceptions about such countries.

With regard to financial support, the visitors may be able to bring money with them, but where they will be supported by friends or relatives here, proof may be demanded from them. This would normally be a letter from the people here confirming that they are able and willing to support the visitor for the period of stay but also proof that they are able to do so, for example, a recent bank statement or recent pay slips showing that they have enough extra money. They may also be telephoned (or written to) by immigration officers to ask for further confirmation of their financial status.

People may come in for visits for private medical treatment provided they can show that they have the money to pay for their treatment as well as for the other expenses of their stay. Visitors are not entitled to National Health Service medical treatment, except for emergencies, so immigration officers may refuse entry to people who they suspect are coming for medical treatment but cannot afford it. There were complaints when it was revealed in July 1991 that port medical inspectors had instructions to give estimates of the cost of treatment for people seeking entry to the UK who have or are "suspected of having" Aids or HIV infection to see whether the passengers could afford any medical treatment.

If it appears that there is, or may be, a romantic relationship between the visitors and the people here sponsoring them to come, this can lead to intrusive personal questioning from immigration officers to see whether "something more than a visit" is intended. This may be a problem for people of opposite sexes, in case they have any marriage plans in which case the visitor should have gained entry clearance as a fiancé, or for lesbian or gay couples, if this is known to the immigration officer, as they could not fit into the rules to stay here together but immigration officers may think that they are trying to do so. Immigration officers have the power to ask any questions, and to look at any documents being carried by the visitor, in order to further their inquiries.

Visitors can be allowed in for six months. It is not possible under the rules to be granted an extension of this six months, except if the person is a medical visitor and the treatment is still continuing. Visitors may be able to leave the country and to get permission to re-enter for a further visit, but the more often this is done the more suspicious immigration officers may become that the person is really living rather than visiting here. It is possible to apply for an extension of stay, to the Home Office; the application will be refused but as long as the application was made in time, before the initial six months as a visitor had run out, there is the right to appeal against the refusal (although the appeal cannot possibly succeed, because six months is the maximum visit permitted by the immigration rules). However, because of bureaucratic delays both in the Home Office and the immigration appeals authorities, the application and the appeal can take many months, or up to a year, before it is finished and the visitor can stay in the UK for that time.

It is important to note that it is not safe to travel out of the UK and expect to be allowed to re-enter during this time; the visitor would not be let back in. It will also make any future visits to the UK more difficult, as the people have shown that they did want to remain for longer than was allowed in the past and therefore might wish to do so again.

It can be possible for a person who entered as a visitor to apply to change status and to remain longer for a different purpose. However there are several pitfalls in this:

Anyone wanting to work in the UK has to get permission for this in advance of travelling here. The immigration rules specifically forbid visitors from changing to do any kind of work here and exceptions are only very rarely made. This is not really a practical proposition. Work also includes running a business and being self-employed.

Visa nationals who entered as visitors (or on any other basis) are not allowed to change to become students. Others may be able to do so if they satisfy the relevant requirements of the rules.

It is still possible for a visitor who marries while in the UK to apply to stay with his/her spouse but there are worries that this will be the next casualty of the "no switching" requirement. An application could be made completely out-side the immigration rules for a visitor to remain with a lesbian or gay partner; this is likely to take a very long time, if the Home Office gives it any serious consideration at all, and it is unlikely to succeed.

Students

In order to come to study in the UK, students have to satisfy the immigration officers of three things. If they are visa nationals, they have to do this abroad at the British post; if not, they can apply at the port or airport here, or if they are already in the UK they can apply to the Home Office to change their status. They have to prove:

1. They have been accepted for a full-time course of studies at a recognized educational institution. "Full-time" for immigration purposes means at least 15 hours daytime classes per week; if a student wants to study an unusual combination of subjects which means doing two part-time daytime courses which together add up to 15 hours, this may be allowed provided that the student can show acceptable reasons for this way of pursuing studies and that it is not in order to study cheaply.

2. They have the money to pay their fees and to live here without needing to work or to claim benefits. Overseas students have to pay fees which cover the full cost of their courses, usually thousands of pounds a year, and they are not usually allowed to work; even if they do obtain permission to work, the Home Office cannot consider any likely earnings they may have towards the cost of their fees and maintenance here; they have to show that they have enough money without relying on work.

3. They intend to leave the UK at the end of their course of studies. This is subjective once again and can be used as immigration officers think fit — for example, if a student has had other relatives coming here to study who have been able to stay on longer, or who have lived here for a long time, if

they think that studies are not the main reason for the person coming here but that he or she has some ulterior motive, if they think the student is really a refugee who will not want to return after the studies are finished then the immigration officers can refuse entry.

The last requirement may also be difficult for a person already in the UK, for example as a visitor. Visitors have already had to show that they intended to leave at the end of their visit; the fact of applying as a student shows that they have not done this. They will have to show very clear and strong reasons why they changed their minds after coming in as visitors and why they will not change their minds again but will definitely leave at the end of their studies. The other danger is if the Home Office believes that they were never really genuine visitors at all — that they had always considered staying on to study but had not revealed their intentions from the beginning. The Home Office may then treat the person as an "illegal entrant". This means that the Home Office believes the person did not tell the truth on entering the country, that if they had told the truth they would not have been allowed in and therefore that they came in illegally by deceiving the immigration officers on entry. An illegal entrant can be arrested and detained and sent back to the country of origin without any form of appeal before removal, so this is not advised!

Other temporary categories

Young women aged between 17 and 27, who are citizens of any EC country, or Andorra, Austria, Cyprus, Czechoslovakia, the Faeroes, Finland, Greenland, Hungary, Iceland, Liechtenstein, Malta, Monaco, Norway, San Marino, Sweden, Switzerland, Turkey or Yugoslavia, may come here as au pairs, to live with an "English-speaking" family in order to help with housework and childcare and to learn the English language, in return for pocket-money. This can be permitted for up to two years.

Commonwealth citizens of either sex, between the ages of 17 and 27, may come here as "working holidaymakers" for up to two years. They need to satisfy the immigration officers that they are coming for an extended holiday, that they will only be taking work "incidental to their holiday" and that they have enough money to get home again. This provision was intended for Australians and New Zealanders "doing Europe" and it is unusual and difficult for a person from a Third World Commonwealth country to gain entry under this provision.

Commonwealth citizens who had a grandparent born in the UK can be allowed to come to live here because of this fact. They need to get entry clearance from the British High Commission and show all the relevant birth and marriage certificates to prove their legitimate descent from a person born here, and they can be allowed in for four years, free to work here, and at the end of four years can get permission to stay permanently.

COMING TO LIVE HERE: RELATIONSHIPS

Anyone coming to the UK intending to stay and live here has to get permission in advance of travelling, from the British Embassy or High Commission in their country of origin. This applies to all nationalities, not just visa nationals.

Coming to join a relative who is a British citizen or who has already been allowed to stay here permanently is now the most common way for people to be allowed to live in the UK, but the relationships provided for are very limited. People may come in to join their spouses or fiancé(e)s, their parents (if they are under 18), their children (if they are over 65) and occasionally a more distant relative only in very limited and difficult circumstances. There are no provisions for joining a lover, or for joining a person of the same sex in order to live together as a couple. Even if a "marriage of convenience" is organized, this is no guarantee of being allowed to stay as the immigration rules on marriage are very strict.

Marriage

In order to grant permission to someone to come to join a spouse or fiancé(e) here, (unless the spouse is a citizen of another EC country working here) the entry clearance officer at the British post has to be satisfied:

1. The couple have met each other. This provision is aimed specifically against Asian arranged marriages, to ensure that the extra trouble and expense of a visit has to take place before the application can be considered.

2. The couple intend to stay together permanently as husband and wife. This is a subjective test giving entry clearance officers vast amounts of discretion.

3. The primary purpose of the marriage or intended marriage was not immigration to the UK. This is used mainly against men from the Indian subcontinent, but also increasingly against women from the Philippines and Thailand, when it is thought that this particular marriage was undertaken in order that a person might have better economic prospects in the UK, or wanted to come here for any other reason and knew that marriage was the only way that s/he might qualify. The use of this rule means that women living here who wish to marry a man from the Indian subcontinent have less than 50 per cent chance of being able to live here with their partner.

4. The couple can support and accommodate themselves here without needing to have recourse to public funds.

5. The person living here is a British citizen or is settled (allowed to stay permanently) in the UK.

If all these criteria are satisfied, a fiancé(e) will be allowed in for six months, with a prohibition on working, and expected to marry within that time and then to apply to the Home Office for permission to remain as a spouse. A spouse will be given a year at first, and is free to work. Near the end of the year, an application can be made to the Home Office for permission to stay permanently. The Home Office can then check to be sure that the couple are still together (and will probably want a letter from the partner originally living here to confirm that the marriage is still continuing) and that they can still support themselves, before granting permission to stay. Thus it is important that any couple planning to marry are fully aware of the immigration rule consequences and that they will have to remain together for at least a year (probably longer, given the present and long-standing Home Office delays in dealing with applications) if they are to be allowed to stay. It is also possible, if a couple split up soon after one of them has been allowed to stay and the aggrieved partner tells the Home Office, that further investigations may be made. If the Home Office believes that the marriage was never intended to be "genuine" or permanent, it is possible for a decision to deport the partner from abroad to be made, on the grounds of deception and that it is "not conducive to the public good" that the person be allowed to stay. This Home Office action is rare.

Applications to remain in the UK because of a lesbian or gay relationship, which is seen in the same light as marriage, do not fall under any immigration rule. Even if a marriage has taken place in a country which recognizes a gay or lesbian marriage, like Denmark or the Netherlands, it will not be recognized in Britain. Any couple applying to stay here together on the grounds of their relationship will probably face a long and uphill fight, and will have to put forward a strong case, based on the length of their relationship and the difficulty or impossibility of it continuing in the partner's country for immigration or other reasons. Only one couple have so far tried to fight their case through the courts, a Swedish man, Lars Wirdestedt, and his British partner; although they lost in the Court of Appeal in 1984, the Home Office decided not to pursue the case further after over four years and allowed Wirdestedt to remain. The Home Office has stated in conversation that a gay or lesbian relationship in itself would not usually be enough to grant a person permission to remain unless there were other exceptional circumstances, for example, nursing a partner with Aids.

Children

Children may be allowed to join their parents if both parents are settled here, if the children are under 18 and if there is adequate support and accommodation for them. The major problems for children are in countries where there is no detailed system of registering births and marriages, as it can then be difficult to satisfy an immigration officer that the children are actually "related as claimed" to the parents. It has been to counter these suspicions that the growth in DNA fingerprint testing of children and parents, particularly families from Bangladesh, has grown up, so that this complicated and sophisticated medical test is becoming almost an essential part of immigration control procedures.

When only one parent is living here (unless the other parent is dead) it is very hard to bring a child here. It has to be shown then either that the parent living here has had the "sole responsibility" for a child's upbringing (clearly impossible to prove literally when someone else, by definition, has had day-to-day care of the child) or that there are "serious and compelling family or other considerations rendering the child's exclusion undesirable". This means that the child must be living in absolutely intolerable conditions and cannot be expected to continue, and this has to be in relation to the general standard of living in the country of origin, not the UK. In practice, the Home Office has an unpublished concession which may permit children under 12 to come to join a lone parent here, provided support and accommodation is available and, if the relative is the father, that there is a "female relative living in the household who is able and willing to care for the child". However, not all British posts abroad appear to know about this and it does not always happen.

Adopted children do not automatically qualify as children of the family, as they do in other areas of the law. If an adoption takes place in the UK, that automatically gives the child the right to remain here, and to have British citizenship, if one of the adopters is a British citizen. If the adoption takes place abroad, it may not be legally recognized here and even if it is, it gives the child no right to come here unless it can be shown that the adoption took place "because of the inability of the natural parents to care for the child" and not as a device for getting round the immigration rules. Thus it is very hard for, say, an Indian couple to adopt their nephew or niece, as agreed within the family because they can have no children of their own, but comparatively easy for a white couple to adopt a child from an El Salvadorean orphanage and bring it here. Where the adoption overseas is not recognized under UK law there is a complicated and long-drawn-out procedure for bringing a child here for adoption, which involves detailed medical and social reports on the child and the adoptive parents; it is more common for the parents to return here with the baby and then dare the immigration service to send it back on its own. This can only work with non-visa national babies.

Parents

Parents have to prove many things to be able to come to join their adult children settled here. They must show:

1. That one of them is at least 65. If a widowed mother is applying to come on her own, she can be younger; this does not include divorcées or separated women or women who have never been married. Widowers have to be 65.

2. They must have been wholly or mainly financially dependent on their children before they came here. This means it must be shown that money was sent from this country to support the parents and that this was necessary and important to them. If they were mainly living off their own property or a pension, for example, they do not qualify.

3. They have no other close relatives in their country of origin to whom they can turn for support. If close relatives are physically or financially unable to help, this must be proved.

4. They can be supported and accommodated here without recourse to public funds.

If they can show all this, parents will be allowed to stay permanently on arrival in the UK.

COMING TO WORK

It is difficult to do this. People wanting to come here in order to work must have obtained a work permit before coming. This entails finding a job here and then persuading the prospective employer to apply to the Employment Department for a work permit to employ the person. The work permit system exists in order to protect jobs in Britain for British citizens and residents, not to help people to come to work — so the employer normally has to show that the job was widely advertised, that all the other people who applied for it were unable to do or to be trained to do the job and that the person from abroad's experience, qualifications, training etc. are precisely what was required. The majority of work permits are granted for entertainers and sports people or for people already employed in transnational companies having short-term work experience in the UK; otherwise, work permits are normally only granted for highly skilled unusual professional jobs or where there is a shortage here, though sometimes nurses or teachers have been able to get them.

A few jobs do not require work permits — the immigration rules list them. These include missionaries, ministers of religion, monks and nuns, overseas journalists based here temporarily, the private servants of diplomats — all people who are unlikely to wish to settle here and who will not be taking jobs away from settled people. It is always necessary to get permission in advance of travelling here to come to do any of these jobs.

People can come to do business here or to be self-employed, if they can show that they are bringing with them capital of at least £200,000 to put into the business or self-employment, and satisfy other requirements. People may come to live off their capital, as persons of independent means, if they have at least £200,000 or a guaranteed annual income of at least £20,000 and can show that they have close connections with the UK. Very few people can qualify under this. A close connection accepted in one case was that the person was in a gay relationship with a man here.

Writers and artists, who can show that they will be making enough money to support themselves from their art or writing and will not need to take any other paid employment, may be able to come in without showing this huge amount of capital. Writers can include freelance journalists; artists do not include artistes (performers, who need work permits) but are painters and sculptors and, probably, photographers.

All people coming for work will be admitted for a period of either one or four years on arrival. After they have been allowed to stay in this category for four years, they can get permission from the Home Office to stay permanently.

REFUGEES

Refugees are people who cannot return to the country in which they were living because they have a "well-founded fear of persecution for reasons of race, religion, nationality, membership of a particular social group or political opinion". This is the definition in the United Nations Convention relating to the Status of Refugees, which the UK has signed. However, British immigration officials do their best to stop refugees from coming here to seek asylum and do not consider their cases sympathetically should they manage to get here.

Most refugees now are from Third World countries where people are in danger because of wars, both civil and external. Many countries have ex-colonial connections with Britain and people may therefore seek refuge here. Many Tamils from Sri Lanka, for example, travelled here — until Britain made Sri Lanka into a visa country in 1985 so they could not travel without obtaining visas from the British High Commission in Colombo. There is no provision in the rules for a visa to be given to come as a refugee; it is all discretionary. The process was repeated for Turkey in 1989, when many Kurds from south-eastern Turkey sought refuge here, and for Uganda in 1991.

When people still managed to get on planes without visas, or their desperation led them to forge visas, the government's next step was to pass the Immigration (Carriers' Liability) Act 1987, which fines airlines £2,000 for each passenger they bring in without the correct documents. This has made airlines into agents of immigration control, checking to see whether people have visas before letting them buy tickets or get on planes.

Even when people get here and seek asylum, their applications are not considered sympathetically. Many asylum-seekers are detained for months while their cases are being considered; there have been two suicides of detained asylum-seekers in the past year. Many people are not granted asylum; some are given "exceptional leave to remain" when it is accepted that they should not be returned at present but not that they qualify for full refugee status. This is a much more insecure status, as it is entirely at the discretion of the Home Office and could be revoked. It also does not give people any claim to be joined by their families; the Home Office has stated that they will consider this after four years.

There are no records of people being granted asylum because of their sexuality, though applications have been made for this when people have come from a particularly homophobic country. There are reports that some gay men from Argentina and from Iran have been granted exceptional leave to remain for this reason. Applications can be made on this basis but it will always be at the discretion of the Home Office. The courts decided in *ex parte Z. (QBD 25.7.89)* that it would not be necessary for a gay man to show or "practise" his homosexuality in Cyprus and he would not therefore have to face persecution, so did not qualify for asylum.

AFTER-ENTRY IMMIGRATION CONTROL

Any person who is not a Commonwealth citizen and not an EC citizen and who has been allowed to remain in the UK for more than six months can also be legally required to register with the police. This is a hangover from the Aliens Restriction Act of 1914, passed at the outbreak of the First World War in order to control foreigners here, but has continued since. If a person's passport is stamped requiring him or her to register with the police, this should be done, as it is a criminal offence not to. People have to tell the police their name, address, occupation, marital status and any changes in these, and pay £27.50 for a police registration certificate. No recorded use is made by the police of this information.

If a person is admitted for a temporary period and wants to remain longer or to change the conditions of stay, an application has to be made to the Home Office for this. It is very important that an application is made before the person's permission to stay runs out! This is because as long as an application has been made, and is under consideration by the Home Office, it does not matter that the time given runs out, the person is still legally in the UK. If the application is refused, there is a formal right of appeal; all this can keep a person legally in the country for another year or more. If the application is made even one day late, the person is here illegally, is liable to arrest for overstaying even if an application is made later, and if the application is refused, there is no formal right of appeal. This means, of course, that the Home Office can be less careful in dealing with the application as it knows there will be no formal outside review.

The criteria for dealing with applications in the UK are the same as those outside; the Home Office considers the same things to see if people qualify to remain as entry clearance officers or immigration officers do to see if they qualify to enter. There are added complications; if the person is in the UK illegally, any application is at the discretion of the Home Office, which has to decide whether it will overlook this breach of the rules or not. There are certain things for which entry clearance is necessary and the application made in the UK can automatically be refused. Although the rules may permit fewer things in the UK the fact of being here can also be helpful, as there is generally more bureaucracy and more work to be done in forcing someone out of the country than in not letting someone in at all.

A person who is refused an extension of stay can appeal

against this as long as the application was made in time. When the refusal letter comes from the Home Office, it comes with forms to fill in, which must be sent back to the Home Office and received there within 14 days of the decision, to appeal. With an appeal pending, the person may remain in the UK and there are also no restrictions on working during this period. Income support may be claimed (though will be paid only at the reduced Urgent Cases rate). If the appeal is lost, there is the right to apply for a further appeal to a higher level court, the Immigration Appeal Tribunal, if there is a legal point to be argued. Once these two appeals are over, if the person still remains here, he or she is here illegally and could be treated as an overstayer.

IMMIGRATION OFFENCES

People remaining longer than they have been allowed, or breaking a condition of their stay (usually, working without permission) are committing an immigration offence and, if caught, can be dealt with in two different ways:

1. By being arrested by the police and being charged with the criminal offence. People would then appear before a magistrate's court charged with the offence, which carries a maximum fine of £2,000, and/or up to six months' imprisonment and/or a recommendation for deportation. A court cannot actually deport people but it can recommend to the Home Office that they should be deported. The Home Office then has to consider this recommendation as well as any representations it receives on the person's behalf, in deciding whether or not to carry it out.

2. By the Home Office dealing with the person administratively. The Home Office has its own powers to make decisions to deport people for breaking a condition of their stay. If this is done, the person has the right to appeal against the decision. However, since 1 August 1988, if the person has been in the UK for less than seven years, the appeal is only on the facts of the case, not on its merits. This means that the appeal can only consider whether the Home Office took a

correct legal decision on the facts — whether the person really had stayed longer than allowed, whether or not the person was working. Any other reasons against deportation — that the person has a family or other connections here, or is in the middle of a degree course here — cannot be considered at the appeal. The only exception to this is where the person claims to be a refugee, as then the merits of the refugee claim can be considered at appeal. This reduction in appeal rights has meant that the Home Office has made many more decisions to deport on these grounds, now that there is no formal scrutiny; in 1987 there were 794 such decisions, in 1991, 3,173. Most people who are deported have been here for less than seven years; those who have been here that long do still have a full appeal and can put forward all the compassionate and family reasons why they should not be deported.

It is always very important to make representations to the Home Office as to why a person should not be deported, as it has to consider them. Things like close ties and relationships here or difficulties that would be faced abroad should be listed. If a deportation order is actually made, it is still possible, though more difficult, to argue that it should be revoked. This can also be done after a person has been deported, if he or she wants to try to come back, but the immigration rules say that revocation will normally be considered only if the person has been out of the country for at least three years.

What to do on arrest

If people are arrested on suspicion of having committed an immigration offence, it is very important to get competent legal advice before saying anything to an immigration officer or police officer about it. This is because, as explained earlier, if the authorities believe that they can show that the person did not tell the truth, or did not reveal the full facts, to an immigration officer on arrival, s/he can be treated as an illegal entrant. A visitor who is found working, for example, may be coerced into stating that s/he had always intended to work here from the beginning, and thus be treated as an illegal entrant, as visitors are not allowed to work. A competent adviser will explain the dangers of being verballed in this situation.

Police and immigration officers may also threaten people with long periods in detention. This is a possibility; there is no time limit as to how long a person may be detained for immigration purposes. However, if the person has the right of appeal against the immigration decision being made, there is also the right to apply for bail. Normally two sureties are needed, people who are settled (allowed to stay permanently) in the UK and who can guarantee at least £1,000 or £2,000 as bail should the person disappear. Immigration officers often do not tell people about their right to bail. It is also possible to argue with the Home Office that the person should be released, rather than detained, while the case is being considered. The main place of Immigration Act detention for men from the London area is at HM Prison Haslar, near Gosport, Hampshire; people are also detained in prisons all over the country and at the special immigration detention centres at Gatwick and Heathrow and Harmondsworth, near Heathrow.

OTHER CRIMINAL OFFENCES

People who are not British citizens, and not Commonwealth citizens who were settled in the UK before 1973 and have lived here at least five years since then, are liable to deportation if they are convicted of a non-immigration offence for which they are, or could have been, sentenced to imprisonment. In practice, courts most commonly recommend deportation for people convicted of bringing in or supplying drugs, or of violent offences. There are no known instances of people being deported after conviction on charges frequently made against gay men, e.g. gross indecency. It is unusual for a person settled in the UK to be recommended for deportation and the Home Office has to consider any representations made on the person's behalf. In 1991, 405 people were recommended for deportation; the Home Office decided not to deport 22 of them.

CONCLUSION

Immigration laws give the Home Office and the immigration authorities very wide powers to deal with people subject to immigration control and these powers are not generally used for the benefit of those who are subject to control. The law and rules discriminate against lesbians and gay men by ignoring their existence and making no provision for a gay man or lesbian from abroad to remain in a relationship in the UK. The way the rules are operated is also discriminatory, as the Home Office uses discretion much more widely in favour of unmarried white heterosexual couples than lesbian or gay couples and in most areas it is harder for black people. Persecution or harassment on grounds of sexuality is not recognized as a ground for asylum, and again discretion is rarely used in people's favour.

It is therefore important for people to understand what the law and rules say in order to have some idea whether or not they may qualify for what they want here, or whether there is likely to be any other way round the rules to be able to stay or to come here. However, it is always important to get advice, because the rules can be changed so quickly and easily and because so much depends on knowledge of day-to-day activities and how the Home Office is behaving at a particular time.

CRIME

"The buggers are legal now, what more are they after?" — Tom Robinson, "Glad to be Gay"

The first part of this chapter discusses the various criminal offences with which lesbians and gay men are most likely to be charged. The second section has information about police powers, practical advice about your rights and what to do if you are arrested by the police. We give brief details about how to complain about police misconduct. The next parts discuss how to handle a case and some particular rules of evidence that may be important if you have been charged with a criminal offence. We then outline the different penalties which courts can impose and describe some problems which gay and lesbian prisoners may face.

Because the law in Scotland differ substantially from that in England and Wales, it will be discussed separately.

It is commonly thought that homosexuality was legalized in 1967. The other chapters of this book make it clear that the oppression of lesbians and gays extends far beyond the criminal law. Even within the criminal law, sex between men remains illegal except in certain narrowly defined circumstances — broadly speaking between consenting adults in private. Lord Reid succinctly expressed the legal system's predominant attitude towards "homosexuality". "There is a material difference between merely exempting certain conduct from criminal penalties and making it lawful in the full sense . . . indulgences in these practices . . . is corrupting." (This quotation is from his House of Lords judgement at the trial of *International Times* for conspiracy to corrupt public morals, discussed in more detail below.)

The paradoxical result of this "legalization" of gay sexuality is that the 1980s saw a renewed emphasis on the criminality of gay sex. Perhaps in response to the increasingly vocal homophobia of the press and Tory politicians, the police intensified their surveillance of the gay community. This reached a crescendo in 1989, when the police recorded more offences of "indecency between males" (2,022) than in any year since the 1950s, and indeed the third highest figure since the offence was introduced into the law in 1885. In addition there were 1,138 reported cases of buggery (the highest level in 50 years) and 2,878 of indecent assault on a male. In fact the number of gay men (and to a lesser extent lesbians) facing criminal charges arising from their sexuality is higher even than these figures suggest, as other charges do not appear in the official statistics. The vast majority of these offences relate to consensual sex between men over the heterosexual age of consent (16).

Although many of these offenders were punished by a fine, during the 1980s 2,561 sentences of imprisonment were imposed for gay crimes (buggery, soliciting, indecency and procuring). Nearly all of those imprisoned were convicted of consenting homosexual behaviour.

In Scotland, as in England and Wales, it is virtually impossible to obtain exact statistics about the number of people convicted of crimes arising from lesbian and gay lifestyles. Charges may be brought under broad offences such as breach of the peace, which can include anything from being drunk in the street to public displays of affection by lesbians or gays. Statistics from the Scottish Home Office for 1988 show 70 instances of illegal homosexual acts being reported to the police, of which 57 resulted in convictions.

While citing statistics we should not overlook the effects that so-called minor offences can have on the lives of those involved. Precisely because of the broader oppression of gay men and lesbians, the publicity surrounding criminal charges can have a devastating effect on their lives, often out of all proportion to any penalty actually imposed by the courts. In 1989 for example there were six known suicides of men arrested for "cottaging" offences. Fear of publicity makes lesbians and gays particularly vulnerable to police intimidation and results in a high proportion of guilty pleas and "confessions". This, in turn, encourages the police to give free rein to their homophobia, and improve their conviction rate at the same time.

Aside from laws specifically aimed at criminalizing lesbian or gay behaviour many other laws have been enforced through the courts in such a discriminatory way that behaviour considered completely acceptable in heterosexuals becomes a criminal offence when performed by gays or lesbians. The most extreme example of this double standard is the conviction of lesbians and gays for Public Order Offences, ("insulting behaviour") merely for kissing in public.

In similar fashion, it is doubtful whether the judge in the notorious "Operation Spanner" trial, in which several gay men who had engaged in sado-masochistic sex were convicted of indecent assault (despite the fact that they were all consenting adults and the acts took place in private) would have felt free to interpret the law in this way and to hand out severe prison sentences if the participants had been heterosexual.

Because gay sex has never been legalized, and in the absence of any laws affirming the equality of lesbians and gays or protecting them from discrimination, they are vulnerable to the whims of homophobic politicians, judges and police. A recent political example is Clause 30 of the Criminal Justice Bill 1991 providing for harsher sentences for consensual gay offences. Tory politicians exploited and propagated the stereotypical association of homosexuality with the "corruption of youth" to bolster support for their law and order policies. By describing consensual gay offences such as gross indecency and soliciting as "serious sexual offences" this measure, despite a subsequent concessionary amendment, is likely to encourage increased police activity and lead to more arrests and harsher sentences.

It is not only specifically sexual offences that have been used to harass the gay and lesbian communities. A bewildering variety of bye-laws and antiquated offences (such as the Vagrancy Act of 1824 and the Town and Police Clauses Act 1847) together with the politically controversial Public Order

Act 1986 have also been invoked.

At times the targets have been prominent gay institutions. Most notoriously, the archaic charge of blasphemy was brought (by Mary Whitehouse in a private prosecution) against *Gay News* in 1978. The House of Lords upheld this conviction for publishing a poem by a professor of poetry about a centurion's homosexual fantasies about Christ. In 1984 Gay's The Word bookshop in London was attacked by means of the outdated and illogical obscenity laws, as was Lavender Menace bookshop in Edinburgh. As we will see later these laws, though not specifically aimed against gays or lesbians, have been enforced by the courts in a discriminatory manner.

In summary, the "legalization of homosexuality" still remains to be accomplished and would require not only a thoroughgoing law reform but a complete overhaul of judicial attitudes and police practices.

LESBIANS

The existence of lesbianism is not specifically acknowledged by the criminal law but far from indicating a greater acceptance of lesbians this is an expression of the law's general denial of active female sexuality, particularly one which is independent of men. The social process by which lesbianism is rendered invisible has been analysed as a particularly powerful and insidious means of suppressing lesbian identities.

At times this refusal to acknowledge the existence of lesbianism has been explicit. In 1921 there was an attempt in the House of Commons to insert a clause into a bill which would have made "gross indecency between female persons" illegal. The bill was not passed in the Lords because they were concerned that legislation would bring the "horror" of lesbianism "to the notice of women who have never heard of it, never thought of it, never dreamed of it."

Although there are no criminal laws against lesbian sex, there are some offences with which lesbians could be charged (indecent assault, indecency with children, public order offences, obscenity). These are mentioned in the relevant sections.

The intense hostility towards lesbians within the legal system, despite the absence of explicit criminalization, was made all too clear in an extraordinary case which received a great deal of press attention in 1991. Two women alleged that they had had sexual affairs with another woman in the belief that she was a man. This alleged "male impersonator" was charged with indecent assault on the basis that the consent which the other women had given to sex was invalidated by this deception.

The allegations concerning the "deception" strained credulity, and the fact that both women had repeatedly consented to sex was questioned, but nevertheless a guilty verdict was brought. With a logic more in place in a medieval philosophy debate than a modern criminal court, the act to which the women thought they consented was held to be fundamentally different to the one which actually took place. However the rationale behind the judgement was not so much based on academic reasoning about the nature of reality as on brute prejudice. The judge made this clear in his summing up, saying that he suspected that the victims "would rather have been raped by some young man . . . you have called into question their whole sexual identity." And that of course is what was at stake — the policing of sexual identity. Heterosexual sex and lesbian sex must never be confused.

The most shocking aspect of the case was the vicious sentence of six years imposed by the judge. This was subsequently reduced on appeal, on the basis of the girl's youth, but only after she had spent several months in prison.

GAY SEX IN ENGLAND AND WALES

The first secular law against homosexual activity (in 1533) imposed the death penalty for the "detestable and abominable vice of buggery". It was the act of anal intercourse which was outlawed, regardless of whether it took place with man, woman or indeed animal. Anal intercourse is still regarded by the law as far more serious than any other form of homosexual behaviour. Other forms of gay sex were not illegal until the Criminal Law Amendment Act 1885 which created the offence of "gross indecency". This phrase has been interpreted in the courts as meaning any other form of sexual contact between men.

The current law against gay sex is contained in Sexual Offences Act 1956. The Sexual Offences Act 1967 amended the previous Act by providing that where sex takes place in private, between two men both of whom are over 21 and consenting, then it is not illegal (we examine these conditions below). In all other circumstances it remains an offence.

This "liberalization" did not extend to Scotland until 1980, nor to Northern Ireland until the European Court of Human Rights forced the British government to change the law in 1982. Pressure on Britain to abide by the European Convention of Human Rights was also responsible for the Channel Islands (in 1990) and the Isle of Man (in 1992) reforming their laws along the lines of the English practice. Also in 1992 sex for lesbian and gay members of the armed forces was formally decriminalized.

WHAT THE LAW MEANS BY "PRIVATE"

If more than two people are involved in gay sex the law does not regard this as "private", and therefore "orgies" are illegal for gay men (but not for lesbians or heterosexuals). In 1989 the police raided a private leather party in east London and arrested several people. The arrests were made for gross indecency, though no charges were subsequently brought.

In addition, places which by any commonsense definition would be termed as private are not legally classed as such. If you are having sex with one person in your own room behind closed doors but there is someone else present in another room of the flat then you are not legally in "private". Saunas and health clubs are also not classified as private — the managers of such establishments may face charges for keeping a disorderly house (see below).

In practice most charges for gross indecency arise out of casual sexual encounters in streets, parks or toilets.

The Sexual Offences Act 1967 specified that lavatories were not "private". An unknown amount of police time is wasted "staking out" public lavatories, waiting for gay men to commit this victimless "crime". Often it is precisely the most vulnerable and isolated gay men who are caught in this way.

One line of defence, if you are caught cruising outdoors, is to argue that the place was in fact "private", because in practice no member of the public was likely to come along. The leading case on this question is R v. Reakes 1974 in which the judge said, "You look at all the surrounding circumstances, the time of night, the nature of the place including such matters as lighting and you consider further the likelihood of a third person coming on the scene." The question of whether or not a place is "private" is determined by the jury, or magistrates (depending on the type of court).

Proof of actual physical contact is not necessary, provided that more than one of you willingly participated in the activity. For instance if you are both wanking in front of each other with the intention of exciting each other this will be "gross indecency", if it is in a "public" place (R v. Preece 1970).

Barely one per cent of men convicted for public sex are given prison sentences. The Court of Appeal said that a sentence of immediate imprisonment for an offence of this sort, committed by a man of "previous good character" was "inappropriate and excessive" (R v. Clayton 1981).

Buggery

If two men have anal intercourse the legal term for this is buggery. If one of the parties is under 21 or does not consent, or if the act does not take place in private, then both parties can be charged with the crime (except that boys under 14 are not legally deemed capable of this offence as an active partner). The maximum prison sentence that can be imposed is:

- life imprisonment where the boy is under 16
- ten years where one partner was over 16 but did not consent
- five years where both partners consent but one is aged between 16 and 21

- two years in the above case if the convicted man is under 21.

In 1989, 76 per cent of those found guilty of buggery were sent to jail. This figure is particularly high because it appears that buggery charges (as opposed to charges of gross indecency) are most likely to be brought by the police where one of the partners to sex is under 16. (An estimated 70 per cent of these buggery convictions relate to consensual gay sex with boys of 13 to 16.) Prison terms for men convicted of buggery with boys in this age group average between three and four years.

Gross indecency

Any sexual act between men is termed gross indecency, and is a crime if one or both men are under 21, if it does not take place in private or if it is not consensual. As we explain below both parties are liable to prosecution for under-age sex, although in practice a younger partner will probably be seen as a victim and not charged.

The maximum prison sentence is two years, unless the offence involves a man who is over 21 having sex with a man under 21, in which case the maximum penalty is five years.

In cases including gross indecency and buggery, no charge can be brought more than 12 months after the offence as long as the other party consented and was over 16 (Section 7 SOA 1967).

Under 21

If the offence of buggery or gross indecency involves a man who is under 21 the Director of Public Prosecution's consent is required before a prosecution can be brought.

Sentencing — Clause 30 Criminal Justice Act 1991

In 1988, 23 men were sent to prison for sexual contact with a consenting male partner aged between 16 and 21. Six men were jailed for buggery, four for attempted buggery and 13 for gross indecency. Eight were jailed for up to one year, seven for up to two years, six for up to three years and in two cases of attempted buggery between three and four years. In 1989, six were jailed for soliciting and 73 for procuring.

In the past, although prison terms were a real possibility, particularly where the offence involved young men and/or the defendant had previous convictions for gay sex, they were relatively rare. There is a real fear that the passage of Section 30 of the Criminal Justice Act will increase the number of custodial sentences for gay offences, and lead to harsher penalties generally.

Section 30 gives courts the power to impose longer prison sentences for so-called "serious sexual offences", if there is a possibility that the offender might re-offend and cause "serious personal injury, whether physical or psychological". The section classifies as "serious sex crimes" the predominantly consensual offences of buggery, gross indecency, soliciting and procuring. The phrase "serious personal injury, whether physical or psychological" was an amendment to the bill, which Lord Ferrers, speaking on behalf of the Home Office, claimed "makes it clear that minor and victimless homosexual activities cannot be used in order to justify a heavier sentence."

However the amended Section remains dangerously vague, particularly in the context of the still prevalent stereotype of homosexuals as dangerous predators. Comments by the Home Secretary in a letter to the National Association of Citizens Advice Bureaux graphically illustrate the potential dangers. He argued that it was right to include gross indecency in the Section, since this might involve "seduction, exploitation and corruption of young people." Peter Tatchell, writing for *Capital Gay*, received an alarming confirmation of this approach from a Home Office spokesperson, who stated that in certain circumstances homosexual seduction "might sometimes result in serious psychological harm." "Vulnerable young people may need to be protected from older men who have a way with words, and who may seek to charm them into a sexual situation."

It is difficult to predict the exact effect of Section 30 but its mere existence has a powerful symbolic value in reinforcing the anti-gay bias of the criminal justice system.

IMPORTUNING — CRUISING

> "The offence of persistently importuning for an
> immoral purpose has been called the gay sus law
> because it is used in a completely discriminatory
> way to harass gay men, not for what they do but for
> what they are. Like the use of the old sus law
> against black youths it is used not to enforce the
> law, or to stop crime, but to regulate social behav-
> iour in public that the police do not approve of. In
> short it is used to keep us off the streets as a visible
> presence" — GALOP Annual Report 1984

The grudging acceptance of gay sexuality in the criminal law
is nowhere better illustrated than in the "crime" of importuning. It is a crime for a man "persistently to solicit or importune another man in a public place for immoral purposes".
The Court of Appeal has ruled that lawful gay sex can be an
"immoral purpose" in this context, and therefore it can be
illegal to ask someone to do this legal act. Nevertheless the
jury have to decide in each case whether or not something
amounts to an "immoral purpose", and so it will still be worth
arguing that your "purposes" were "moral".

As the quotation from GALOP suggests, this law has been
very widely used against gay men and the terms of the
offence have been defined by the courts in a way which can
only encourage police abuse of this contradictory and victimless offence .

To "solicit and importune" has been interpreted as meaning anything which would commonly be termed "chatting up"
or making a pass, which can of course be any word or gesture
depending on the context.

It has been further decided by case law that "persistently"
can mean either more than one invitation to one person or
separate invitations to more than one man. These invitations
can even be on different days and still constitute an offence.
The case of Dale v. Smith 1967 illustrates the weak evidence
that can be used to convict someone. In this case a man
merely walked up to a group of youths and said "hello".

Case law has also established that the prosecution does

not need to show that any member of the public was disturbed, nor even to produce the person who has allegedly been solicited. Almost invariably cases are based on police evidence alone.

The term "public place" means anywhere except a private home or hotel room. So in theory it is a criminal offence to chat people up at gay discos or pubs, or even in a private members club.

In practice, this offence is mainly used to control and harass gay men on the streets.

The maximum sentence if the case is heard in a crown court is two years imprisonment. In a magistrates' court the maximum sentence is six months imprisonment or a fine of £2,000, however the sentence is usually a small fine of £50 to £100.

PROCURING — INTRODUCING

The narrow limitations of the "liberalization"of the law in 1967 produce this further illogical offence. Section 4(1) the 1967 Act makes it an offence for a man to "procure" or bring about an act of buggery with anyone other than himself, regardless of whether or not the sex which they have is "lawful"under the 1967 Act, but only if the procurer is a man. (The section specifies that it is not a crime for a woman to "procure" such behaviour.) Procuring gay sexual acts other than buggery will only be unlawful if the sex falls outside the 1967 Act's liberalization (i.e. not between two men in private who are over 21). So if you introduce two gay friends hoping they will hit it off and they then have sex together you may have technically committed a criminal offence.

Although in practice this charge is normally used in connection with gay prostitution, it is not necessary for the "procuring" to have been done for payment in order for an offence to be committed.

ENTRAPMENT — PRETTY POLICE

There have been numerous complaints of police entrapment in the context of "cottaging" offences. Indeed, on some occasions the police have, in the process, themselves committed a crime. The other crime into which gay men are not infrequently "entrapped", is soliciting. Indeed, the "pretty policeman" has become a regular customer at certain gay venues.

The principle in English law is that where police officers set-up or incite someone to commit a crime (entrapment) this has no effect on that person's guilt or innocence before the law. This was clearly stated in the case of R v. Sang 1980. However it might be possible to argue that evidence from agents provocateurs should be excluded under the courts' new broad discretion (under Section 78 Police and Criminal Evidence Act 1984) to exclude evidence which would have an adverse effect on the fairness of the proceedings.

If you have been "entrapped" you can use this as "mitigation" (see page 270), which means that if you are found guilty you can argue that you should be given a lower sentence to reflect your lesser culpability because you were led into crime.

Sometimes the police will go even further and fabricate evidence where no "crime" has been committed. Thus even if you managed to resist the pretty young constable in ripped jeans you may still find yourself charged with soliciting or even indecent assault. This latter possibility was publicized when a Tory MP was arrested on this charge for making a pass at an undercover police officer in a gay bar! Note that it is a defence to a charge of indecent assault if you believed that the other person consented to the "assault" (R v. Kimber 1983), as would in most cases be reasonable in a gay bar! (This will not apply if the alleged "victim" is under 16 as he or she will be assumed to be incapable of consent, see page 229.)

If you have done nothing that even under the homophobic criminal law constitutes a crime then you should plead not guilty and get yourself a good solicitor who is prepared to go painstakingly over the police evidence. For example it is not uncommon for such meticulous reviewing of the case to reveal that what the police claim to have seen would have been impossible from their vantage point.

Various police guidelines have forbidden entrapment. A 1969 Home Office circular stated that "no member of the police force . . . should counsel, incite or procure the commission of a crime." However, there is abundant evidence that it occurs on a wide scale. Indeed as long as the police continue to be rewarded with convictions they have no incentive to observe these guidelines.

OTHER OFFENCES USED TO SUPPRESS PUBLIC GAY SEX

In their vigorous efforts to contain public expressions of gay sexuality (and notch up increased arrest figures for themselves) the police have been inventive in their utilization of outdated laws, originally intended for other purposes. One such archaic offence is "outraging public decency", extensively used during a surveillance operation at the toilets in Hyde Park in 1989. There is no maximum penalty.

Often these offences will only attract small fines, however the danger of publicity for such charges remains. It is not possible to run through the list of potential offences here, and indeed different offences may apply to different parts of the country, but it might be worth consulting a solicitor to assess the validity of the charges and your chances of acquittal. The police may even drop the charges if it is clear that you intend to vigorously defend the charges.

Bye-laws

Recently police forces, particularly in London, have begun to make extensive use of local bye-laws, whether local council bye-laws, railway bye-laws or park regulations, for prosecuting cottaging. Since these are local laws they will vary from one part of the country to another. They were often passed decades previously and some of them are quite outrageous: for instance the Richmond bye-law against staying in the toilet for longer than is necessary for the purpose, which was actually used 1989 to arrest more than 50 men.

Police are probably choosing to charge men under bye-laws rather than the Sexual Offences Act because a charge under the bye-laws cannot be heard by a jury and the police are therefore more likely to get a conviction. Gay men are also more likely to plead guilty to a bye-law offence.

You can sometimes simply plead guilty by post, which avoids the publicity which is often the most dreaded consequence of a charge. The penalty will probably only be a small fine. However we would advise caution as it is not clear whether bye-law offences are recorded as criminal offences on police computers — with possibly disastrous employment consequences.

The police do not have the power to arrest for a bye-law offence. The police will ask for your name and address and will send you a summons by post. If you refuse to give your address you can be arrested and charged. Avoid arguing with the police if possible, otherwise you are likely to be arrested, and charged with obstruction of a police officer in the course of his duty.

Public affection

Bye-laws have also been used to control gay and lesbian behaviour in public. Two men were charged in 1986 under the Metropolitan Police Act 1839, Section 54, for kissing and cuddling in the street. The police argued that this was insulting behaviour. The men argued that it was not insulting but the Court of Appeal disagreed, and upheld the conviction.

Public Order Act 1986

This Act revises and extends the old offence of "insulting behaviour liable to cause a breach of the peace" (Public Order Act 1936) and creates a new offence of disorderly conduct. This new offence provoked great opposition from civil liberties and gay groups because it extended the criminal law into areas of annoyance and disturbance not hitherto punished as crimes. The lack of a tight definition for "disorderly conduct" was felt to allow the police too much discretion, and with it a broad scope for harassment of "minority groups" such as black people and gays.

Insulting behaviour

A person is guilty of an offence if:
- s/he uses threatening, abusive or insulting words or behaviour towards another person or
- s/he distributes or displays to another person any writing, sign or other visible representation which is threatening, abusive or insulting *and*
- s/he intends that person to believe that immediate unlawful violence will be used against him or anyone else by him or by anyone else or
- s/he intends to provoke the immediate use of unlawful violence by that person or anyone else or
- whereby that person is likely to believe that such violence will be used or
- whereby it is likely that such violence will be provoked [this could be used to charge gays or lesbians who are displaying their affection in public].

In practice, public affection and "insulting" messages have been charged under Section 5, "disorderly conduct" (see below). Nevertheless, this Section means that lesbians or gays can theoretically be prosecuted on the basis that they might provoke violence against themselves by the open expression of their sexuality. This is a classic example of "blaming the victim" which can only serve to encourage "queerbashing" by endorsing this reaction.

Disorderly conduct

A person is guilty of this new offence by Section 5 or the 1986 Act if:
- s/he uses threatening, abusive or insulting words or behaviour or
- s/he uses disorderly behaviour or
- s/he displays any writing sign or other visible representation which is threatening, abusive or insulting *and*
- s/he does so within the hearing or sight of a person likely to be caused harassment, alarm or distress by the above conduct.

As we mentioned above "disorderly conduct" is a vague and undefined term. The courts have been ready all too often to accept the police assessment. The police have been using this Section to prosecute alleged sexual offences in public toilets. A police officer may be the person caused alarm or distress, although you should use the argument that police officers should be less susceptible to such reactions than ordinary members of the public (DPP v. Orum 1988).

It is a defence to the charge if you had no reason to believe that anyone was within sight or hearing who would be harassed etc. Thus presumably you could claim that overt sexual behaviour at an exclusively gay or lesbian gathering would not constitute a crime.

Both offences can be committed in either public or private places. However behaviour in a dwelling house cannot be an offence unless the behaviour has an effect outside the house (e.g. someone shouting insults into the street).

People charged with these offences do not have the right to a jury trial. As we will discuss below, magistrates are much more likely to accept the word of the police than are juries, and so your chance of acquittal are lessened.

SEX WITH YOUNG PEOPLE

As is clear from the sections above, if you have sex with a man under 21 you can be charged with buggery and/or gross indecency, depending on the sexual acts involved, and the attitudes of the prosecution. Gross indecency is seen as a less serious charge, and, if the young person is over 16, the prosecution may agree to bring this charge rather than buggery. It is at their discretion. They may offer to do this in exchange for your co-operation — always consult a solicitor before agreeing to such deals.

Indecent assault

If the young person is under 16 you may also be charged with indecent assault. Young people under 16 are legally incapable of consenting to any form of sexual activity, and therefore any sexual contact with them, be it heterosexual, lesbian or gay, is termed an assault. It remains a crime even if the young person in fact consented to or possibly even initiated, sex.

Whilst young people are undeniably entitled to protection from abusive adult sexuality, this law is enforced in a discriminatory way which serves to control and suppress the sexual expression of young gays.

The police will refrain from investigating most under-age heterosexual sex, and often caution rather than charge heterosexual male offenders, unless there is a large age discrepancy, a family relationship or the girl is under 14.

On the contrary, where homosexual contact is involved they will be keen to investigate and charge this because it is seen as a serious offence. The maximum penalty for an indecent assault is ten years imprisonment, and prison terms are much more likely to be imposed for consensual gay or lesbian sex than for heterosexual sex.

The law against sexual contact with young people under 16 applies equally to lesbians, although prosecutions are very rare (under ten per year).

Sentencing guidelines were laid down in the case of R v. Willis 1975. This stated that the penalty should be more severe in cases where there had been an abuse of authority or trust; where the boy had been physically, emotionally or psychologically damaged, or where there had been "moral corruption".

The Indecency with Children Act 1960

It is a criminal offence, punishable by a maximum of two years imprisonment, for a person (male or female) to commit an "act of gross indecency with or towards a child of 14 or under" or to encourage such a child to commit such an act towards them. This law was created to close the legal loophole created in the case where a man who asked a child to touch his penis was found not guilty of indecent assault because he himself had not actually performed an action.

YOUNG PEOPLE WHO HAVE SEX

We set out the position for young gays and lesbians who have sex in the chapter on Young People. The theoretical position is that young boys or men involved in sexual activity are just as guilty of gross indecency or buggery as their older partners. Indeed it is theoretically possible that where both partners are under 16 young lesbians or gays could be prosecuted for indecent assault, because neither of them is legally capable of consenting to sex. We should emphasize that this is unlikely; if any legal action is taken it is more likely to involve care proceedings.

SEX AND PEOPLE WITH SEVERE LEARNING DIFFICULTIES

People with severe learning difficulties are treated by the law in many situations in the same way as children. The "liberalizing" of the law concerning sexual activity does not apply to people "suffering from a severe mental handicap", because they will be deemed legally to be incapable of consenting to sex, and therefore any sexual activity remains illegal. However charges (of gross indecency, indecent assault or buggery for men, and sexual assault for women) cannot be brought if the partner had no reason to suspect that the other person had such a "handicap".

A severe mental handicap is defined as "a state of arrested development of mind which includes severe impairment of intelligence and of social functioning."

SADO-MASOCHISTIC SEX

Until December 1991 it was not thought that any special legal restraints applied to S&M sex. The conviction and imprisonment of the defendants in the "Operation Spanner" case established a legal precedent that, in a sexual context, a person's consent to an assault does not prevent it being a criminal offence. The term "assault" refers to a range of activities — flogging, branding, cutting etc. It is not clear how trivial the injuries inflicted must be before the activity can be considered legal — canes, ropes which cause reddening of the skin?

The judge was, in fact, less concerned with the harm inflicted upon the individuals involved in the case (indeed the harm inflicted by taking criminal proceedings greatly exceeded the physical harm to which the men in question had consented) than with controlling unacceptable sexuality. He stressed that "the courts must draw the line between what is acceptable in a civilized society and what is not."

A particularly ludicrous aspect of the judgement was that the men who consented to having physical violence inflicted upon them were convicted of aiding and abetting "actual bodily harm" upon themselves!

The defendants in this case received a series of prison sentences, some of three or four years. Such sentencing for activity which had previously not been thought a crime is staggeringly unjust.

This ruling is currently under appeal. In the meantime if you are engaging in S&M sex you should be extremely careful to leave no records — such as diaries, photos or videos — and be aware that you may be placing yourself at risk of blackmail, particularly if a younger man is involved.

GAY MEETING PLACES — DISORDERLY HOUSES

Some of the defendants in the S&M case referred to above were charged with keeping a disorderly house, receiving sentences of up to four and a half years in prison. British gay saunas have been the subject of frequent police raids and have, on occasion, similarly been charged with "keeping a disorderly house".

The use of the Disorderly Houses Act 1751 is an excellent example of the revival and use of an antiquated law for purposes other than those for which it was originally designed. It is a very vague offence, originally created to control entertainments which got out of hand and created a public nuisance. Under this Act the manager (not necessarily owner) of an establishment can be prosecuted if it is "not regulated by the constraints of morality . . . so as to violate law and good order".

In the case of R v. Quinn & Bloom 1961 this definition was explained by the court to mean a "house conducted contrary to law and good order in that matters are performed or exhibited of such character that their performance or exhibition in a place of common resort: a) amounts to an outrage of public decency or b) tends to deprave or corrupt or c) is otherwise calculated to injure the public interest so as to call for condemnation and punishment." In practice grounds b) and c) are seldom relied upon. No unruly behaviour is necessary to bring a "house" within this definition, nor is it necessary for the prosecution to show that prostitution was occurring.

The establishment must be a place of "common resort". It is for the jury to decide whether or not this applies, but it has been held that merely charging an entrance fee does not protect you from this offence. However a well-regulated club might not be considered to be an "open house".

Although such charges against gay pubs and clubs are quite rare the existence of such potential charges adds to the insecurity of the gay and lesbian world. A draconian sentence was made on the owner of Brownies sauna: six months in jail and £5,000 fine. Another sauna in Manchester was raided in 1989.

MALE PROSTITUTION — RENT BOYS

It is not a crime to be a male prostitute. The laws criminalizing prostitutes are specified to apply to women only. However the Sexual Offences Act 1967 makes it a crime to "procure others to commit homosexual acts", and also makes it an offence to live wholly or partly on earnings of male prostitution (Section 5). It is also an offence to be involved in running a brothel.

In practice those found guilty of organizing male prostitution are likely to be given very stiff prison sentences. The maximum sentence for living off the earnings of male prostitution is seven years.

Rent boys themselves are likely to be charged with soliciting. Their clients may be charged with offences relating to under-age sex or public sex, depending on the circumstances. The penalty is likely to be more severe where prostitution is involved.

CENSORSHIP

Without engaging in a theoretical debate concerning pornography and censorship, the law has been used to censor items which are only considered obscene because of their representation of a strong lesbian or gay identity. Although nowhere made explicit in the legislation, a different standard has been applied to representations of heterosexual and homosexual sexuality.

As we mentioned above, the obscenity laws have been used to target and attempt to control important community resources, such as Gay's The Word bookshop in London. They have also been more generally used to harass members of the gay and lesbian communities, providing an excuse to raid homes, demand lists of friends, or stop and harass people at customs. This is one of the commonest categories of call received by GLAD (Gay and Lesbian Legal Advice — helpline).

Generally speaking the purchase and possession of material which might be termed pornographic is not illegal (unless it is child pornography). It is the distribution of such material which the law seeks to control. However, the police have distorted the law by extensive operations on private homes, charging individual consumers, for instance, with smuggling an obscene video into the country or procuring obscene material to be sent through the post.

OBSCENE PUBLICATIONS ACT 1959

This Act makes it a crime to "publish" any "article" which the court decides is likely to "deprave and corrupt" those who are likely to see, hear or read it. "Publishing" in this context is defined as distributing, circulating, giving or lending as well as selling or hiring for a profit. In the case of videos or films this term includes showing or projecting.

The word "article" is also given a very broad meaning in this Act: any "article containing or embodying matter to be read or looked at . . . any sound record and any film or . . . pictures."

The meaning of the phrase "deprave and corrupt" is very much open to the interpretation of the jury (this charge is triable in the Crown court) within broad guidelines laid down in the case of DPP v. Whyte 1972. In particular this case discounted the argument that the people who were likely to read the book were already "in a state of depravity" and therefore unlikely to be corrupted further. It also said that this term referred to states of mind and therefore the prosecution did not have to show that the "article" stimulated antisocial behaviour.

The material must go beyond merely shocking or disgusting readers. The Court of Appeal quashed the convictions of the editors of *OZ* because the judge had misdirected the jury by suggesting that the legal meaning of "obscene" was "repulsive, filthy, loathsome, indecent or lewd". The actual meaning is much stronger than this. Similarly "corrupt" means more than leading morally astray. In addition the items must be considered liable to have a corrupting effect on a significant proportion of persons liable to read or view it.

It is a defence to this charge if you can convince the jury that the distribution of the article in question is for the "public good". This means that the work has intrinsic literary or artistic merit, and you are allowed to call experts to support you on this question. The case of DPP v. Jordan established that this defence does not include articles which claim to have therapeutic value.

You are entitled to a hearing in the Crown court and the maximum penalty is three years imprisonment and/or a fine. A prosecution cannot be started more than two years after the alleged offence.

Under Section 3 of the Act the police can apply for a warrant to search and seize obscene items kept for publication for gain. The items are then passed to the Director of Public Prosecutions, who decides whether they should be returned with no further action or a prosecution for obscenity instituted or the items destroyed. Before the articles can be destroyed the magistrates must issue a summons and give the owner of them an opportunity to show why they should not be destroyed (a forfeiture hearing).

In practice the local police force have a great deal of discretion about how this law is enforced. They tend to use a "shopping list" approach, where certain acts or images will automatically be prosecuted. For example an erect penis or oral sex. Often this will be a matter of degree (how close is the mouth to the labia?).

CINEMA AND THEATRE

Before a prosecution for obscenity can be brought against either a play or a feature film the Attorney General must give prior approval. Videos and 8-mm films are not protected from prosecution in this way.

Several other layers of censorship however apply to feature films. District councils can refuse exhibitors a licence to show a particular film and the British Board of Film Censors may insist on cuts before certifying it fit for public performances. In addition the import regulations set out below will apply to foreign films.

The Obscene Publications Act has applied to television since 1988. Although no prosecutions have yet been brought, in 1991 the Obscene Publications Squad recommended that the Director of Public Prosecutions take legal action against Channel Four for screening a clip of a Derek Jarman film showing an erect penis. Ironically the program was itself about the censorship of sex. No action was taken but a complaint to the British Broadcasting Standards Council was upheld. This body is responsible for monitoring the portrayal upon television of "violence, sex and matters of taste and decency". It has rejected several other complaints about gay programs, however the potential for complaints, and possible adverse effects on their licences, undoubtedly leads to some self-censorship among television companies.

VIDEO RECORDINGS ACT 1984

This Act was brought in as a response to the public concern about so-called "video nasties". It requires all videos (except educational ones or those concerned with sport, music or religion) to be submitted to the British Board of Film Censorship for classification as appropriate for sale to particular age groups and for censorship if deemed unsuitable for viewing at home.

It is illegal for any video to be sold or distributed unless it has an official certificate from the BBFC. Fines of up to £20,000 can be imposed on distributors of unclassified videos. It is not, however, illegal merely to possess an unclassified video.

This legislation is in addition to any potential charges under the Obscene Publications Act.

CUSTOMS LEGISLATION

The Customs Consolidation Act 1876 (as amended by the Customs and Excise Management Act 1979) imposes a ban on the importation in to the United Kingdom of "indecent or obscene prints, paintings, photographs, books, cards, lithographic or other engravings or any other indecent or obscene articles." The ban is far broader than the material prohibited by the Obscene Publication Act, and there is no "public good" defence.

This anomaly resulted in the ludicrous situation in 1984 where Gay's The Word had large numbers of books confiscated which were quite legitimately on sale in this country, including books by Oscar Wilde, Christopher Isherwood and Jean Genet. The directors were charged with conspiracy to import indecent and obscene material.

In 1986 the charges were dropped as a result of a decision in another case by the European Court of Justice. This decision stated that British customs could not apply a more stringent test (i.e. the test under the Customs and Excise Act of indecency rather than obscenity) to goods imported from EC countries than to goods produced within Britain, since this would be in breach of the requirement in the Treaty of Rome for free trade between countries within the EC. Illogically however, a court refused in November 1989 to allow expert witnesses to be called about the literary merits of books seized by Customs officials under this Act, despite the fact that such witnesses would always be vital to a defence under the Obscene Publications Act.

However, Customs are still entitled to impose the weaker, indecency, test on items imported from countries outside of the EC. The law in this area is in complete disarray and cries out to be revised.

In practice

Customs officers can either seek forfeiture of the items without criminal consequence to the importer or can charge him/her with the criminal offence of "smuggling". Guidelines state that a criminal charges should only be brought where someone is importing material on a large scale. However GLAD (Gay and lesbian legal advice — telephone service) and GALOP (Gay policing project) both report numerous calls from individuals who have had small quantities of magazines or videos, intended for their own use, confiscated and some criminal charges of importing have been brought. It appears that videos are particularly likely to be confiscated. The only safe option if you are bringing such items into the country appears to be to declare them at Customs. You may then have them confiscated but you cannot be prosecuted for illegally importing them.

People have also been prosecuted after raids on their homes revealed that they owned copies of videos which had been imported. In 1990, for instance, *Gay Times* reported a nationwide operation, involving police raids on private homes in London, Manchester, Liverpool, Gloucester, Swindon, Humberside and Scotland. One man was fined £3,000 for importing indecent material, while another was fined £1,000 for having imported an allegedly obscene newsletter.

Since it is not illegal to own pornographic material (unless it includes pictures of children under 16) you should not answer police questions about how the items came into your possession as the answers can only incriminate you and possibly others. (See section below on the right to silence).

When goods are seized the importer is notified and has one month in which to notify the Commissioners that s/he intends to challenge their claim to forfeiture, otherwise the goods will be destroyed. If the importer disputes the seizure either the commissioners can change their minds and return the goods or they must institute proceedings before magistrates or a High Court judge (sitting with or without a jury). However, particularly if the non-EC rules apply, you are likely to find it very difficult to win.

A prosecution for smuggling must be brought within three

years of the alleged offence. The maximum penalty is two years imprisonment and/or an unlimited fine.

CHILD PORN — PROTECTION OF CHILDREN ACT 1978

It is an offence to take, or permit to be taken, any indecent photographs of a child under 16, to distribute such photographs or to have them in your possession with a view to their being distributed or shown. It is also an offence to publish, or cause to be published, any advert likely to be understood as conveying that the advertiser distributes such indecent photographs. Offences can be punished with a short term of imprisonment and/or a fine.

It is a possible defence to such a charge that you had not seen the photographs and did not know or suspect them to be indecent.

In addition, Section 160 Criminal Justice Act 1988 makes it illegal to possess pornographic pictures of children under 16.

POSTAL REGULATIONS — POST OFFICE ACT 1953

Section 11 of this Act makes it an offence to send or attempt to send, or procure to be sent, a postal packet which encloses any indecent or obscene article (again defined very widely so that it includes videos, written or pictorial material) or has on the cover any words or designs which are "grossly offensive" or "of an indecent or obscene character."

The courts have given a wide interpretation to these terms, in effect any sexually explicit material comes within the definition. There is no defence that the material is for the "public good".

It follows from the wording of the Act that the subscriber to such material is as guilty of an offence as the person or organization which sends the material, and no profit need be involved. In practice, however, most charges are brought against people who openly advertise such material for sale.

You have a right to choose a jury trial. This offence can be punished with a short term of prison or a fine.

In 1981 the Director of Public Prosecutions indicated that as a matter of practice, prosecution for this offence would only be brought where indecent material was written on the outside of envelopes or was sent to unwilling recipients. Unfortunately these guidelines have not been followed where gay pornography is concerned. One of the common charges which police have brought following systematic raids on private homes of gay men, is the charge of procuring indecent material to be sent to them — an indefensible legal anomaly where the same material could have been legally bought in a shop.

This charge has also been used against *Gay Times* and *Zipper*, whose directors were fined £5,100 in 1985 for this offence.

TELEPHONE CALLS

Section 66 of Post Office Act 1953 makes it an offence to send any message by telephone which is grossly offensive or of an indecent, obscene or menacing character.

PUBLIC DISPLAY

A wide range of publicly displayed items deemed to be disturbing to the "ordinary citizen" are prohibited by a variety of unnecessarily repetitious and vague Acts and bye-laws, once again giving the police and courts broad scope for the control of harmless behaviour which they find offensive (often on the basis of homophobic prejudices).

Section 4 of the Vagrancy Act 1824 punishes "every person wilfully exposing to view in any street, road, highway or public place, any obscene print picture or other indecent exhibition." Section 28 Town Police Clauses 1847 (which applies outside London) creates an almost identical offence and many local bye-laws overlap with this provision by prohibiting "indecent behaviour". For good measure the Indecent Displays (Control) Act 1981 also makes the display of indecent material in public a criminal offence.

Finally the Local Government Act 1982 allows local councils to refuse a licence to shops which sell a significant proportion of books, magazines, films or other items portraying or used in connection with sexual activity.

CONSPIRACY TO CORRUPT PUBLIC MORALS — OUTRAGING PUBLIC DECENCY

Last, but not least, in this overview of the criminal law as used against lesbians and gay men, we come to the vaguest crimes of them all. In the case of DPP v. Knuller in 1973 the House of Lords found the publishers of the magazine *International Times* guilty of conspiracy to corrupt public morals for publishing gay "contact ads". Clearly this has not stopped other magazines including these adverts, although one further charge has been brought since this case (in 1986 in Birmingham, against publishers of a contact magazine).

The offence of "outraging public decency" is a similarly imprecise offence which is not defined by any statute. It has been used to prosecute for "cottaging offences" and (in 1989) to prosecute an artist who exhibited art which included earrings fashioned from human foetuses. In this case the judge directed the jury to decide whether the offence had been committed on purely subjective grounds — whether the display outraged their emotions.

The vagueness of these offences threatens not only contact ads but any other gay or lesbian activity or publication which a court decides can be brought within their broad scope. The danger lies not so much in the number of actual prosecutions but the ever present possibility that they can be brought. This is the clearest example of the courts "making it up as they go along" in order to achieve the suppression of lesbian and gay identities because of the danger which they are seen as creating for "society". The mere existence of this, and the other relatively rare offences mentioned above legitimizes homophobia.

GAY SEX IN SCOTLAND

The situation with regard to sex between men is broadly similar to that in England and Wales — i.e. all such sex is illegal unless it falls within the exception created by Section 80 (7) of the Criminal Justice (Scotland) Act 1980, covering consensual sex in private between two men, both of whom are over 21. There is one, narrow respect in which the Scottish law is more lenient than the English one: if the sex was consensual and private, but one of the parties was under 21 it will not be a crime if the older party is under 24 and had not previously been charged with such an offence and had reasonable cause to believe that his partner was over 21.

Private is not defined, save that public toilets are explicitly stated not to be private. It is likely that the definition will be interpreted in the same way as in England (see pages 217–218). Where more than two people are present, this automatically is not private sex.

The 1980 Act itself makes it a crime for men to "commit" a homosexual act otherwise than in private where both parties are over 21 and consenting. A "homosexual act" is classified as either "sodomy" or "gross indecency" (see below). Alternatively charges of shameless indecency, lewd practices or breach of the peace may also be brought. The definitions and applications of these crimes are often very unclear, and there is much overlap between them. Effectively they amount to a selection of charges from which the police can choose to penalize behaviour which they regard as unacceptable.

Briefly at the end of 1991 it looked as though Scotland might advance beyond England and Wales with regards to tolerance for gay sexuality. It was announced that the Lord Advocate of Scotland was devising new guidelines which would halt all prosecutions for consensual sex involving men under the age of 21, provided that they were over 16, the sex was in private, and that there was no "corruption, seduction or abuse of trust".

However, this announcement was followed by a retraction of this policy, as the result of protest by MPs, including some from the Labour Party.

Sodomy

Sodomy is narrowly defined in Scots law as anal intercourse between two men, whatever the degree of penetration. Both men are liable to prosecution. The fact that they are consenting is irrelevant. Proceedings are brought in the High Court, and the offence is punishable by an unlimited prison sentence.

Gross indecency

This is a broad offence, covering any sexual activity between two men which does not fall within the Section 80 exception. Such sex may also lead to charges of shameless indecency, or if it involves a boy under the age of puberty (usually 14), as lewd or libidinous practices.

Shameless indecency

This crime broadly covers any sexual contact which the courts regard as "shamelessly indecent". There is no specific definition of the crime, and its application very much depends on prevailing social practices. It cannot be brought if the Section 80 criteria apply, but has been frequently used against gay men. It applies in theory to lesbians as well, but we know of no cases involving lesbians. The scope is extremely broad and vague, and there is no maximum penalty for this crime.

The leading case (dating back to 1934, McLaughlan v. Boyd) involved a publican who was convicted after groping various men in his pub. He had clasped their hands, and placed them on his groin. For this behaviour he received a prison sentence. In the 1970s the scope of the crime was significantly extended to cover the showing of obscene films or the selling and distributing of obscene material. In Watt v. Annan 1978, the court held that the crime had been committed when a film showing masturbation, oral sex and various other "unnatural practices" was shown to a group of adult men in a private club.

In 1980 a crime was likewise held to have been committed where articles were sold to the public which were obscene and liable to corrupt morals and instil in the public "inordinate and lustful desires". It was no defence that the materials for sale were kept out of sight.

Although it has never been precisely defined, indecency is generally regarded as being something which is "likely to corrupt and deprave people's moral standards".

Despite the above cases, the use of this charge to censor sexual material has slowed down, such material now being dealt with more appropriately through the statutory obscenity laws (see below). Moreover, its use to penalize gay sex is now relatively rare, charges more frequently being brought under the 1980 Act. However, such charges are still occasionally brought.

CRUISING — IMPORTUNING AND SOLICITING

The law against soliciting and importuning is used in the same way as in England (see page 221). It covers any sort of chatting up or verbal or physical pass at another man with the view of having sex with them.

The law is set out in Section 80 (12) of the 1980 Act, which makes it an offence to "solicit or importune" another man for the purpose of a homosexual act. The action must be a personal one (i.e. a notice in a shop-window would not count). A homosexual act includes any sexual contact between men. The exception for consenting adults in private does not apply to this section. The actions need not take place in public (as is the case in England) and a one-off action is sufficient to commit the offence (unlike in England where the soliciting must be "persistent").

The maximum sentence is two years in prison plus a fine, but it is usually punished by a caution or a fine, at least on the first occasion. Proceedings must be brought within 12 months of the incident.

Circumstances giving rise to this charge could also lead to a charge of shameless indecency or breach of the peace.

INTRODUCING — PROCURING

The law in this area is in practice the same as in England and Wales (see page 218). Section 80 (9) makes it a crime to bring about the commission of a homosexual act. Again the exception for consenting adults in private does not apply. Procuring can be committed by either a man or a woman, and is punishable by a maximum of two years in prison plus a fine.

LESBIAN SEX IN SCOTLAND

There is no specific law against lesbian sex in Scots law, and to our knowledge there are no recorded convictions under other offences for such sexual acts. The 1980 Act described above does not apply to lesbian sex. On the other hand this means that the exception contained in that Act, permitting sex between consenting adults in private, similarly does not apply to lesbians. This theoretically leaves open the possibility that a charge of shameless indecency could be brought in such circumstances.

However, this is extremely unlikely. In practice, the most likely charge that might arise out of lesbian activity would be breach of the peace, arising from explicit sexual conduct in public, or if a girl of under 16 was involved (see below).

BREACH OF THE PEACE

As Lord Justice General Emslie said in the Scottish Court of Appeal in 1977, "there is no limit to the kind of conduct which may give rise to a charge of breach of the peace." There is no statutory definition of this offence and, like shameless indecency, it is used to penalize behaviour which is regarded by the police and the courts as disruptive, annoying, dangerous or just plain wrong. Generally charges arise from threatening or abusive words or disorderly conduct in public, but they can also be brought for any behaviour which could reasonably be said to disturb, alarm or upset a member of the public, even if it has not in fact done so. In practice, it is regularly used against gays, particularly those having sex in public toilets.

One particularly alarming case extended the scope of this charge to private situations, where no member of the public had access. Thus in one well-publicized case (Young v. Heatley 1959) a deputy headmaster made some remarks to some male students aged 16 and 17 regarding their sexual experiences. He did this on three occasions in his office and on each occasion the deputy head and the students were the only people present. There was evidence that the students were not alarmed, nor even were their parents upset, by these conversations, but the deputy head was nevertheless convicted.

Breach of the peace has also been used to penalize any display of public affection between lesbian and gay couples — on one occasion for kissing on a bus. It was also recently used to punish a male transvestite entering a red light district, even though there were no members of the public present in the street at the time (Stewart v. Lockhart 1991).

Although breach of the peace can, and occasionally does lead to imprisonment, the penalty is far more likely to be a fine.

PUBLIC AFFECTION

As we set out in the section above, public affection between gays or lesbians is most likely to be charged in Scotland as a breach of the peace. Some parts of the Public Order Act 1986 (see page 227) apply to Scotland, but not those sections concerned with public affection, insulting behaviour or disorderly conduct.

INDECENT ASSAULT

In Scotland a charge of indecent assault may be brought wherever there is violent sexual assault or some lesser form of sexual contact, such as touching, or where there are threatening gestures by one party accompanied by some sort of explicit sexual gesture or suggestion. The essence of the crime is that the person touched does not consent to the behaviour.

The matter has not been decided in Scotland but a child's consent would probably be regarded as a defence to assault. This offence has no maximum penalty, and sentences are likely to be severe where the other party is young.

SEX WITH YOUNG PEOPLE — MEN

Gay sex between two consenting men under 21 (unless they come into the "under 24" exception outlined above) is a crime, and may lead to charges of sodomy, shameless indecency, or lewd and libidinous practices where one of the parties is under the age of puberty.

In theory there is no lower age limit for these offences, except that in Scots law a child under eight is deemed incapable of committing a crime. In practice, young boys or men under the age of 17 are more likely to be referred to local authority supervision or a Children's Hearing.

Where one party is an adult over 21 and the other is under age the position is different. If the younger is aged between 14 and 21, then the adult may be charged with shameless indecency or sodomy. If the other party is aged under 14, then the charge will probably be sodomy or lewd practices. The younger party, although in theory also committing a criminal offence, in practice will not be charged, being regarded as a victim. The younger the other sexual partner the heavier the sentence is likely to be.

If the under-age partner is not consenting to sex, this will probably be charged as sodomy or indecent assault and the penalties are likely to be severe. For example, in Lilburn v. HMA 1990 a man with a previous record of sex with boys had his sentence of five years in prison upheld on appeal.

SEX WITH YOUNG PEOPLE — WOMEN

Lesbian sex, although not itself a crime, may lead to charges of lewd practices if one or both parties are under the age of puberty (usually 12 for girls). Once again, the consent of the girl is irrelevant to the commission of the offence. As with the situation for men, although technically liable to prosecution, the younger party is likely to be treated as a victim, and will not be charged with an offence. Where both parties are under 16 if any legal action is taken this is likely to take the form of a referral to the local authority for supervision.

Where either party is not consenting, the charge of indecent assault could be brought, with generally severe penalties, particularly if the victim is young.

Quite separately , Section 5 of the Sexual Offences (Scotland) Act 1976 states that it is an offence punishable by up to two years in prison for anyone, man or woman, to use lewd, indecent or libidinous practices on a girl between 12 and 16. If both parties are under 16 once again a referral to the local authority is more likely than criminal charges.

In practice, any charges for lesbian sex are extremely rare.

SEX AND PEOPLE WITH LEARNING DIFFICULTIES

It is an offence under Section 80 (3) of the Criminal Justice (Scotland) Act 1980 for a man to have sex with, or "to participate in gross indecency" with, another man who is mentally ill or handicapped to such an extent as to be incapable of leading an independent life or guarding against serious exploitation, on the basis that such a person cannot be said to be truly "consenting". It is a defence if you did not know, and had no reason to suspect, that this was the case.

There are equivalent provisions for women under the Mental Health (Scotland) Act 1984, and sex with women who are mentally ill could also be treated as lewd practices, or, if the woman was so handicapped as to be incapable of truly understanding or consenting, it could amount to an indecent assault.

PROSTITUTION

Prostitution, in itself, whether heterosexual or homosexual, is not illegal, but various offences place restrictions on it. Under Section 46 of the Civic Government (Scotland) Act 1982 it is an offence for a prostitute, whether male or female, to "loiter, solicit or importune in a public place for the purposes of prostitution." "A public place" can be anywhere to which the public have access, including, in particular, public toilets and also places which charge an entry fee, as well as places which, although themselves private, can be seen from a public place. This offence is punishable by a fine.

Section 46 is aimed at any sort of prostitution. Section 80 of the Criminal Justice (Scotland) Act dealing with soliciting and procuring (see above) will also apply to rent boys and their pimps. There is also a separate offence of living wholly or partly off the earnings of a gay brothel, for which the maximum penalty is two years imprisonment.

CENSORSHIP

As in England and Wales, the obscenity laws in Scotland primarily apply to material which is "liable to deprave and corrupt". They have often been used against lesbian and gay material regarded as pornographic.

Although charges of shameless indecency could still be brought for showing "obscene and indecent" books, magazines or films, they are now more likely to be brought under the Indecent Displays (Control) Act 1981 or the Civic Government (Scotland) Act 1982.

The 1981 Act applies to Scotland in precisely the same way as in England (see page 239). The 1982 Act, applying only to Scotland, makes it an offence to display in a public place, or to publish, sell, distribute or, with a view to eventual sale, to make, print, or have any "obscene" material. In this context, a public place includes anywhere to which the public have access, whether or not they have to pay to do so. "Material" includes any book, newspaper, magazine, film, photo, drawing, painting or recording, and "publishing" covers all forms of reproduction except television broadcasts or performances in the theatre. The word "obscene" is not defined, being expressly left to the courts to interpret in the light of the prevailing moral consensus. The interpretation is likely to be broadly similar to the English one. However it is the practice of the Scottish courts themselves to decide what is obscene and not to rely on expert evidence (unlike England and Wales). There is no equivalent in Scotland to the public good defence described on page 233.

It is a defence under the 1981 Act if there are adequate warnings as to the indecent nature of the display. Nevertheless, a display will still be criminal if it is obscene under the 1982 Act, since warnings do not provide a defence to this Act. In practice, of course, the distinction between "indecent" and "obscene" is very blurred; it appears to centre on ability to deprave and corrupt, which must be present if something is to be obscene rather than merely indecent.

A recent instance of the control over gay expression resulting from the 1982 Act involved an art student in Edinburgh
who was prevented from showing four of his works for public
exhibition on the basis that if the pictures had been displayed
the organizers would have been prosecuted under the 1982
Act. The pictures depicted sex between men. They were kept
under lock and key in a separate room, and access to them
was only allowed on supplying written reasons for viewing
them in advance to the appropriate authority.

There is also a further, common law crime of publishing
and advertising work with the intention of corrupting public
morals. Other Acts regulate the sending of indecent or
offensive material through the post and the taking of indecent pictures of children. The customs legislation (described
on pages 235–236) applies equally to Scotland.

PRACTICAL ADVICE

POLICE POWERS AND YOUR RIGHTS
— ENGLAND AND WALES

We set out below an outline of police powers and your rights.
We should warn that even the limited legal protection set out
below is sometimes ignored in practice. It is useful to know
your rights, but it can be of limited assistance when you are
in the police station and police are ignoring all your requests
to contact a solicitor or friend, and possibly even assaulting
you. Each individual situation will vary and we can only
really give a general overview and a few practical suggestions.

Evidence obtained in breach of limitations
on police powers

The flouting of legal restraints by the police is encouraged by
the fact that evidence obtained in breach of the police codes
of practice is not automatically excluded from a court hearing. The defendant has to show that the evidence would have

such an adverse impact on the fairness of the trial that it should be excluded.

Confessions

The refusal of your right to a solicitor, failure to advise you of your right to silence and other breaches of your rights can add significantly to the pressure to admit an offence which you have not committed. RESIST THIS PRESSURE. It is very hard to retract confessions of guilt made to the police.

Any confession, verbal or written, which you make to the police will be used against you in a prosecution UNLESS you can convince the court that the circumstance in which you made the confession was oppressive, or likely to make your confession unreliable. These are vague terms and in practice it is very difficult to persuade the court to exclude evidence.

On the streets

The golden rule is to KEEP CALM. Try and remember everything that happens and get as many witnesses as possible. You can refuse to answer questions but this increases the likelihood of arrest. A limited form of co-operation is advisable. Think carefully before you answer any questions. Anything you say to the police at any stage can be used against you in a prosecution. Beware casual chats: it is not only answers in a formal interview that can be used in evidence.

Stop and search

The police can stop and search you in the street without arresting you if they have reasonable grounds for suspecting that you are carrying drugs, a weapon or a stolen item. They should explain to you why they are searching you and cannot ask you to take off more than your outer clothing in public. They can strip search you in a van but can only conduct intimate body searches in the police station (see below). They can also search you after arresting you for material evidence, means of escape or harming yourself, items obtained by an offence or weapons.

Arrest

You can be arrested in order to prevent a breach of the peace or for a variety of other offences which the law specifies — mainly, but not exclusively, serious offences that carry a maximum of at least five years in prison. The police can also arrest you for any offence which they reasonably believe you have committed if they doubt the address which you have given them or if you have not given them an address. This is because the alternative way to charge someone with a crime is to send a summons with a date to appear at court. It is therefore sensible to give the police your name and address.

Finally, the police can arrest you if they think you have committed an offence and they believe an arrest will prevent harm to yourself or others, damage to property, obstruction of the highway or an offence against public decency (a particularly dangerous ground for lesbians and gays).

The police should tell you what you are being arrested for and should "caution" you (i.e. warn you that although you do not need to say anything, whatever you do say may be taken down and used in evidence against you).

They may use reasonable force to arrest you. It is probably unwise to resist, even if you doubt the legality of their actions. You may otherwise find yourself charged with obstruction of a police officer in the course of his/her duties or even assaulting a police officer.

WHAT TO DO IF YOU HAVE TROUBLE WITH THE POLICE

Keep calm

Try to remember as much as possible about events and write them down as soon as possible. If this account is signed and dated by you shortly after the event (preferably in front of a witness), then you may be able to refer to this account in any court proceedings, which may often take place months later.

At the police station

The chief purpose in keeping you in a police station is usually to question you in the hope that you will incriminate yourself. The police often do not otherwise have sufficient evidence to bring charges.

Do not trust the police

It is crucial that you:
- Refuse to answer questions!
- Insist on seeing a solicitor!

The police will try all sorts of tactics to get you to speak. They may say that they have evidence from friends or "accomplices" which prove your guilt. They may say that it will be much better for you at court, and in terms of avoiding publicity, to admit guilt. They may even say that they are not interested in prosecuting you but some nasty accomplice of yours. Do not believe them! Even if you are sure that you have committed no criminal offences (and as we have seen above the law criminalizes a wide spectrum of gay behaviour which for heterosexuals is completely acceptable and legal) resist any temptation to explain your actions or to prove your innocence! This can be distorted and used against you. Keep quiet unless advised by a reliable solicitor to do otherwise.

Detention — how long can they keep you?

The police can keep you for up to 24 hours without charge, or 36 if they suspect you of a "serious arrestable offence". After that they can apply to the court for an extension of time up to 96 hours.

Serious arrestable offence

This is a term used frequently in the Police and Criminal Evidence Act 1984 to define police powers. Some offences are always considered serious — most relevantly buggery without consent or with a boy under 16. Other offences which are defined by law as "arrestable" are termed "serious" if they lead to serious consequences such as grave injury or serious financial loss.

At the end of their investigation they may charge you with an offence. They may decide to "caution" you instead. This means that you are accepting that you are guilty of the charge but for some reason (usually because it is a first, and not very serious, offence or you are under 17) the police do not prosecute. A caution will stay on your record, and so you should think carefully and consult a solicitor before you accept one.

If you are charged with an offence you will normally be "bailed" — allowed to leave the station on the condition that you turn up at court on a certain date. The police may refuse to grant you bail if they think you are likely to abscond, commit further offences, interfere with witnesses, or harm yourself or others. If they do not release you after charging you they must take you to court at the earliest opportunity. At court you can have legal representation to try to persuade the magistrates to grant bail. There are "duty solicitors" at the court who will represent you.

The police may decide that they do not have enough evidence to charge you but wish to continue their investigations. They may ask you to return to the police station at a later date. They cannot force you to do so but, since they could simply re-arrest you at a later date, it is wise to agree to return and arrange for a legal adviser to go with you.

RIGHTS IN THE POLICE STATION

Your right to have others notified

You have the right to have one person informed of your whereabouts as soon as practicable.

You have the right to make one phone call

If you are held for an arrestable offence the police can refuse these rights for to 36 hours if they think that it may hamper the investigation or cause harm to others.

Parents of young people must be informed

If you are under 17 years old then your parents must be notified immediately. If you indicate that you are estranged from your parents and object to them being notified then some other responsible adult will be informed. The same applies to people with learning difficulties.

Your right to a solicitor

You have a right to consult a solicitor in private. You can however be denied this right for up to 36 hours if you are being held for a serious arrestable offence on the same basis as you can be denied the right to a phone call.

There is a 24-hour solicitors' rota, about which the police will tell you, but you cannot be sure that the solicitor on this rota will be gay-positive. If you do not know a good solicitor we suggest that you contact a friend (with your one telephone call) and ask them to telephone the London Lesbian and Gay Switchboard and be referred to a solicitor from their nationwide list. This is a 24-hour service.

If you have asked for a solicitor the police should not interview you before s/he arrives unless the 36-hour ground above applies or the superintendent believes that delay would risk harm to others or property "or would unreasonably delay the investigation". They can also question you without your solicitor being present if you give your consent in writing or on tape. You are strongly advised not to do this.

QUESTIONING

The right to remain silent

You have the right to remain silent but if you answer some questions and leave others unanswered then the court can be asked to make its own inferences. It is generally best therefore to answer no questions except for your name and address. If you feel that you have a good explanation, discuss with your solicitor first whether you should answer questions. You can always put your explanation forward at a later stage.

Young people, mentally ill people or people with learning difficulties

These people should always have a parent or a responsible adult present during questioning, but this is not a statutory right and is often ignored by the police.

People with sight, hearing or language difficulties

People with serious visual difficulties should be allowed somebody with them to assist with documentation. If you have a hearing difficulty or do not speak English very well then you should have a signer or interpreter when you are questioned.

Intimate body search

An intimate body search (i.e. of nose, ears, anus or vagina) can be made for drugs or dangerous items (which could be used to harm yourself or others) if a senior officer believes these may be concealed. Young people, and adults who are mentally ill or have learning difficulties should only be searched with a responsible adult present.

All searches should be carried out by officers of the same sex as the person being searched. Reasonable force can be used if you resist.

Intimate body samples such as semen or urine can be taken if you are suspected of a serious arrestable offence and it is believed that the sample will prove or disprove your innocence. The samples can only be taken with your consent but if you refuse, this can be mentioned in any trial and the court invited to draw its own conclusions. You should therefore consult your solicitor before you refuse.

Non-intimate body samples such as hair (other than pubic hair) can be taken without your consent but only if you are suspected of a serious arrestable offence and they are thought likely to determine your guilt or innocence.

Fingerprints

These can be taken without your consent if you have been charged with an imprisonable offence or you have not yet been charged and a senior police officer believes that the fingerprints will prove or disprove your innocence.

Photographs

Your written consent is necessary for a photograph unless you have been arrested at the same time as others (e.g. after a demonstration) and a record is necessary of who has been arrested where etc. They can also be taken without your consent if you have been charged or reported for a recordable offence or if you have been convicted.

Note that photographs, fingerprints etc. should be destroyed if the prosecution is not proceeded with or if you are cautioned or you are found not guilty.

ENTRY AND SEARCH OF BUILDINGS

The police can enter and search buildings in a wide variety of circumstances including: to investigate an offence; to arrest someone (either for an arrestable offence; for a public order offence; for criminal trespass; to prevent "a breach of the peace"); if they have arrested you elsewhere; if there is an emergency or with a specific warrant. (A warrant is a document authorizing an arrest or a search, issued by magistrates on the application of the police. You are entitled to a copy. It should not be dated more than one month earlier than the search or it is invalid.)

The police should provide you with a notice of their powers and your rights, before a search, unless the officer in charge believes that it would frustrate the purpose of the search or endanger people.

Ask the police on what grounds they want to enter and search.

If none of the above circumstances apply they cannot enter without your consent. You would probably be best advised not to allow them in. Unless you are sure the police are acting unlawfully (i.e. by insisting on entering when none of these situations apply) do not use physical force to resist.

Searches should be at a reasonable hour.

If one of the above grounds for searching applies then the police can use reasonable force to enter your premises even if you are out. They must attempt to contact you or someone else in charge unless they believe it will prejudice the investigation. They should leave the premises secure.

The search should be limited to such places as the item being searched for could be found.

Try to get witnesses to the search.

The police should normally allow this, unless they claim that delaying a search for their arrival would seriously hinder the investigation. You should make a note of any reasons they give.

Seizure

The police are entitled take away more or less anything they find which they suspect to be evidence. You are entitled to a receipt for any items seized.

The police can keep seized items for as long as is necessary for the investigation.

If the police have caused any damage to the items or your premises you should take photographs and make a note of what has happened.

Items under legal privilege

The police are not entitled to seize items protected by legal privilege (e.g. solicitor–client correspondence). They can seize confidential material if they come across it in the course of a search and believe it to be evidence of an offence.

POLICE POWERS — SCOTLAND

Police powers are less regulated in Scotland than they are in England. Although the same general principles apply, the specific rules governing police behaviour which exist in England do not extend to Scotland. This means that although most of the general advice in this chapter about how to deal with the police applies equally on both sides of the border, in certain areas, particularly as regards procedure, the rules are different.

STOP AND SEARCH

The police can stop and question you in Scotland if they have reasonable grounds for suspecting that you have committed or are committing a criminal offence, or if they believe that you have witnessed a crime. Also if you have been convicted of theft in the past and this is known to the police, they may stop you at any time and question you as to what you are doing and ask you to explain any item in your possession.

They must tell you whether you are being stopped as a suspect or as a witness, and you should ask them if they do not tell you this.

You must give the police your name and address: if you refuse, or if you give a false name and address, then you will be committing a criminal offence. If you are a suspect, but not if you are a witness, the police are entitled to make you wait while they check that the information is correct. You need not give them any other information.

As well as being stopped you may also be searched in the street if the police have obtained a warrant from the court. In addition, they may also search you without a warrant if you are carrying an offensive weapon, stolen property, drugs, or, probably, if for any reason they consider that there is a risk of any evidence being lost if they do not search you immediately.

Unless you consent, or they have obtained a warrant, the police have no power to take fingerprints or other body samples (such as blood, hair or nail clippings) before they arrest or detain you (see below). However, in cases of emergency, where they consider that evidence may be lost if they delay, they can probably take finger or palm prints without your consent or a warrant.

DETENTION

The police have powers, short of arrest, to detain you where they have reasonable grounds for suspecting you of being involved in certain offences (basically all those offences for which you can be imprisoned) and wish to question you. They cannot detain you just to obtain information without first of all having reasonable grounds for suspicion.

You can be detained and questioned on the street, at the police station, or elsewhere. In any event, the reason why you are being detained must be made clear to you. Detention can last up to six hours, after which you must be released. Further detention arising out of the same circumstances is not allowed, except with the authority of a magistrate.

On being detained you must be advised of your right to silence, and told of your right to have a solicitor informed immediately of your detention. You may also have one other person notified immediately, though the choice of person must be reasonable, and if the police believe that it would hinder their enquiries they may delay informing that person. This could happen if, for example, they thought that the person was also involved in the crime for which you had been detained. However, although you have the right to have these people informed, you do not have an immediate right to see them.

If, at the end of their enquiries, or after six hours detention, the police think that they have enough evidence with which to charge you, then they will arrest and charge you. Otherwise, they must release you.

Arrest

You can be arrested, as opposed to being just detained, if the police think that they have enough evidence to charge you with an offence. You may be arrested either with or without a warrant. They also have wide powers to arrest without a warrant, for example, if they suspect you of having committed a serious offence such as indecent assault or theft, or if they believe you are actually committing, or about to commit an offence. This includes arrests for quite minor offences such as breach of the peace, or being drunk in a public place.

The police can also arrest you without warrant if they believe that you are carrying stolen goods, have no fixed address or are known to have been convicted of another offence in the past. Because of their very wide powers of arrest it is, in practice, very hard to challenge the police on the grounds that they arrested you without a warrant in circumstances when they ought to have had one.

When arrested you will normally be taken to the police station, where you will be cautioned as to your right to remain silent and charged. If you are charged with a serious offence you will probably be kept in police cells until your first court appearance, when you can apply to be released on bail. If you have been charged with a minor offence then you will be released from custody straight away on the basis that you must reappear at court on a later date.

If you are kept in custody, you will appear in court as soon as possible, probably the next working day after your arrest. Since most courts do not sit at weekends, if you are arrested on a Friday your detention could last until Monday morning. There is also an intermediate situation in which the police release you on an undertaking, "ordaining" you personally to appear at the next court. In this situation although you are at liberty, you are technically still in custody.

On arrest you have an immediate right to have a solicitor, and one other person reasonably named by you, notified of your arrest. As with detention the police may delay notifying the other person if they consider that it might hinder their enquiries. You are entitled to, and should see a solicitor before your first court appearance. If you do not know of a solicitor then you should ask to see the duty solicitor, who is available to see you if you are being kept in custody. Duty solicitors' services are free of charge (regardless of your financial circumstances).

Arrest and detention

For both arrest and detention the police have the power to search you, take your fingerprints and photographs without your consent, and, if necessary, can use reasonable force to do so.

Probably (although the law in this area is not clear) they have no right to take tissue samples (such as hair or blood) without your consent unless they have a warrant or it is an extreme emergency and evidence would otherwise be lost.

If you have just been detained, and the police decide not to charge you, they must destroy the samples and photographs. If you are charged then, whatever the outcome of the case, even if the charge is eventually dropped, the fingerprints remain on file.

Young people

If you are under 16 and are arrested or detained, then the police must, without delay, inform your parents or guardian (if they know who they are). Your parents are entitled to visit you in the police station, unless the police believe that they are involved with the offence for which you are being detained.

Entry and search of buildings

The position in Scotland is broadly the same as in England and Wales (see page 257).

Helping the police with their enquiries

Instead of arresting or detaining you the police may simply ask you to help them with their enquiries. This may mean that they suspect you of committing an offence but do not have much evidence against you. It is entirely up to you whether or not you assist them. If you do agree to help, then remember that you are free to leave at any time. However, if you attempt to leave the police may decide to detain or arrest you.

Police questioning

The general principle is that the police must act fairly in the way that they question you. They should not intimidate or put pressure on you. They should also allow you breaks in questioning from time to time, though there are no specified time limits as there are in England.

This duty to act fairly applies particularly if you are young or in ill health. If you consider that the police have acted unfairly, then you could consider making a complaint against them and any confession which they may have obtained from you may be excluded from evidence at your trial. However, the courts retain a large degree of discretion to listen to improperly obtained evidence, and in practice the police tactics would probably have to be extreme before such evidence was excluded.

WHAT YOU CAN DO ABOUT POLICE MISCONDUCT

England and Wales

If the police mistreat, harass or assault you then on an individual level you have three potential legal mechanisms for complaining: the police complaints procedure, suing the police in the civil courts and/or starting a private criminal prosecution. We would certainly suggest that you discuss the matter with GALOP and possibly your local law centre before deciding on any course of action. If there is a local police monitoring group or local authority police committee support group they might also be able to help.

If these organizations cannot deal with your case themselves they can give you initial advice and refer you to local solicitors who are experienced in this sort of work. These agencies do not charge for their help. Solicitors will charge but you may be eligible for free legal advice under the Green Form Scheme.

Some general points that will apply whatever you decide to do about the police misconduct:

1. Try and memorize the appearance of the officer(s) involved, and if possible the number(s) on their shoulder and the registration number of any police vehicle involved. But be aware that if the police see you making notes of these details they may be more likely to arrest and charge you, for instance, with obstructing the police.

2. Take details of any other witnesses of the incident.

3. Afterwards, as soon as possible, write up a full account of the incident.

4. If you sustain any injuries you should see a doctor as soon as possible so that there is a medical record. It is helpful to take photographs of the injuries.

Police complaint or civil action?

The advantage of the police complaints procedure is that you can complain about a wide range of behaviour for which you cannot bring court proceedings, for instance breach of your various rights while in a police station. In addition, the process is taken out of your hands so that you will not require much legal advice (although we would suggest that you should have some).

Complaints rarely produce satisfactory action against the officers concerned whilst civil proceedings may not only produce a satisfactory finding of guilt against the police involved but can also result in large amounts of compensation (some awards have been as much as £25,000) for victims of police misconduct. In addition to suing the police this means that there is a public forum where their misconduct is judged by an impartial authority. In contrast the police complaints procedure involves the police investigating their own misconduct.

The standard of proof in police disciplinary procedures is higher than in civil actions. Wrongful conduct must be established "beyond reasonable doubt", while in civil proceedings it must be shown "on the balance of probabilities".

Police complaints procedure

If your complaint arises from an incident as a result of which you have been charged with a criminal offence, then you should say nothing to the police complaints officers until that charge has been dealt with, in order to avoid incriminating yourself.

To start a complaint against the police you or your legal adviser should write a brief letter to the local Chief Constable and the Police Complaints Authority setting out the details of the incident. (You can get the address from the local library.)

Your complaint is then dealt with by a local senior police officer, unless it is considered a very serious complaint in which case the police complaints authority will investigate. The officer investigating your case will want to see you to take full details of your complaint; make sure your legal adviser is present during this interview.

In most cases the officer investigating the complaint decides that no criminal proceedings should be taken and tries to persuade the complainant to accept an "informal resolution". This usually means an apology on behalf of the police force, while the officer involved may him/herself remain completely unrepentant and indeed continue to deny the allegation. If you accept this informal resolution no action will be taken against the officer(s) involved and your complaint will not even be recorded in the statistics of the Police Complaints Authority.

If you refuse this "informal resolution" (or if the PCA consider your complaint serious enough in the first place to itself supervise investigations) an officer from the Area Complaints Branch will investigate. Again you should only talk to this officer if your legal adviser is present. The police officer who is the subject of the complaint will also be interviewed, as will any other witnesses.

If the investigating officer considers that a criminal charge may be justified by your complaint then the papers are passed to the Director of Public Prosecutions, who must agree before criminal prosecutions against the police are started. It is very rare for criminal prosecutions to be brought in this way. In 1991 only two to three per cent of police complaints were upheld and of these substantiated complaints only 15 per cent led to disciplinary proceedings.

Disciplinary proceedings against the officers involved may be taken instead, but again this is very rare, even where the complaint investigator has found the complaint to be proved. Where disciplinary proceedings are taken you will only be notified of their result, unless you are asked to give evidence at a hearing.

Because the police are responsible for investigating complaints against themselves, predictably the complaints procedure seldom produces satisfactory results. Without a witness your complaint will invariably be found to be "unsubstantiated".

Private criminal prosecution

It has to be said that unless you have very strong evidence, you are unlikely to get much satisfaction from these proceedings either. No legal aid is available, so you will either have to pay lawyers privately or conduct the case yourself — which is extremely difficult. Always consult a lawyer before starting such a prosecution. The mechanisms for starting such a prosecution are discussed in the section of this book concerned with violence (see page 93).

Suing the police in civil courts

Although this procedure is very slow, for the reasons discussed above we would suggest that in many circumstances it is the mechanism most likely to produce a satisfactory result. If you suffer loss, damage, injury, discomfort or emotional shock at the hands of the police you may be able to sue them and, if you are successful, be awarded financial compensation (damages) by the courts.

If you have been arrested and imprisoned without a lawful reason you may be able to sue for "false imprisonment". If you have been prosecuted and found not guilty in circumstances where the police have lied and clearly manufactured the evidence against you then you may succeed in a claim of malicious prosecution. If you have been assaulted or your goods damaged, or the police have forced entry into your home without lawful excuse then you may be able to sue them for trespass to your person, goods or land.

Proceedings are (as always) expensive, and so will probably only be possible if you are eligible for legal aid. If you are facing a criminal charge as a result of the incident you should wait until you have been found not guilty before you start proceedings. You will normally only succeed in a claim if you have been found not guilty or if the charges were withdrawn. You can also lodge a complaint with PCA but should insist on waiting until your civil proceedings have been completed before you agree to be interviewed.

TAKING ACTION AGAINST POLICE MISCONDUCT IN SCOTLAND

The general principles set out above with regards to England and Wales apply equally to Scotland, but the procedure is different.

Complaints can be made in person at the police station, but it is much better to set them out in a letter, and perhaps get a lawyer or Citizens Advice Bureau adviser to write on your behalf. The letter should set out in detail the circumstances of the incident, including, if possible, the names and numbers of the police officers involved, the place it happened and the names and addresses of any witnesses. The letter should be sent to the Chief Constable of the local area, whose address can be obtained from a police station, CAB or library.

Your complaint will then be passed to the Deputy Chief Constable, and will be investigated by a senior police officer, or, if it involves criminal allegations, it may be passed to the Procurator Fiscal. You will probably be interviewed. You can ask to be interviewed at home, if you feel more comfortable there, and are entitled to have a friend or legal adviser with you. You should read over your statement carefully to ensure that it is complete and accurate. A report is then prepared, which you are not entitled to see, and a decision taken about whether the matter should be taken further. You will be informed of this decision by letter, and there is no appeal against the decision.

If the Deputy CC or the Procurator Fiscal decide to take the matter further, the police officers involved may be given a formal warning or be charged with a disciplinary or criminal offence, and you will be called as a witness at the hearing.

POLITICAL ACCOUNTABILITY?

The police have a wide discretion as to how they enforce the law and where they choose to target their activities. Chief Constables are effectively unaccountable to either local or national government.

As Lord Denning put it: "No minister of the Crown can tell him that he must or must not keep observation on this place or that; or that he must, or must not keep observation on this place or that . . . Nor can any police authority tell him so. The responsibility for law enforcement lies on him. He is answerable to the law and the law alone."

Each police district has a "police authority" comprising of local councillors and magistrates. However their powers are extremely limited. Local accountability of the police force is needed to make them focus on the real needs of the communities who they supposedly "serve" — for instance protection from queerbashing or racist attacks or male violence.

The impotence of local authorities and the deep-rooted bigotry within the police force were graphically exposed by James Anderson, Chief Constable for Manchester. In December 1987 in a talk to members of the emergency services he described Aids as a "self-inflicted scourge" and said that "people are swirling around in a cesspit of their own making." Despite being reprimanded by the police authority for these and other remarks he proceeded to give an interview in January 1988 in which he called for the recriminalization of homosexuality and declared that "Sodomy between males is an abhorrent offence condemned by the word of God."

There are some tentative suggestions that the police may be improving their attitudes towards lesbians and gay men. The adoption of a policy of recording incidents of gay-bashing, in the same way that racial assaults are monitored, is one such indication. Another is the formation of the first association for lesbian and gay police officers. However any such improvements are still at a very early stage, and have a long way to go before they can tackle the entrenched prejudices of the police.

HANDLING A CRIMINAL CASE

ENGLAND AND WALES

Our advice would be to contact a solicitor as soon as possible, you do not need to wait until you have been charged with an offence. A solicitor can advise you on whether, and to what extent, to co-operate with the police investigations and generally answer your questions.

The police may take many months after initiating their investigations to actually charge you, especially if they need permission from the Director of Public Prosecutions. You can either be charged at the police station or you may receive a summons through the post. You will receive a date to appear at court.

FIRST COURT APPEARANCE

This will always be at a magistrates' court. When you are charged with certain offences you will be entitled to choose to have your case heard in a Crown court, if you wish. We discuss this decision below. Generally speaking Crown courts have the power to impose higher penalties, although this does not necessarily mean that they will do so in practice. For this reason certain serious cases (e.g. buggery) have to be heard in a Crown court and in some instances the prosecution may ask or the magistrates may themselves decide that the case should be heard in a Crown court.

In any event even if the case has to be heard at the Crown court there will be a first hearing at the magistrates.

Request a solicitor

If you do not have a solicitor, apply for an adjournment to get one. We strongly advise against pleading guilty in a panic to get it over with. Even if you are in fact guilty you may have a technical defence and, at any event, you will have someone to present "mitigation" for you (we explain this term below).

A duty solicitor will normally be available at court — you may feel happy to allow him/her to advice you on a guilty plea and present mitigation. But you will not have much time at court and both you and your solicitor will be able to consider the situation better with a bit of extra time. The court will almost always grant a first adjournment.

If the police have kept you in custody and not granted you bail you can ask the magistrates to do so. The police can oppose bail if the charge is particularly serious, if you have no permanent address or if they allege that you will interfere with witnesses or commit further offences. The duty solicitor should be able to answer these objections, perhaps by suggesting that bail is given on certain conditions.

If you choose to go to Crown court then at your second court appearance there will be a formal hearing in front of the magistrates (called a committal) at which your case is referred to the Crown court. It will only last a few minutes generally.

Publicity

The law's respect for the freedom of the press means that there are few circumstances in which the press will be restricted from printing information about criminal charges and trials, even if you are acquitted.

Choosing your court: magistrates or Crown court

It is generally accepted that if you are pleading not guilty and can elect to go to the Crown court you will stand a much greater chance of being found not guilty there, because you will be tried by a jury rather than by magistrates.

It is a common misconception that, because Crown courts try the more serious crimes, you are more likely to receive press publicity if your case is heard in these courts. This is not necessarily true. One disadvantage with going to the Crown court is the delay involved, which can last months.

Crown court proceedings are more expensive. This may affect you even if you have full legal aid, because if found guilty the judge may order you to pay part of the prosecution costs.

Pleading guilty

As we suggested above it is always advisable to get good advice before pleading guilty. The offence may not be what you think it is, or the prosecution may not have a strong case against you. They have to prove your guilt "beyond reasonable doubt".

The police may suggest that you will be subjected to less publicity if you plead guilty. This is not true.

The only good reason for pleading guilty is that you will often "be given credit" for this when you are sentenced. This means that you will get a lower fine or other form of sentence as a reward for "owning up". If you are facing a first offence which is a minor one, like gross indecency or importuning, you will probably only get a small fine in any event — and this is unlikely to be affected by your pleading guilty.

If you plead guilty to a minor offence you will not normally get legal aid to pay for a lawyer to present your mitigation, but you may be able to get advice under the Green Form Scheme about how to do it yourself or you may want to pay a solicitor privately.

You will get legal aid if it is a more serious matter.

Mitigation

The procedure for a guilty plea is that the prosecution gives a brief account of the offence and details of any previous convictions. You then have your chance to put your version of events and a general account of your background and character. This is known as mitigation. It is your decision whether or not you make excuses for your actions. Suffice to say that magistrates will very seldom be influenced by political speeches about the injustice or discriminatory effects of the law. What they may be influenced by is hearing that you regret your action, that you have been punished in other ways (e.g. effects of police custody, publicity etc.) and that you will not repeat your action.

IN SCOTLAND

Criminal cases are usually dealt with by one of three courts: the District court (for minor offences such as breach of the peace), the High Court of the Judiciary (for serious offences, including sodomy and serious assaults) and the Sheriff court for everything else. The choice of court is entirely a matter for the prosecution, who will decide according to the gravity of the offence, any previous criminal record which you have, and the sentencing powers of the different courts.

Criminal cases may follow either a solemn or a summary procedure. Solemn procedure is for more serious matters, and so will be used by the High Court or the Sheriff court. Summary procedure is for less serious offences, and is used in the District or Sheriff court without jury. Again the choice as to which procedure to use is entirely up to to the prosecution, and so in Scotland, unlike in England, there is no right to a trial by jury.

SUMMARY PROCEDURE

Summary procedure starts when you have a copy of the police complaint served on you. You may already have been arrested and charged, or, in less serious cases, you will have been reported to the police and will have a copy of the complaint sent to you through the post. The complaint sets out the substance of the charge against you.

The next stage is your first court appearance, which if you are in custody will follow soon after your arrest. Before the first court appearance you are entitled to see a solicitor and discuss with them the questions of bail and whether to plead guilty.

The advice given on pages 267–270 above applies equally in Scotland. If you plead guilty, then the magistrate, justice of the peace, or sheriff can proceed to sentence you, after hearing mitigation (see page 271), or have the case postponed for a short period while a social report is prepared for the court.

If you plead not guilty, then a date in the future will be fixed for a trial.

For charges based on statute (as opposed to common law offences, like breach of the peace) there is generally a time limit of six months within which the complaint must be brought.

Solemn procedure

Solemn procedure starts with a petition being served on you, which sets out the nature of the offence. Whether or not you are being kept in custody, you must be brought to court as soon as possible. You should immediately seek legal advice. At the first hearing you will either be detained for seven days for further enquiry or committed to trial. Usually you will not plead guilty or not guilty at this stage, though you may ask for bail.

POSSIBLE SENTENCES

The Criminal Justice Act 1991 formalized the principles of sentencing. It also contained the notorious Section 30 which gives the courts power to impose longer prison sentences for so-called "serious sexual offences" if there is a possibility that the offender might re-offend and cause "serious personal injury, whether physical or psychological". Buggery, gross indecency, soliciting and procuring are all classified as "serious sexual offences". This provision is particularly dangerous in the light of the judiciary's overwhelming homophobia, in particularly the tendency to regard under-age partners as victims of seduction. As it only came into force in October 1991 it is difficult to say exactly how much difference the Act will make in practice.

Generally the sentence is supposed to relate purely to the seriousness of the offence. This sounds reassuring for lesbians and gays convicted mainly for consensual sexual activities — until you remember that Jennifer Saunders (see page

216) and the defendants in Operation Spanner (see page 231) received heavy prison sentences for consensual sex. The sentence can be reduced where there are "mitigating factors" — such as previous good character (see page 271 for mitigation).

The sentences described below all apply to Scotland as well as England and Wales, except that prison sentences cannot be suspended in Scotland.

Community sentences

A community sentence consists of one or more of the following: probation, supervision, community service, curfew or attendance centre. Community sentences are only supposed to be imposed where the offence is sufficiently "serious". When a community sentence appears to be justified in principle, the choice of sentence is made in the light of which restrictions on liberty are justified by the seriousness of the offence and which are relevant to the particular circumstances of the individual.

Curfew orders were introduced for the first time by the Criminal Justice Act 1991, but at the time of publication of this book had not yet been put into effect. Such orders require an offender to remain at a specified place at specified times for up to 12 hours at a time. An imaginative magistrate faced by someone convicted for a cottaging offence might well be tempted to use such as order to wreck an offender's social life!

A probation order should only be imposed if the court considers that it will secure the "rehabilitation" of the offender or protect the public from harm or prevent the offender committing further offences.

Fines

If it is a first and minor offence you will almost certainly be made to pay a fine. The magistrates will want to know detail about your income and expenditure in order to assess how much you can afford to pay. The amount of the fine is calculated according to the seriousness of the offence and the offender's ability to pay. You can ask to pay the fine in instalments.

Discharges

If you are lucky you may receive either a conditional or absolute discharge.

A conditional discharge lasts for a fixed length of time. If you commit any other offences during this time you will also be re-sentenced for the original offence.

An absolute discharge means that although the court agrees that you are technically guilty it feels it would be wrong to punish you. It has no practical effect, apart from appearing on your criminal record.

Prison sentences can be suspended

This means that if you do not commit further offences for a fixed period of time (normally a year or two) you will not go to prison. But if you do commit any other offence, no matter how minor, your prison sentence will be automatically activated. The Criminal Justice Act 1991 specifies that sentences should only be suspended in exceptional circumstances.

Youth offenders institutes

These are alternatives to prison for people under 18, but over 15.

Deferred

Your sentence could be deferred for a fixed period. Basically to give you an opportunity to show that your behaviour has been improved. You will then have to return to court after this fixed period to be sentenced.

Bind-overs

The distinctive feature of a bind-over is that it can be imposed without a finding of guilt. A bind-over is a promise to "keep the peace" for a fixed period of time. If you "break the peace" you will have to pay a fine. Magistrates will sometimes try to impose a bind-over where they feel that the prosecution has been unable to prove their case but that the defendant was "up to some mischief". This is a purely subjective evaluation, and magistrates appear more likely to leap to this conclusion because of their prejudices about the defendant (i.e. because s/he is gay, lesbian, black etc.).

This legal device goes contrary to the principle that if the prosecution does not prove its case beyond reasonable doubt then the defendant is not guilty and should not suffer any sanctions. Sometimes at court the prosecution offers to drop all charges, if you agree to a bind-over. We would advise you to instruct your solicitor to resist a bind-over. In general bind-overs are not regarded seriously by prospective employers, but explaining the circumstances in which one was imposed could be embarrassing.

REHABILITATION OF OFFENDERS ACT 1974

For some purposes you are entitled not to declare criminal convictions after a fixed amount of time has passed. (For more details see Employment chapter.)

A FEW RELEVANT RULES ABOUT EVIDENCE

What the prosecution can use as evidence

The prosecution must concentrate on the facts of the specific incident for which you have been charged and not drag in evidence merely to persuade the court that you are the type of person likely to commit this crime.

Previous criminal convictions cannot normally be mentioned in court unless you have already been found or pleaded guilty. Nor should the prosecution be allowed to ask questions about your character. In particular they should not ask if you are gay (R v. Horwood 1969). This rule is designed to prevent the court being prejudiced against you.

However, if you attack the character of a prosecution witness or you claim to have a good character then the police can bring up previous convictions and other details about you.

The rule concerning attacks on prosecution witnesses' character has been interpreted in a particularly oppressive way against gay defendants. In the case of R v. Ford 1977 the prosecution produced as evidence against a man accused of buggery, a medical statement showing that the young man whom he was alleged to have "buggered" had had sexual intercourse that day. The defendant then said that this young man had told him that he had already allowed an act of buggery on his person that day and would do the same for him for a fee. This was held to be an attack on the character of the young man, thereby allowing the prosecution to inform the jury of the defendant's previous convictions.

The issue of consent may be crucial in a lot of cases but there appears to be a danger that merely suggesting that someone consented to a homosexual act will be regarded as a slur on his character.

Even if questions about homosexuality are allowed then the judge must warn the jury that admissions of homosexuality in no way show that the defendant committed any offence.

In addition, evidence of an offence against one victim is admissible in a criminal trial for an offence against another victim if the probative value of the evidence sufficiently outweighs its prejudicial effect (R v. P HL 1991). This replaces a previous rule under which the two alleged offences had to bear a striking similarity before evidence of one could be admitted in the trial of another. This might still be relevant in assessing its probative value.

There is a danger that under this rule evidence of sex with one under-age young man might be admitted as evidence of a further offence. The vagueness of this rule makes it more open to prejudicial use against gay defendants.

Before the type of evidence which we describe above is mentioned in court there will be a discussion about whether it is legally admissible. If you are in a Crown court the jury will be sent out so that if the evidence is held inadmissible, they will never hear it, and cannot be prejudiced by it. However in a magistrates' court this is not possible so that even if the magistrates rule that certain evidence is not admissible they will still have heard it and may be prejudiced by it. This is another reason for opting for the Crown court if you can.

Unfair evidence

Whether or not evidence which has been obtained unfairly (for instance in breach of the police rules of behaviour set out in the previous section or possibly obtained by the use of an agent provocateur) should be excluded from use in a trial is decided by the judge with reference to Section 78 Police and Criminal Evidence Act 1984. The question to be decided is whether having regard to all the circumstances the admission of the evidence would have such an adverse effect on the fairness of the proceedings that it should be excluded (R v. Quinn 1990, CA).

Where there has been serious police misconduct, evidence may be excluded on this basis. For instance in one case police officers pursued a man into his own backyard and demanded a breath test. They were not legally entitled to do this because he was on private property. They were said to have acted oppressively and in bad faith and the evidence was excluded.

In some cases confessions obtained where suspects have been refused access to a solicitor have been excluded.

It is unfortunately difficult to make hard and fast rules about when judges will agree to exclude evidence. It is certainly worth a try where police have behaved unfairly.

SEPARATE TRIALS

If you are being tried for offences against several different people you should try and argue that these charges should be heard separately because hearing the evidence in respect of one charge may prejudice your chances with respect to the other charges.

If you are being charged with an offence arising from an incident for which other people have also been charged you will normally be tried together. However if you can show that the effect of a joint trial would be extremely prejudicial to your case you are entitled to a separate trial (R v. Glover 1987).

WHERE TWO MEN HAVE BEEN CHARGED WITH GROSS INDECENCY

When this occurs, the fact that one of them has pleaded guilty should not be given in evidence at the trial of the other except in exceptional circumstances (R v. Mathison 1990). However the converse side of this is that if your alleged "accomplice" has been found not guilty the police are still entitled to prosecute you — that verdict is simply a particular jury's opinion of the facts.

YOUNG PEOPLE AS WITNESSES

Children giving evidence

The judge must warn the jury of the risk of convicting on the child's evidence alone, without any corroboration.

Men under 21

Young men may find themselves in the appalling position of being called to give evidence against an older lover charged with gross indecency, buggery or indecent assault. The law regards the young person's consent as irrelevant to the issue of guilt. As we have said, it is legally possible for the younger partner, whom the law is allegedly designed to protect, to be charged with offences in these situations but it is more likely that the older partner alone will be charged.

The police will question you. If you do not wish to have charges brought against your sexual partner say nothing. You are entitled to do this.

If you have given a statement to the police they will ask you to go to court. You will not have to give evidence if the defendant pleads guilty, but you will probably not know this until the actual day of the hearing. The police can serve a subpoena on you to force you to go to court. If they have not done this there will be no consequences for you if you do not attend.

Once at court if you refuse to answer questions you can be found in contempt of court and sent to prison. If you give a different version of events from the one which you originally gave to the police you must be prepared to explain why you originally gave a false version.

If the police consider that you are lying while giving evidence in court you could be charged with perjury.

SCOTLAND

The general rules of evidence in Scotland differ from those which apply in England, but the principles set out above will apply equally in Scotland. One major point of difference is the law relating to unsupported ("uncorroborated") evidence. In Scotland you cannot be convicted on the basis of evidence from only one source. Thus you cannot be convicted solely on the basis of your own confession or evidence from just one witness. This tends to be particularly relevant to cottaging offences, or sexual offences generally, where the acts complained of are usually witnessed by only one other person.

However, there are exceptions to this rule about uncorroborated evidence. One of these is known as the Moorov doctrine. This states that if a person is charged with two or more similar offences, for each of which there is only one witness, then each of those witnesses can support and corroborate each other. For this to be permissible, the offences must be similar in time place and character. This was applied, for example, in a 1989 case where a previous act of sodomy evidenced by only one witness was used to corroborate a later charge of attempted sodomy by the same person, again witnessed by only one person (Munn v. Jessop). Another example (Hay v. Wither 1988) involved a charge of breach of the peace where a verbal suggestion to a 16-year-old that they have sex was held to be sufficiently corroborated by a later, physical, advance to a 14-year-old boy in a public toilet. On both occasions the boys were the only witnesses.

Another special exception is the "self-corroborating" or "special knowledge" confession. Here the detail of the confession, if that detail can only be known by the guilty party, may in itself provide adequate corroboration for a conviction.

In practice, very flimsy evidence can be held to amount to corroboration, so that the rule against self-corroboration is often of little practical significance.

PRISON

The difficulties experienced by all prisoners are accentuated for gays and lesbians. Probably the most frightening aspect is the hostility which they face from both the inmates and the guards. Rule 43 offers segregation to those prisoners suffering persecution from other inmates. The Rule does not automatically apply to certain categories of offenders, prisoners will generally request segregation for themselves. It is normally applied to sex offenders. However most homosexual offences would not be considered likely to attract the level of animosity that would justify this segregation, and the rule would probably only be applied to those found guilty of sex with young boys.

In any event, segregation under Rule 43 is unlikely to help you if you are experiencing hostility because of your sexuality. Rule 43 prisoners face particularly appalling conditions and still experience a high level of abuse from other prisoners. Prisoners who have been segregated under this rule are often shut up in their cells for 23 hours a day. The director of the Prison Reform Trust, Stephen Shaw, commented: "Rule 43 may be part of the problem rather than the only possible solution. Its existence may stigmatize and perpetuate the persecution of sex offenders . . . The Home Office should expand schemes . . . which encourage integration rather than segregation."

Difficulties arise for lesbian and gay prisoners because the supervision and control of every aspect of their lives allows the prison authorities plentiful scope for venting their prejudices. One example is the censorship of incoming mail. Gay and lesbian magazines are routinely withheld from prisoners. Standing Order 4 provides that newspapers or magazines can be withheld only if their contents would "present a threat to good order and discipline" or they could have "an adverse effect on the inmate from the medical point of view."

Prison authorities argue that "excessively pornographic work" could present a threat to order and discipline. However *Gay Times* has been withheld despite its complete lack of pornographic content, and a magazine such as *Him* does not contain any more explicit material than magazines such as *Penthouse* which are freely available within the prison.

Other problems may arise because the prison authorities are refusing to make certain types of allocations available to gay prisoners — most commonly they are not allowed to be transferred to open prisons if these have dormitory accommodation.

AIDS AND PRISONS

The provision of condoms and needles to prisoners to restrict the spread of HIV is the area of prison policy upon which the most vocal pressure for reform has focused. However there are other issues which need to be addressed in this area, and about which organizations such as the National Aids Trust and Prison Reform Trust have been campaigning.

HIV highlights problems which already exist in an overcrowded and insanitary service. Prisoners who develop full blown Aids or Aids-related complications face particular problems because of the generally low level of medical care within prisons, while the unhygienic slopping-out procedures clearly raise particular dangers for spreading infection.

Prisoners, like the general population, cannot be tested for HIV infection without their explicit consent. In some prisons the authorities try to pressurize those who they consider to belong to high risk groups — such as men convicted of gay offences — to take the test. The advantage of taking the test is that it may provide the opportunity for proper counselling and care. Even if most prisons do not offer adequate facilities for supporting HIV-positive prisoners the Terrence Higgins Trust and Body Positive are now allowed access to prisoners, and offer support both directly and through letters.

Some prisons (Bristol and Saughton in Edinburgh) have developed progressive policies, offering adequate care and counselling, and acting to quell hostility from other prisoners and staff. However the report, "Prisons, HIV and Aids: Risks and Experiences in Custodial Care" (by the Centre for Research on Drugs and Health Behaviour) found that most prisons had less progressive policies, resulting in testimony such as: "No-one would talk to us. No-one would even eat dinner with us" and "I was only allowed to slop out once a day, I had to use drinking water to wash."

The Viral Infectivity Regulations, which set the framework for prison policy towards HIV and Aids, allow doctors to segregate HIV-positive prisoners and to reveal their status to non-medical staff. This segregation cannot be justified on medical grounds and often leads to increased discrimination. This policy is said to be prevalent in most British prisons.

Confidentiality is essential for HIV-positive prisoners because of the animosity which they encounter from other prisoners and staff if their status becomes known. Obviously this is difficult to achieve within the prison service, because of the closed nature of the system, but more could be done to improve policy in this crucial area. Prisoners are simply not going to consent to being tested if they know that they are making themselves vulnerable to victimization.

In addition a better national programme of Aids education and training for both staff and inmates is the essential first step for improving conditions and promoting safety.

THE LEGAL SYSTEM

LAWYERS

There are two types of lawyers: solicitors and barristers. Barristers specialize in representing people in court (although solicitors can also represent people in court sometimes). You cannot approach barristers directly but must go to a solicitor first. Whether or not your solicitor instructs a barrister to represent you in court will depend on the type of case and court. If the case is a fairly straightforward one in the magistrates' court, or if the solicitor is particularly experienced at advocacy, then s/he will probably represent you in court him/herself.

If you want your solicitor to instruct a barrister to represent you s/he should do so, but it is more expensive and, if your case is being paid for by legal aid, the legal aid board may not agree to the added expense. If you have heard of a particular barrister that is experienced at your type of case, do ask the solicitor to try and get him/her for you.

The best way to locate a good, gay-positive solicitor, experienced in your sort of case, is to ask either a local or national gay organization for advice. Failing that, ask your local Citizens Advice Bureau or law centre for suggestions. Not all firms of solicitors do legal aid work, so if you want to try and claim legal aid make this clear.

Citizens Advice Bureaux can normally offer initial free advice but not follow through complicated cases or cases involving court proceedings.

Law centres can represent you in court, depending on the type of case (usually not criminal or family ones) and do not charge, but are usually selective about the types of cases they take on. You should contact the Law Centres Federation (see Listings) and ask them if there is a law centre near you.

LEGAL AID

Legal aid (with the exceptions of police station and child care work) is subject to means-testing. There are different means-tests depending on the different types of legal aid, the Green Form Scheme being the most restricted. Certainly if you are receiving income support you will be eligible. Otherwise the income and capital limits vary according to whether you have any "dependants" and the level of your certain or eligible regular outgoings (e.g. rent).

The legal aid may be granted on the condition that you pay a certain amount of the costs of your case.

If you get legal aid it will always apply to the particular firm of solicitors which you have consulted. This can make it difficult and time consuming to change. This is why it is important to ask around and get the right one first time.

The Green Form Scheme

This is available to cover a wide range of matters. It pays for the solicitor to give you initial advice and assistance, but will not pay for the lawyer to appear in court for you, and only initially covers a few hours worth of work (although extensions are possible).

CRIMINAL LEGAL AID

At your first court appearance (which will invariably be at a magistrates' court) you, or the solicitor who has been advising you, apply to the magistrates for legal aid. They will only grant legal aid if they consider the charge sufficiently serious. Different magistrates will have different attitudes. We would argue that all "gay offences" are serious, because the potential impact on the accused's life extends far beyond any penalty that the court might impose. However, many magistrates will refuse legal aid for gross indecency, importuning and public order offences. Certainly if you are trying to defend a bye-law offence you will not be able to get legal aid.

Criminal costs generally

If you are acquitted the court can order either the prosecution or central government to pay your costs. Often however (and again this varies from court to court, and is probably more likely if the magistrates or judge disapprove of your "lifestyle") they make no order, so that you are left to pay your own legal costs, which can be very steep if you have not got legal aid. A Crown court is more likely to make an order providing for an acquitted defendant's costs to be paid than is a magistrates' court.

If you are found guilty

If this happens the court also has a discretion about who pays what costs: they may make an order that you pay a contribution to the costs of the prosecution.

CIVIL LEGAL AID

This is restricted to people within the financial limits, and also to those cases which are considered sufficiently serious. Legal aid is not available for representation before tribunals (employment and immigration cases) or for suing people for slander or libel.

You will have to fill in application forms in your solicitor's office and these are then sent off to the legal aid office which will generally take months to reach a decision. (There is an emergency procedure but this is not often available. It applies mainly to cases of domestic violence.) You will subsequently be sent a further form asking in great detail about your financial circumstances. You should return this promptly.

If you win any financial compensation, or gain any property (e.g. in divorce disputes over property), then the legal aid fund is entitled to claim back the money it has paid in legal fees.

CIVIL COSTS GENERALLY

Broadly speaking if you win a civil case (that is to say if you successfully take action or if you are successful in resisting the action) the other side will be ordered to pay your legal costs. The court may decide not to do this if you are legal aided, if it thinks that your case was a frivolous one or that you were unreasonable in refusing to settle earlier. It is rare in family disputes (i.e. divorce, custody, access etc.) for the court to make any order other than that each side should pay his/her own costs.

COURTS

Generally you will start your case off at the lowest tier of courts and can appeal against their decision to the next court up the scales. Basically the higher up the scale, the more expensive and formal the proceedings become.

In the civil system most cases are started in the county court. Most divorce cases are heard in county courts. Some family disputes can be heard in the magistrates' court, while others may be heard in the county court. Care proceedings are — usually heard in the magistrates' court.

In the High Court and the county court cases are decided by a judge. In the magistrates' court three lay justices of the peace make decisions.

The magistrates' courts also form the lowest tier of the criminal system. As we explain in the criminal law section some cases can only be heard in the magistrates, others can only be heard in Crown courts, but in many criminal cases the defendant can choose the venue. Crown courts have a judge and jury. The jury decide on your guilt or innocence while the judge rules on points of law and determines the sentence if you are found guilty.

Youth courts deal with criminal cases including young people under 17, except where these are considered serious enough to be heard in the Crown court or where an adult co-defendant is involved.

The courts are supposed to follow principles laid down in decisions which were made in the higher courts. So if a decision has been made in the House of Lords or Court of Appeal this decision will have more weight attached to it.

SCOTLAND

LAWYERS AND LEGAL AID

The position in Scotland regarding the relationship between solicitors and advocates is similar to that in England, though in Scotland barristers are referred to as advocates. A solicitor will normally represent you in the District and Sheriff courts, with advocates also being instructed in the High Court and Court of Session.

The principles of legal aid are again similar in the two countries. Legal advice and assistance is available in Scotland and is know as the Pink Form Scheme

In criminal solemn procedure cases, it is for the courts to decide where to grant legal aid. In summary cases, application is made by applying within 14 days to the Scottish Legal Aid Board.

With civil claims where you are seeking less than £750 compensation, you cannot be awarded legal aid, though the more limited Pink Form Advice Scheme maybe of some assistance.

COURTS

Criminal cases may be brought in any one of three courts: the District court, Sheriff court, or High Court. A case in the District court will be heard by a magistrate or justice of the peace. Cases in the Sheriff court, where the majority of criminal cases are heard, will either be before a sheriff alone or a sheriff and a jury of 15 members. High Court cases are before a judge and jury of 15. Verdicts are by a majority, and can be either guilty, not guilty or not proven. The latter two will both result in acquittal.

Appeal from both the District and Sheriff courts is to the High Court of Appeal. Appeal from the High Court as a Court of Trial is again to the High Court of Appeal. There is no further right of appeal thereafter.

Civil cases may be brought either in the local Sheriff court or the Court of Session in Edinburgh. There are various different procedures in both courts. Small claims, where you are looking for compensation of under £750, will generally follow the Small Claims procedure in the Sheriff court which is designed for people to use on their own without any legal advice or representation. Claims of more the £750 but less than £1,500 may follow the Summary Cause procedure in the Sheriff court (which again may be used by people without any legal advice or representation, though in practice people do tend to use solicitors). Claims for over £1,500, or for other matters such as divorce and custody cases or claims between landlords and tenants, follow the Sheriff Court Ordinary procedure.

The Court of Session hear the more complex civil cases where the legal issues are more complex or where compensation is likely to be substantial. Where there is a dispute in a divorce or child custody case then this may also be brought in the Court of Session. Some civil cases in the Court of Session, such as certain personal injury compensation claims, may be heard before a judge and jury of 12 members.

Appeals from Sheriff court decisions may be made, sometimes only with leave, either to the Sheriff Principal and then on to the Court of Session, or directly to the Court of Session. Appeal from a Court of Session decision is to the Inner House of the Court of Session, and then, with leave, to the House of Lords in London.

SECTION 28

The National Council of Civil Liberties describe Section 28 as "an extraordinarily badly drafted piece of legislation", asserting that "some have argued that it is unlikely ever to be used to any effect because of its narrow scope and the difficulties of its interpretation." Section 28 nevertheless remains particularly dangerous because these ambiguities mean that, without cases ever coming to court, it is misinterpreted, and used to justify acts and decisions which result in censorship and discrimination. In addition to promoting local authority cut-backs in services to our community, Section 28 by its ideological nature promotes and legitimizes bigotry and is therefore widely regarded as a major and shameful attack on civil liberties.

WHAT IS SECTION 28?

Section 28 of the Local Government Act 1988 applies to England, Scotland and Wales, but not Northern Ireland. It forbids local authorities from acting in certain ways. It prevents local authorities from engaging in any of the following three courses of action: intentionally promoting homosexuality; publishing material with the intention of promoting homosexuality; or promoting the teaching in any maintained school "of the acceptability of homosexuality as a pretended family relationship."

The Section explicitly states that it should not prevent anything being done to treat or prevent the spread of diseases including Aids.

The Section does not create a criminal offence. It simply states that local authorities do not have the power to do certain things. If they attempt to act in any of these ways, which are outside their legal powers, then any local member of the public can legally challenge this action. If the court agrees that the policy is outside the local authority's powers it will order that the policy be discontinued. To date there have been no legal challenges of any policies on these grounds.

The Section applies only to local authorities. There is no question of voluntary groups, or indeed individuals, of being legally liable for "illegal" acts under this Section. This Section could, however, have a major, indirect effect on voluntary organizations as it means that local authorities cannot legally fund any activity banned by the Section.

The political context

To understand the legal meaning and the actual impact of Section 28 it is essential to locate it within the political context in which it was framed, and to look at the real aims of those responsible for this measure. This Section was the culmination of a series of cynical Tory attempts to tap popular homophobia and use it to taint the Labour Party with a "loony left" image on the basis of its alleged support for gay rights. In the run-up to the 1987 General Election the Conservative Party ran an advertising campaign using billboards featuring books with the titles *Young Gay and Proud* and *Black Lesbian in White America*. Unsubstantiated allegations were made that Labour councils were promoting homosexuality, particularly in schools.

The reality is that in the past local authorities have always based their service provision on the assumption that all the local inhabitants were heterosexual. This has meant that lesbians and gays have been, and still are, unfairly treated. A few Labour authorities had made tentative initiatives to correct this bias and attempt to provide equal services.

Shortly before the 1987 General Election a Private Member's Bill restraining local authorities from promoting homosexuality had been introduced in the House of Lords by the Earl of Halsbury and adopted by Dame Jill Knight in the

House of Commons. The Conservative government opposed this bill on the basis that it was unnecessary and open to harmful misinterpretation. In the event it failed because of the announcement of the General Election.

Section 28 itself emerged as an amendment to the Local Government Bill in December 1987. Only six months after declaring such a measure unnecessary the government now supported and adopted essentially the same provision.

The reason given for this change of policy was that "there was growing concern in Parliament and in the country as a whole about the use of ratepayers' money by some local authorities intentionally to promote homosexuality" — Margaret Thatcher. The government was however unable to provide the slightest shred of evidence of these alleged activities. In this context therefore it is not surprising that no cases have been brought under the Section, since the "evil" against which it purports to legislate is a fictional creation of right-wing ideologues. Nevertheless the hidden agenda of Section 28 has been achieved in that popular homophobia has been stirred up and political points scored.

The Parliamentary debate itself produced some vicious comments by Members of Parliament inciting hatred of lesbians and gays, most notably when the Conservative MP Elaine Kellet-Bowman refused to condemn an arson attack on the offices of *Capital Gay* saying "It is quite right that there should be an intolerance of evil."

The narrower purpose of the Section was to promote and defend "traditional" family values, particularly in schools and through attacking the existence of an alternative to heterosexuality in the form of a strong lesbian and gay movement. The success of this goal has been more contradictory. Self-censorship, bureaucratic timidity, fear of politically damaging publicity and ignorance of the law have extended the impact of the Section far beyond its strictly legal scope, which is actually very limited.

The unintended effect of Section 28, however, has been to stimulate the renewal and politicization of the lesbian and gay movement, leading to a series of marches around the country which culminated in April 1988 with 30,000 taking to the streets. As we shall see below, in several cases concerted action by lesbians and gays has defeated attempts to use Section 28 as a justification for cuts and bans. Some commentators have suggested that Section 28 has had the contradictory effect of promoting homosexuality by this stimulation of the lesbian and gay movement. However the fact remains that lesbians and gays have been forced onto the defensive and had to struggle to maintain their rights while the attempt to move forward by equal opportunities policies and positive images campaigns has been blocked.

WHAT THE SECTION MEANS

Promotion of homosexuality

The promotion of homosexuality logically appears to mean the encouragement of individuals to "become" homosexuals or to experiment with homosexuality. This suggests that homosexuality is an abstract identity, outside an individual which can be imposed on them rather than, as most lesbians and gays experience it, something that is intrinsic and natural to ourselves.

Many lesbians or gays have always been aware of their sexuality while few, if any, feel that their homosexuality has been promoted by external forces. On the contrary most have experienced a great deal of hostility and opposition to their sexuality.

Few would therefore deny the value of having a supportive, or at any rate non-hostile environment, in which to acknowledge this aspect of sexuality. The extent of suicides amongst young lesbians and gays testifies to the urgent need for such an environment. However such an environment could also be said, in broad terms, to promote homosexuality. When the Section was passed it was feared that the repressive effect would be to make the fostering of such a supportive environment unlawful.

The consensus of legal opinion appears to be that the promotion of homosexuality should not be confused with the discouragement of forms of discrimination against lesbians and

gays. The most obvious example of anti-discrimination policies is the provision of equal opportunities in employment,
but they also include the provision of services on the basis of
equal access to lesbians and gays and the funding of organizations which provide advice, assistance and counselling
services for lesbians and gays. All these measures are in line
with local authorities' overriding duty to exercise their powers
without discrimination between different groups of people in
their area and there appears to be nothing in the wording of
the Section itself to suggest that these activities are now
unlawful.

This view is supported by various government assurances.
The Earl of Caithness, during the bill's debate in the House
of Lords, on the government's behalf said of equal opportunities policies: "This clause is not about banning employment
of homosexuals by local authorities. Like all public bodies,
local authorities should be, and I am sure are, equal opportunities employers." He also stated that: "Some local authorities have tried to ensure that the services provided by the
Councils serve the needs of homosexuals as much as the
needs of the community. There can be no objection to such an
aim."

The Arts Minister, Richard Luce, wrote in April 1988 to
the Association of Metropolitan Authorities, concerning their
fears of censorship in the arts: "If, for example, an authority
clearly had a policy of seeking to bring the work of all sorts of
artists and playwrights before the public . . . the fact that the
artists concerned include some who were homosexual would
not put the local authority at risk under this section." He
went on to assure them that: "If an authority stocks books of
every kind in its libraries, the fact that a particular book
deals with the topic of homosexuality or is written by a
homosexual does not put the authority at risk."

A circular from the Department of the Environment in
May 1988, clarifying the implications of Section 28 echoes
these assurances: "Local authorities will not be prevented by
this Section from offering the full range of services to homosexuals, on the same basis as to all their inhabitants. So long
as they are not setting out to promote homosexuality they
may, for example, include in their public libraries books and

periodicals about homosexuality or written by homosexuals, and fund theatre and other arts events which may include homosexual themes."

Intentional

It is clear that the crucial question in determining whether or not an activity is illegal is the intention of the local authority. This Section is thus unusual amongst limitations on local authority powers by making an otherwise lawful act unlawful depending on the intention of the local authority. A course of action will be illegal if there is an explicit desire that it should have the result of persuading individuals to experiment with homosexual relationships, or if it was known that such a result was highly likely.

It is difficult to envisage exactly how such an intention might be proved in court. Statements of councillors and the contents of reports prepared for them would presumably be scrutinized. The NCCL therefore suggests that when decisions are made in this area care should be taken to make explicit the goals of a particular decision and the factors which were taken into consideration (i.e. the likely percentage of the local population that are lesbian/gay, what, if any, general provision there is in the area under consideration which includes gays/lesbians, how the measure fits into equal opportunities policies etc.). The process by which a decision is taken is likely to be crucial in defeating challenges to council policies.

In practice

Unquestionably a whole range of measures, services and policies have been restricted as a result of Section 28. Policies have to face new internal hurdles with delays, demoralization and defeatism the likely results. There are many cases where council officers and councillors have been more cautious in interpreting Section 28 than is necessary. It is likely that only a fraction of these have come to light.

Examples of this discrimination include the banning by East Sussex County Council of a booklet by National Youth

Bureau because it listed the London Lesbian and Gay Centre as one of 100 agencies where young people could volunteer.

In March 1989 John Carlisle, Conservative MP for Luton, called for the production of *The Normal Heart* (a sell-out play about gay men and Aids) to be banned from a council owned theatre. He claimed that the play would "bring shame on Luton" and would be "illegal" under Section 28. The council ignored Mr Carlisle's advice and proceeded with the play.

The most outrageous attempt to "enforce" Section 28 took place by the police, who have no responsibility or power to enforce this law since it is not a criminal one, before the law had even been brought into effect. The Woolwich police threatened to close down the Greenwich Lesbian and Gay Centre on the grounds that it was illegally funded by Greenwich council.

In April 1989 Wolverhampton Council banned a video entitled *Get the Clause Off Our lives* from being shown at a council-funded arts centre, alleging that they would otherwise be in breach of Clause 28. Voluntary groups in the area who received council funding also refused to show the video, intimidated by the council.

One London authority wrote to its staff saying that it would hold them personally liable for breaches of Section 28. Hardly an attitude likely to sponsor new initiatives for lesbian and gay equality! Strathclyde Regional Council wrote to all Colleges of Further Education stating that grants to student associations would be withheld unless they agreed to cease all lesbian and gay-related activities. Essex County Council issued a directive to all principals of Further Education Colleges instructing them to ban lesbian and gay groups from meeting on their premises. These last two directives were defeated by a combination of lobbying, campaigns and legal advice to the effect that these actions were not justified under Section 28.

Voluntary groups whose funding is threatened should first of all get the local authority to make their reasons explicit and then challenge them by a similar combination of legal and political action.

Education

> "There was a real concern that local authorities were targeting some activities on young people in schools and outside, in an apparent endeavour to glamorize homosexuality" — Margaret Thatcher

> "Sixty per cent said that the topic was not mentioned in any lesson at school. Of those who said that the topic was talked about 80 per cent said that they did not find it helpful" — *Something to Tell You* — London Gay Teenage Group

The effect of Section 28 on education has probably been stronger than on local authority policies. Teachers as employees have always been under intense pressure to remain in the closet and keep quiet on the issue of homosexuality (see Employment chapter). Section 28 has unquestionably increased that pressure, once again less by reason of what the law actually says than by what it is believed to say. The one positive effect of Section 28 is that it has for the first time brought out the major teaching unions in support of lesbians and gays. National Union of Teachers and National Association of Teachers in Further and Higher Education both passed resolutions at their 1988 conferences opposing Section 28.

Of the three prohibitions contained in Section 28 the third one (against the promotion of the teaching of the acceptability of homosexuality as a pretended family relationship) specifically applies to maintained schools. However the other two broader restrictions against the promotion of homosexuality also apply to schools.

Pretend families

Local authorities are prohibited from teaching the "acceptability of homosexuality as a pretended family relationship." Logically this prohibition makes even less sense than the other two. Homosexuality is a form of sexuality and not a family relationship and it is difficult to understand how a family can be "pretend" rather than real. The emotive force of this section however is clear — children are not to be taught that families based on homosexual relationships are acceptable.

Once again the point needs to be made that these prohibitions only apply to local authorities. Recent changes in education have divided the responsibility for education in a complex way. To understand the limited legal impact of Section 28 we must look at this division of responsibility.

General curriculum

Education (No 2) Act 1986 gives English Local Education Authorities (LEAs) the duty to determine and keep under review their policy in relation to the secular curriculum of schools maintained by them. In relation to everything except sex education it is the duty of the head teacher to ensure that the schools curriculum is in line with their policy. Education Reform Act 1988 qualifies this responsibility by giving the Secretary of State new powers to establish a national curriculum which override local authorities' responsibilities.

In Scotland, the curriculum is determined by local education committees who have to comply with Section 28.

Sex education

Education (No 2) Act 1986 provides that in England and Wales while the local authority may propose a policy with regard to sex education the ultimate responsibility for this part of the curriculum lies with school governing bodies. The governing bodies of state schools have the duty to consider whether sex education should be part of the curriculum and to keep a written statement of their policy on the content and organization of such education, if any. The head teacher must ensure that the sex education is compatible with the governors' policy. Section 28 does not apply to either school governors or teachers and therefore sex education remains paradoxically unaffected by the Section.

However the moral content of sex education had in any event already been amply legislated for. Section 46 of 1986

Act stipulated that where sex education is provided the local authority, the school governors and head teacher have to ensure that it "encourages pupils to have due regard to moral considerations and the value of family life."

Department of Education circular 11/87 expands on this subject. While it states that controversial sexual matters cannot be avoided and should be discussed in a factual and balanced way, it also states that "there is no place in any school in any circumstances for teaching which advocates homosexual behaviour, which present it as the 'norm', or which encourages homosexual experimentation by pupils." It goes on to emphasize that encouraging or procuring under-age homosexual acts is a criminal offence.

DISCIPLINARY ACTION AGAINST TEACHERS

LEAs have the power to dismiss and discipline all staff, (except staff schools which have "opted out") subject to various requirements for consultation with the governing body and head teacher. Section 28 would impose a responsibility on LEAs of using their power to take disciplinary action to ensure that staff did not promote homosexuality or the acceptability of pretend homosexual families. We shall see below the actual effect of this. In schools which have "opted out" the school governors and head teacher are responsible for staff. As we have seen, they are not affected by Section 28 which only applies to local authorities.

These restrictions on what may be taught must be placed within the overall context of a teacher's duty to promote the welfare of their pupils and the LEAs' duty to afford a rounded education for all pupils bearing in mind their specific individual characteristics.

Department of the Environment circular 12/88 explains that Section 28 does not "prevent the objective discussion of homosexuality in the classroom, nor the counselling of pupils concerned about their sexuality."

The Earl of Caithness, in debates on the proposed section, stated on behalf of the government that the Section "in no way prevents local authorities from advocating a tolerant and non-discriminatory approach to children living in such [i.e. homosexual] relationships."

Bullying can therefore be countered, counselling for pupils who feel they are lesbian or gay can continue to be provided and homosexuality can be discussed both within sex education and in the curriculum as a whole provided that homosexuality is not promoted. If the question of a gay or lesbian teacher's sexuality is raised by pupils it may in some circumstances be appropriate to respond honestly in the interests of fostering a relationship of trust. This would not necessarily be contrary to Section 28. In practice, of course, teachers have in the past has difficulties in this area, and these will certainly be intensified by Section 28.

In practice

While Section 28 was still being debated in Parliament Dr Allen, a supply teacher in Bradford was told that his contract would not be renewed because he had answered direct questions from pupils about his lifestyle. Clause 28 was used in support of this decision. Support from the head teacher, chair of the governors and the NUT eventually forced the local authority to back down and renew his contract.

In a separate case, Robert Nicholson was sacked by Birmingham Education Authority for supposedly promoting homosexuality. Mr Nicholson is heterosexual but was roused to include discussions of homosexuality in his lessons following the suicide of two former pupils because of problems with their sexual orientation. An industrial tribunal upheld his claim for unfair dismissal in 1989 accusing the Birmingham senior schools advisor of adopting a "secret and furtive approach to sex education." Mr Nicholson was awarded £12,000 compensation. However an Employment Appeal Tribunal subsequently reversed this decision on the basis that Birmingham City Council had acted reasonably in sacking him.

EUROPE

While the British government has sanctioned and promoted homophobic attitudes by Section 28 of the Local Government Act 1988, most other countries in Europe have been progressively liberalizing their laws concerning lesbians and gays, and indeed many of them have passed protective anti-discrimination measures. This has led some lesbian and gay lobbyists to seek the use of these developments to promote change within Britain. There are two separate sets of European institutions through which British lesbians and gays can attempt to utilize the more progressive attitudes within the rest of Europe — the European Court of Human Rights and the European Community.

EUROPEAN COURT OF HUMAN RIGHTS

The European Convention of Human Rights is an international treaty which provides basic guarantees for a number of fundamental human rights. States which sign the treaty are under a duty to ensure that their laws comply with the Convention. Although the Convention is not part of British law it allows individuals an opportunity for legal redress for breaches of the rights guaranteed. It can also be used by British courts when interpreting national law, since the presumption is that British law does not conflict with the Convention.

The following articles have been invoked in support of lesbian and gays rights:

Article 14 states that the enjoyment of all the rights contained in the Convention should be without discrimination on any ground. This could reasonably be expected to be interpreted as an indirect commitment to non-discrimination against lesbians and gay men. But so far lack of political will has meant that it has not been interpreted in this way. The International Lesbian and Gay Association is currently campaigning to get consultative status with the Council of Europe and to secure amendments to the Convention so that there is an explicit statement that rights apply irrespective of sexuality.

Article 8 states that everyone has the right to respect for their private life, home and correspondence. This Article has been used to order the British and Irish governments to decriminalize male homosexuality. In 1981 Jeffrey Dudgeon won a court ruling that the total ban on consensual sexual relationships between men within Northern Ireland was in breach of this Article and the British government was thus forced to extend the 1967 Act to Northern Ireland in 1982. In 1988 David Norris won a similar ruling against Ireland which is currently expected to reform its laws.

On the other hand applications relating to the law on the armed forces, age of consent, public housing, immigration and the definition of privacy for gay sex (brought by a man whose private party had been raided by the police) all failed.

Procedure

Complaints about violations of the treaty are processed by two bodies, the European Commission of Human Rights and the European Court of Human Rights. Complaints from individuals and non-government bodies must be made first to the Commission, which decides whether an application is admissible. All remedies within the national legal system must have been exhausted before an application is admissible and it must be made within six months of the final national decision.

Applications can be dismissed as manifestly ill-founded or an abuse of the right of petition. In 1982 *Gay News* attempted to use the Court of Human Rights to overturn the blasphemy charge against its editor (see Crime chapter) but the Commission refused to refer it to the Court. In 1984 the Commission rejected a case brought by a gay man about the ban on gay sex within the British army (see Employment chapter).

Once the Commission has ruled that the petition is admissible, the Commission must investigate the facts and attempt a "friendly settlement". If this fails it prepares and sends a secret report to the state concerned. If the state still refuses to compromise the Commission can refer the case to the Court. The Court has the power to award compensation to the individual and, more significantly, to order the state to amend its laws.

The chief drawbacks to such applications are the expense and delays involved. Cases normally take several years to be resolved.

EUROPEAN COMMUNITY

Legislative authority is increasingly being transferred from Parliament to the institutions of the EC. At present the EC has an almost exclusively economic agenda. The push for a single European market in 1992 has been primarily concerned with economic integration. The left in the European Parliament has been struggling to add a social dimension to this integration to counter-balance the present focus on the interests of industry.

As a result of these efforts a Social Charter was adopted in 1989 covering issues such as minimum wages, women's equality and protection for young, elderly and disabled persons. Lesbian and gay movements in different European countries have been lobbying in an attempt to have discrimination against gays and lesbians included in this social programme.

One of the problems faced by campaigners is the undemocratic nature of the European Community. It has three political institutions: the European Parliament, the European Commission and the Council of Ministers. The

Commission is the European civil service, which is responsible for implementing decisions taken by the Council. The
Council is composed of ministers from the governments of the
elected states and is the main decision-making body. The
Parliament has primarily a consultative role.

In 1984, on the basis of the Squarcialupi Report, the
Parliament recommended an equal age of consent for homosexuals and heterosexuals and the banning of workplace
discrimination against gays and lesbians. At this point it
seemed as though the Commission might support the latter
proposal. The Commissioner for Social Affairs said: "The
Commission feels that it is unacceptable that homosexuals
should be refused employment or suffer victimization and
harassment at work on account of their private lives."

However no further action was taken. In 1988 the Presi-
dent of the European Commission, Jacques Delors, stated
that the Community had no powers to intervene to protect
"sexual minorities" against discrimination. The powers of
the EC to pass legislation which is binding on the member
nations derive from the Treaties which established the
European Community. These set out the precise areas of
policy within which the nation-states delegate their powers
to the European Community. These areas are almost exclusively economic, with national states retaining sole authority
over social issues.

Lesbian and gay lobbying intensified and in 1989 the
Buron report on the Social Charter to the Parliament recommended that the Charter should ensure workers the right to
equal treatment despite their sexual preference. However,
once again, this recommendation was rejected by the Council
of Ministers.

Recently there have been signs of a change of heart at the
Commission, but there remains a long way to go in terms of
political campaigning and lobbying. Many groups are critical
of the racist, "Fortress Europe" nature of the European
Community and harmonization in some instances has been
a means of "levelling down" provision (particularly with
regards to immigration controls). For a more in-depth look
into the prospects of using the EC for achieving lesbian and

gay rights see *Europe in the Pink* by Peter Tatchell (GMP, 1992).

If EC legislation seems as though it might help your case (and short of anti-discrimination legislation being instituted you will need to take expert legal advice on this question) it can be quoted in the British courts, which are obliged to interpret British law in the context of relevant European legislation, and in some cases they are legally bound to follow the European law even if it conflicts with British law. You can try to convince a British court to ask for a preliminary ruling on specific points of EC law. This will delay the resolution of your case, and may involve additional legal costs, but may prove advantageous. Once again you should secure expert legal advice before taking such a step.

LISTINGS

If you do not see any useful addresses for your area you should either consult *Gay Times* which has an extensive listing section, or telephone a local gay switchboard or lesbian line. To get their numbers you could contact London Lesbian Line (071 251 6911) or Gay Switchboard (071 837 7324). In Scotland you could telephone Edinburgh Gay Switchboard (031 556 4049, daily 7.30pm–10pm).

You may also find the following specialist contacts useful:

IRISH GAY HELPLINE
BM IGH
London WC1N 3XX
Tel: 081 983 4111

JEWISH LESBIAN AND GAY
HELPLINE
BM Jewish Helpline
London WC1N 3XX
Tel: 071 706 3123

BLACK LESBIAN AND GAY
HELPLINE
Tel: 071 837 5364

REGARD
c/o Camden High Street
London NW1 7JR
For lesbians and gays with disabilities.

• EMPLOYMENT

COHSE
Lesbian and Gay Rights
Group
c/o Glen House
High Street
Banstead, Surrey SM7 2LH

COMMISSION FOR RACIAL
EQUALITY
Elliott House
Allington Street
London SW1

EQUAL OPPORTUNITIES
COMMISSION
Overseas House
Quay Street
Manchester M3 3HV

LESBIAN AND GAY
EMPLOYMENT RIGHTS/
LESBIAN EMPLOYMENT
RIGHTS
St Margaret's House
Old Ford Road
London E2 9PL
Tel: 081 983 0696

ACTT LESBIAN AND GAY
WORKING PARTY
c/o 111 Wardour Street
London W1
Tel: 071 437 8506

AT EASE
28 Commercial Street
London E1 6LS
Tel: 071 247 5164 (Sun, 5pm-
7pm)
Help for lesbians and gay men
in the armed services. Not gay
run, but gay positive.

CIVIL AND PUBLIC
SERVICES GAY GROUP
c/o 160 Falcon Road
London SW11 2LN

GAY MEDICAL
ASSOCIATION
BM/GMA
London WC1N 3XX

LESBIAN AND GAY
WORKERS IN EDUCATION
(Formerly "Gay Teachers")
BM/Gayteacher
London WC1N 3XX

LESBIANS AND GAYS IN
NAPO
3-4 Chiwalty Road
Battersea
London SW11 1AT

LESBIANS IN EDUCATION
(Manchester)
c/o Gay Centre
PO Box 153
Manchester M60 1LP

NALGAY (NALGO Gay
Group)
c/o 71 Mabledon Place
London WC1 9AJ

NUCPS
BM Box 1645
London WC1N 3XX

NUJ
BM Box NUJLGG
London WC1N 3XX

RANK OUTSIDERS
c/o Stonewall Group
2 Greycoat Place
London SW1P 1SB
Tel: 071 222 9007
Support and lobbying organization for lesbian and gay
service people or ex-service
people.

TEACHERS IN FURTHER
AND HIGHER EDUCATION
LESBIAN AND GAY GROUP
c/o 5 Caledonian Road
London N1

• HOUSING

ADVISORY SERVICE FOR SQUATTERS
2 St Paul's Road
London N1
Tel: 071 359 8814 (Mon-Fri, 2pm-6pm)

CARDIFF: TRIANGLE HOUSING GROUP
c/o Cardiff Flatshop
4 Ninian Park Road
Cardiff CF1 8HZ
Working with local housing association to provide permanent housing for lesbians and gay men, may also have temporary hostel space.

CENTREPOINT
33 Long Acre
London WC2 9LA
Tel: 071 379 3466
Runs night shelter, long-term support hostel and lets flats/bed sits for young people.

CENTREPOINT SOHO
Haberdasher's House
306 Queens Road
London SE14 5JN
Gay-positive short-stay hostel (up to three months) for 16 year olds. Will also refer to other projects.

HOUSING ADVICE SWITCHBOARD
Tel: 071 434 2522
Advice and referral agency in London. Has a 24-hour emergency phone line.

PICCADILLY ADVICE CENTRE
100 Shaftesbury Avenue
London W1L 7DH
Tel: 071 434 3773
Gay-positive drop-in advice and referral centre. Aimed at young people who are new to London.

SHAC
The London Housing Aid Centre
189a Old Brompton Road
London SW5 0AR

SHELTER – THE NATIONAL CAMPAIGN FOR THE HOMELESS
88 Old Street
London EC1V 9HU
Tel: 071 253 0202

STONEWALL HOUSING ASSOCIATION
Unit W55 TEC
560 High Road
London N17 9TA
Tel: 081 885 2305
You cannot approach them directly, you must be referred from other agencies such as the Piccadilly Advice Centre.

• HEALTH

COURT OF PROTECTION
24 Kingsway
London WC2
Tel: 071 269 7000

MIND (National Association
for Mental Health)
22 Harley Street
London W1
Tel: 071 637 0741

WOMEN'S HEALTH AND
REPRODUCTIVE RIGHTS
52 Featherstone Street
London EC1Y 8RT
Tel: 071 251 6580

• DEATH

GAY BEREAVEMENT
PROJECT
Unitarian Rooms
Hoop Lane
London NW11 8BS
Tel: 081 455 8894

• WELFARE BENEFITS

CHILD POVERTY ACTION
GROUP
1-5 Bath Street
London EC1V 9QA
Tel: 071 253 6569

• INSURANCE

BOWATER MASSON
Lady Somerset House
58 Lady Somerset Road
London NW5 1TU
Tel: 071 828 1098
Gay-positive company provid-
ing free advice on life insur-
ance, mortgages etc.

• VIOLENCE

CRIMINAL INJURIES
COMPENSATION BOARD
(England and Wales)
19 Alfred Place
London WC1E 7EA
Tel: 071 636 9501

WOMEN'S AID
FEDERATION
52 Featherstone Street
London EC1
Tel: 071 251 6537
Can provide telephone num-
bers for refuges around the
country.

• PRESS

ADVERTISING STANDARDS
AUTHORITY
Brock House
Terrington Place
London WC1

PRESS COMPLAINTS
COMMISSION
1 Salisbury Square
London EC4Y 8AE
Tel: 071 353 1248

• LESBIANS AND GAY MEN AS PARENTS

NATIONAL

LESBIAN ACTION FOR
PARENTING
4 Wild Court
London WC2B 5AE
Tel: 071 281 4834

LESBIAN AND GAY
FOSTERING AND
ADOPTIVE PARENTS
c/o BM Friend
London WC1N 3XX

LESBIAN CUSTODY
PROJECT
c/o Rights of Women
52—54 Featherstone Street
London EC1
Tel: 071 251 6576

PREGNANCY ADVISORY
SERVICE
11 Charlotte Street
London W1
Tel: 071 637 8962

LONDON

LESBIAN MOTHERS
SUPPORT GROUP
South London Women's
Centre
55 Acre Lane
London SW2
Tel: 071 274 7215

MANCHESTER

ALBERT KENNEDY TRUST
23 New Mount Street
Manchester M4 4DE

LESBIAN MOTHERS GROUP
c/o GYM
PO Box 153
Manchester M60 1LP
Tel: 061 274384

• AIDS

ACT-UP
BM Box 2995
London WC1N 3XX
Tel: 071 590 5749
Campaigning group.

AIDS AHEAD
(Aids Health Education and
Advice for the Deaf)
c/o Cheshire Society for the
Deaf
144 London Road
Nanthwich, Cheshire
CW9 51II
Tel: 0606 47047

AIDS HELPLINE
NORTHERN IRELAND
PO Box 206
Belfast BT1 1SJ
Tel: 0232 326117

BLACK AIDS ACTION
Tel: 071 8839

BLACK COMMUNITY AIDS
TEAM
c/o Unity Housing Assn.
115 Chapletown Road
Leeds LS7 3HY
Tel: 0532 621954

BLACK HIV AND AIDS
NETWORK
111 Devonport Road
London W12 8PB
Tel: 081 742 9223

BLACKLINERS
Tel: 071 738 5274 (Tue-Fri,
1pm-4pm)
Advice for black and Asian
people about HIV and Aids.

BODY POSITIVE
PO BOX 493
London W14 0TF
Tel: 071 373 9124
Admin: 071 835 1045
Campaigning and support
group for people who are HIV-
positive.

IMMUNITY
260 Kilburn Lane
London W10 4BE
Tel: 081 968 8909
Law centre advice about HIV
and Aids.

THE LANDMARK
47a Tulse Hill
London SW2
Tel: 081 678 6687
Drop-in centre offering legal,
financial and housing advice,
plus counselling and domestic
facilities.

THE LONDON
LIGHTHOUSE
111 Lancaster Road
London W11 1QT
Tel: 071 792 1200

NATIONAL AIDS HELPLINE
Tel: 0800 567 123

NAZ PROJECT
BM Box 3167
London WC1N 3XX
Tel: 081 563 0191
HIV/Aids counselling for Asian
communities.

POSITIVELY WOMEN
5 Sebastian Street
London EC1V 0HE
Tel: 071 409 5515

SCOTTISH AIDS MONITOR
PO BOX 48
Edinburgh EH1 5SE
Tel: 031 558 1167

SHARE
BM Box 3167
London WC1 3XX
Shakti Aids support for Asian
people.

SITRA HOUSING
16-18 Strutton Ground
London SW1 2HP
Tel: 071 222 5844
Although currently working
only in London SITRA may be
able to put readers in touch
with special needs housing
provision throughout the
country. Local help lines may
have details of special
schemes.

TERRENCE HIGGINS
TRUST
52 Grays Inn Road
London WC1X 8LT
Admin. line: 071 831 0330
Help line: 071 242 1010 (daily
3pm-10pm)

• YOUNG PEOPLE

ADVISORY CENTRE FOR
EDUCATION
18 Victoria Park Square
London E2 9PB
Tel: 081 980 4596

ALONE IN LONDON
190 Euston Road
London NW1
Tel: 071 278 4225
Gives advice to young people
in London.

BLACK AND IN CARE
(see NAYPIC below)

CHILDLINE
Tel: 0800 1111
A free, confidential phoneline
for children in trouble or
danger. They offer advice and
practical help.

CHILDREN'S LEGAL
CENTRE
20 Compton Terrace
London N1 2UN
Tel: 071 359 6251

LESBIAN AND GAY YOUTH
MOVEMENT (LGYM)
BM/Gym
London WC1N 3XX

NATIONAL ASSOCIATION
FOR YOUNG PEOPLE IN
CARE (NAYPIC)
20 Compton Terrace
London N1 2UN
Tel: 071 226 7102

NATIONAL CHILDREN'S
BUREAU
8 Wakeley Street
London EC1V 7QE
Tel: 071 278 9441
Campaigns for and gives
information to children in
care.

NATIONAL UNION OF
STUDENTS
461 Holloway Road
London N7 6LJ
Tel: 071 272 8900

SCOTTISH CHILD LAW
CENTRE
1 Melrose Street
Glasgow G4 9BJ
Tel: 041 333 9305

STONEWALL YOUTH
GROUP (Edinburgh)
Tel: 031 556 4060 (Tues,
evenings)

STREETWISE YOUTH
PROJECT
3b Langham Mans
Earl's Court Square
London SW5 9UH
Tel: 071 373 8860
Advisory centre for young men
involved in the sex industry.
They offer health care, welfare
and legal rights and counsel-
ling.

• IMMIGRATION

JOINT COUNCIL FOR
WELFARE OF IMMIGRANTS
115 Old Street
London EC1V 9JR
Tel: 071 251 8706

LAW CENTRES
FEDERATION
Duchess House
18-19 Warren Street
Tel: 071 387 8570

LESBIAN AND GAY
IMMIGRATION GROUP
(LGIG)
c/o BCM/Welcome
London WC1N 3XX
Tel: 071 388 0241

UKIAS (UK Immigrants
Advisory Service)
2nd Floor
County House
190 Great Dover Street
London SE1 4YB
Tel: 071 357 6917

• CRIME

GALOP
38 Mount Pleasant
London WC1
Tel: 071 278 6215

GAY RIGHTS IN PRISON
c/o LLGC
69 Cowcross Street
London EC1M 6BP
A campaigning group which
also befriends and supports
individual prisoners and
provides information and help
to their family and friends.

• LEGAL RIGHTS AND MONITORING GROUPS

GAY AND LESBIAN LEGAL
ADVICE (GLAD)
c/o LLGC
67-69 Cowcross Street
London EC1
Tel: 071 253 2043 (Mon-Fri,
7pm-10pm)

LAW CENTRES
FEDERATION
c/o Brent Law Centre
190 High Road
Willesden, London NW10 2PB
Tel: 081 451 1122

NATIONAL ASSOCIATION
OF CITIZENS ADVICE
BUREAUX
115-123 Pentonville Road
London N1 9LZ
Tel: 071 833 2181

NATIONAL COUNCIL OF
CIVIL LIBERTIES
21 Tabard Street
London SE1 4LA
Tel: 071 403 3888

NORTHERN IRELAND GAY
RIGHTS ASSOCIATION
PO Box 44
Belfast BT1 1SH

SCOTTISH COUNCIL FOR
CIVIL LIBERTIES
146 Holland Street
GLASGOW G2 4NG

• LESBIAN AND GAY CENTRES

BLACK LESBIAN AND GAY
CENTRE PROJECT (BLGC)
BM 4390
London WC1N 3XX
Tel: 081 885 3543

EDINBURGH
58a Broughton Street
Edinburgh EH1 3SA
Tel: 031 556 2788

LONDON LESBIAN AND
GAY CENTRE
67-69 Cowcross Street
London EC1
Tel: 071 608 1471

MANCHESTER GAY
CENTRE
49-51 Sidney Street
Manchester M60 1LP
Tel: 061 274 3814

NOTTINGHAM LESBIAN
CENTRE
Women's Centre
30 Chaucer Street
Nottingham
Tel: 0602 483697

• POLITICAL GROUPS

CAMPAIGN FOR
HOMOSEXUAL EQUALITY
(CHE)
Room 221
38 Mount Pleasant
London WC1X 0AP
Tel: 071 833 3912

CGHE (Conservative Group
for Homosexual Equality)
Box BM/CGHE
London WC1N 3XX

DEMOCRATS FOR LESBIAN
AND GAY ACTION (DELGA)
National Secretary
SDGR, SDP HQ
4 Cowley Street
London SW1P 3NB

(IRISH) NATIONAL GAY
FEDERATION
Hirschfeld Centre
10 Fownes Street Upper
Dublin 2
Tel: (Dublin) 710608

LABOUR CAMPAIGN FOR
LESBIAN AND GAY RIGHTS
(LCLGR)
PO Box 306
London N5 2SY

LESBIAN AND GAY
COMMUNISTS
16 St John Street
London EC1M 4AY
Tel: 071 251 6160 (Thur 4pm-
7pm, Bob Deacon)

SCOTTISH HOMOSEXUAL
RIGHTS GROUP
60 Broughton Street
Edinburgh EH1 3SA
Tel: 031 557 2625 (women);
031 558 1279 (men)

STONEWALL GROUP
2 Greycoat Place
London SW1P 1SB
Tel: 071 222 9007

●EUROPE

ILGA
c/o 141 Cloudsley Road
London N1 0EN
Tel: 071 278 1496

Also by The Gay Men's Press:

Peter Tatchell
EUROPE IN THE PINK

What does European integration mean for lesbians and gay men in Britain and the other countries of Europe?

  With the move towards a united Europe, the European Community is becoming an important focus for the lesbian and gay rights struggle. *Europe In The Pink* documents the current legal status of lesbians and gay men in 32 European countries, and includes a major survey of anti-gay discrimination in Britain. It records the campaign to win support for homosexual equality from the European Community and the Council of Europe, as well as the struggle of lesbians and gay men in the East European countries.

  Peter Tatchell argues the need for a Europe-wide campaign for lesbian and gay rights, and sets out a radical European agenda for homosexual equality.

ISBN 0 85449 158 9
UK £5.95 US $10.95 AUS $17.95

Richie McMullen
MALE RAPE

In a male-dominated culture, men do not want to accept their role as victims. In this ground-breaking work, Richie McMullen challenges the position of English law that does nothing to recognize the existence of this under-reported but increasingly prevalent crime.

  This critical study argues across thee whole spectrum of abuse cases, identifying possible causes and re-evaluating the threat as a problem for all of us to face, whatever our sex.

  It tackles basic issues of male sex aggression and liberation, concluding with research profiles and counselling advice for victims and those who help them; it courageously foregrounds a crisis few of us want to hear about. And leaves us with a message: By accepting to break the circle of sexual violence, we must educate, train and force for change; and thus redefine what it means to be male.

ISBN 0 85449 126 0
UK £9.95   US $18.95   AUS $29.95

Terry Sanderson
HOW TO BE A HAPPY HOMOSEXUAL
A Gay Man's Handbook for the 90s

This second GMP edition of Terry Sanderson's seminal work contains practical counselling information on topics as varying and relevant as coming out, forming relationships, enjoying safer sex, understanding the place of gays in the law and coping with homophobia. Completely revised and updated this helpful volume reviews the latest in issues surrounding Aids and maintains a realistic, optimistic approach to every relevant subject.

"This is a splendid book, honestly felt. honestly written, honestly presented. It's jam-packed with commonsense advice and should leave its readers feeling much more relaxed about themselves and their lives. I've only one regret...it's unlikely to be read by enough heterosexual people. It should be. They have as much to learn from it as have homosexual people" — Claire Rayner

ISBN 0 85449 191 0
UK £4.95   US $9.95   AUS $14.95

Lorraine Trenchard
BEING LESBIAN

In this insightful, unpretentious guide, Lorraine Trenchard explodes the myths surrounding lesbianism, and encourages her readers to embrace their sexuality with a positive mind.

Drawing on her experiences as counsellor and activist, she examines the needs and realities of loving your own sex, and in practical steps, explains how to encourage self esteem and enjoy a successful lesbian lifestyle.

Being Lesbian points to the needs of all lesbians, their responsibility to themselves and others, and the importance of helping other minorities. It celebrates lesbian identity and unites its factions, asserting the right to stand up to a hostile world.

ISBN 0 85449 113 9
UK £4.95   US $7.95   AUS $14.95

GMP books can be ordered from any bookshop in the UK, and from specialised bookshops overseas. If you prefer to order by mail, please send full retail price plus £3.00 for postage and packing to:

GMP Publishers Ltd (GB),
P O Box 247, London N17 9QR.

For payment by Access/Eurocard/Mastercard/American Express/Visa, please give number and signature.
A comprehensive mail-order catalogue is also available.

In North America order from Alyson Publications Inc.,
40 Plympton St, Boston, MA 02118, USA.
(American Express not accepted)

In Australia order from Bulldog Books,
P O Box 155, Broadway, NSW 2007, Australia.

Name and Address in block letters please:

Name
_____

Address
_____

_____

_____